NEW WORLDS OF
Dvořák

NEW WORLDS OF
Dvořák

Searching in America for the Composer's Inner Life

MICHAEL B. BECKERMAN

W. W. Norton & Company New York London

For information about permission to reproduce selections from this book, write to
Permissions, W. W. Norton & Company, Inc., 500 Fifth Avenue, New York, NY 10110

Manufacturing by Courier Westford
Book design by Chris Welch
Production manager: Julia Druskin

Library of Congress Cataloging-in-Publication Data
Beckerman, Michael Brim, 1951–
New worlds of Dvořák : searching in America for the composer's inner life /
Michael B. Beckerman.
p. cm.
Includes bibliographical references (p.) and index.
ISBN 0-393-04706-7
1. Dvořák, Antonín, 1841–1904—Journeys—United States. 2. United States—
Description and travel. 3. Composers—Czech Republic—Biography. I. Title.

ML410.D99 B42 2003
780'.92—dc21

[B]   2002026590

W. W. Norton & Company, Inc., 500 Fifth Avenue, New York, N.Y. 10110
www.wwnorton.com

W. W. Norton & Company Ltd., Castle House, 75/76 Wells Street, London W1T 3QT

1 2 3 4 5 6 7 8 9 0

To Karen

Contents

Figures 1–25 appear between pages 102 and 103.

Music examples in score may be found and downloaded at
www.wwnorton.com/trade/beckerman

Preface

My first serious interest in Dvořák's music dates back to the 1960s, when, as a teenager, I fell in love with his *Romance* and the Quintet in E-flat. My interest in writing about Dvořák dates back to a seminar I taught at Washington University in the 1980s. We were looking at different kinds of pastorals and I sent a student off to find out what kind of pastoral the Largo from the "New World" Symphony might be. She came back and told me that according to her research, it was not a pastoral at all; rather it was a piece inspired by Minnehaha's funeral from Longfellow's *Song of Hiawatha*. I started wondering: was the Largo a funeral in pastoral tone? A pastoral in funeral tone?

This book represents my attempt to answer these and other questions. As I have worked and reflected I have come to conclude that Dvořák is not exactly what he appears to be. Yet how can I or anyone else discover what Dvořák *is*? Since his music moves us, we have the illusion that he knows us. Can we look backward through the music and come to know him?

I have often sat and tried to imagine what it might have felt like to be Dvořák. What did he feel when his "New World" Symphony took New York by storm, or when he was depressed and homesick in his apartment, or when he finally arrived in Spillville, Iowa, and heard the birds for the first time in months? I have wondered how it came to be so difficult for him to walk alone in New York or Prague and what he must have felt at such times. And finally, I have wondered what any of this might have to do with his music. The questions, and sometimes the answers, are found in the pages that follow.

I have always envied art historians. Though their field is no less specialized than musicology, it has always been easier for them to communicate with a broad public. Almost any intelligent reader can follow the basic argument about a painting by referring to its reproduction. Leonard Meyer's *Emotion and Meaning in Music* has been a popular book, but it cannot compare, either in influence or accessibility, to Gombrich's *Art and Illusion*. The Great Divide between serious books about music and a larger public has always been the presence or absence of music examples. Most might agree that for general audiences in the humanities, music examples lie somewhere between the accessibility of art illustrations and the inscrutability of advanced mathematical equations. It is my view that for most readers, music examples are actually far closer to calculus, and that authors and publishers have tended to overrate the information obtainable from such examples. While the vast majority of musicians and music lovers can easily follow a score, and many can reproduce its contents at a keyboard or other instrument, the number of people able to hear a score in their heads effortlessly and immediately is small indeed. Thus there is, alas, a certain "Emperor's New Clothes" component in the whole process.

Finally, though, we have the technology to remedy this problem. The CD included with this volume contains almost one hundred examples, which range in length from a few seconds to just over five minutes. Some are performed on the piano and others are orchestral. In order to illustrate connections between Longfellow's *Hiawatha* and Dvořák's "New World" Symphony, I have created "melodramas" in which the texts in question are declaimed over the music. A scene from Dvořák's proposed *Hiawatha* opera is realized. All the examples from the article *Negro Music* are reproduced in sound, and several are arranged the way Dvořák might have heard them. It is my hope that these "reproductions" will allow the widest possible audience to be active participants by judging the quality of my arguments with their ears as well as their intellects.

Adding this audio component to the volume would not have been possible without the support of the publisher, W. W. Norton. I am deeply grateful to Supraphon Records for permission to use these examples and to Libuše Schlossbergerová for her assistance in obtaining them. I also thank Luigi Irlandini, who worked with me to prepare the examples, and the recording engineer, Kevin Kelly, at the University of California, Santa Barbara.

It has been difficult to decide precisely what to do with the written examples, traditionally an essential part of any serious scholarly study of musical works. In the end, I decided to play to the ear and not the eye. However, all music examples may be found and downloaded at the following Web site: www.wwnorton.com/trade/beckerman. Once again Luigi Irlandini deserves special thanks for his assistance in preparing the examples.

Acknowledgments

In all my work, I am indebted to the Dvořák scholars who have come before me and to many others as well. Perhaps the first debt of gratitude for anyone studying Dvořák's sojourn in the United States goes to Josef Kovařík, that intrepid young violist who served as Dvořák's factotum. The very careful diary he must have kept has never surfaced, yet in a series of articles in both Czech and English he described his years with Dvořák in America. Particularly beautiful are the letters he wrote to Dvořák's biographer Otakar Šourek. Taken together, these writings provide a chronicle of those times. Although parts of them have been published here or there, they have never been published in their entirety, and they should be.

An almost equal debt is owed to Šourek himself, who solved many mysteries and contributed a few others in his monumental four-volume biography of the composer. Perhaps one day we shall have it translated into English. Also of great importance is Šourek's collection, *Antonín Dvořák: Letters and Reminiscences*, a gold mine of recollections. If Šourek is the Jovian elder statesman of Dvořák biography, Antonín Sychra is the quicksilver Hermes of the field. His absorbing and sometimes visionary insights are essential reading for anyone interested in the subject. Another invaluable source is the *Correspondence and Documents*, edited by Milan Kuna. That the volumes have continued to appear through all the difficult times over almost fifteen years is a tribute to the determination of the editor. The two books and many articles of John Clapham have blazed the path in English-language Dvořák studies, and I recall my personal association with John Clapham with pleasure and many fond memories.

On the specific topic of Dvořák in America we are all indebted to Merton Robert Aborn for his splendid groundbreaking work on Dvořák's American years, particularly his time at the National Conservatory. I also thank the conductor and scholar Maurice Peress, who helped me greatly with my work on Henry Krehbiel. It was to Peress's comprehensive knowledge of the American years that I have aspired.

Several colleagues have been working in this area together for several years. Warmest thanks to Robert Winter, whose masterly efforts created one of the most underrated music history projects, the brilliant and astonishing CD-ROM on the "New World" Symphony. Working with him on a variety of projects has been pure pleasure. Trying to keep one step ahead of James Hepokoski has also been a challenge, and his stimulating response to my first article on Dvořák and Hiawatha has set a high standard for any further work. I must also thank Joseph Horowitz for generously sharing all his exciting ideas about Dvořák and for being such an important force in the field, for arranging festivals, for writing books, and for bringing some of this information to public school students. He loves the New World of Columbus and the New World of music as much as I do. Special thanks to him for giving me information about Anton Seidl's Hiawatha opera.

I am grateful to David Beveridge for reading parts of this manuscript and making many important comments; his eleventh-hour contribution to this study was a lifesaver. Among other living Dvořák scholars, there are none so generous and continually helpful as Jan Smaczny. I am indebted to him for many reasons, but in particular for showing me the unfinished manuscript of his book on the Cello Concerto and for cheerfully answering my many nagging e-mails about various topics over the years. Warm thanks to Alan Houtchens for his assistance and friendship over the years.

Several others helped me with this project in various ways. Almost ten years ago, Leon Botstein invited me to arrange a conference on Dvořák in connection with the Bard Music Festival. Many of the wonderful opportunities I have had in the past few years clearly date from that moment, and I am indebted to Leon for his support and advice. My friend and colleague Laurence Dreyfus is always a shining example of incisive thought, and I thank him for his interest and support. I also express my great thanks to Richard Taruskin. Not only are his industry and his intellect an example for all of us working in Slavic music and elsewhere, but he has served as a mentor to me many times and in many ways.

I owe a great debt to the staff of the Dvořák Museum in Prague. First I would like to thank Markéta Hallová for her deep knowledge of Dvořák's music, life, and materials, for her friendship, and for the access she has always given me to documents, even when she was unhappy with the direction of my research. Special thanks to Jarmilá Tauerová, who has always been a model professional and a source of support. Also thanks to Paní Tomkinová, who made studying at the Museum the greatest pleasure. To all the rest of the staff of the Dvořák Museum, sincere thanks.

I can mention with gratitude several of my Czech friends and colleagues. Special thanks to Aleš Březina, who first invited me to give a paper on Dvořák and anxiety, and who has been a remarkably generous collaborator and supporter. Jiří Fukač has long been a friend and mentor. I also thank Prof. Jiří Vyslouzil for his help over the years. Alena Němcová, friend, supporter, and scholar, has always looked out for me, even in the bad old days, and Eva Drlíková has been a wonderful friend and editor. I especially thank Don Sparling, whose life and work have always been an inspiration for me.

My thanks to the music libraries at Stanford University, Washington University, the University of California at Santa Barbara, and UC Berkeley, all of whose staff members were both courteous and helpful. I have nothing but the warmest memories of my work at the New-York Historical Society Library and the special feeling it evokes of the past. I remember in particular spending one January day looking through century-old newspapers. I found that exactly one hundred years before there had been a huge snowstorm. Many woodcuts and etchings in the papers revealed that Central Park had been turned into a winter playland, with sleds and sleighs and thousands ice-skating. When I left the building it had happened! A snowstorm had transformed the park. From where I stood, no new buildings could be seen, and even in the cold I felt a blast of pure warmth. It was the closest I have ever come to living in the past.

I gratefully acknowledge the Stanford Humanities Center, where the basic premise of this book was established, as well as Keith Baker, the Susans Dunn, Sebbard, and Dambrau, and Gwen Lorraine, who all made my experience at Stanford so remarkable. I also thank all my stimulating colleagues at Stanford, in particular Robert Kraut and Celia Applegate.

I would not have been able to complete this book without the help and support of my students, to whom I owe a great debt. Thanks to Erik Entwistle for his assistance in many areas and to Dave Malvinni for his always thoughtful comments. Thanks to Tom Svatos, who went to the Dvořák Museum in Prague at my request and was the first to actually see Dvořák's own copy of "Negro Music," which he faxed to me almost immediately. I thank Derek Katz for his many helpful comments and for reading parts of the manuscript critically. Special thanks to Diane Paige for her research assistance and her marvelous work on this project. She is a virtual coauthor of much of the funeral march material, and her relentless digging was essential to the discovery of the article "Negro Music." Thanks to Judy Mabary for her constant help, her wonderful ideas, and her diligence. I am indeed fortunate to have had such wonderful students, and I thank especially those who survived my first Dvořák seminar at Washington University.

I am grateful to my many teachers for their time, their insights, and their patience: Fritz Whang, Blanche Abrams, William Hettrick, Herbert Deutsch, Albert Tepper, Charles Turner, Ray Kennedy, Emmanuel Green, Rado Lencek, Niels Ostbye, Christoph Wolff, William Harkins, Edward A. Lippman, Peter Kussi, Leeman Perkins, Ernie Sanders, and Fred Kraus, who played the pump organ for us.

Great thanks to my colleagues at UCSB, Bill Prizer, Bob Freeman, Alejandro Planchart, Pieter van den Toorn, Lee Rothfarb, Timothy Cooley, Cornelia Fales, Pat Hall, Dolores Hsu, and Paul Berkowitz; and at Washington University, Marian Guck, John Perkins, Darrel Berg, Dolores Pesce, Craig Monson, and Jeffrey Kurtzman. Thanks also to those who have served as friends, consultants, and mentors at various times: Janet Johnson, Victor Coelho, Christopher Gibbs, Joe Dubiel, Margaret Murata, Judith Shatin, Philip Bohlman, and Michelle Kisliuk. A special thanks to Onno for giving me the wonderful Dutch pop songs—my Burleigh!

Thanks to Mikuláš Bek, Jiří Čtrnáct, Eva Slavíčková, Jakub Skalník, Saul Lilienstein, Petra Šafářová, Mirek Čejka, and Nicole Nadya Taubingerová for their friendship and inspiration, and thanks to Nadya Zimmerman and Maiko Kawabata for their friendship and encouragement.

A special measure of gratitude should go to Roland Huntford, who is an inspiration to anyone writing biography of any sort.

I also thank my now retired editor at Norton, Michael Ochs, for his first-rate work on this project—he will surely be missed—and also his assistant, Allison Benter, for advice and hounding, and all those Nortonians who have worked to make this a better book.

There are two people I must thank most deeply. Jaromil Jireš was a dear friend who has been an inspiration to me from the moment I met him. His films on Janáček and Dvořák bring those figures to life in a special and remarkable way. There is a good deal of him in my book.

Not many people get to have a second father. Jarmil Burghauser was mine, and if there is anything good in this book, it reflects his vision, his gentleness, and his love for Dvořák. He is author of both thematic catalogues, invaluable research tools, and has served as editor of the complete edition of Dvořák's works. When I was banned from Czechoslovakia for several years, this man took the risk of publishing my ideas in scholarly journals. There was always a place set for me at his table, and usually a dinner based on Czech medieval recipes. We often played together on the two grand pianos in his small living room—everything from Dvořák to folk songs from Písek, where Burghauser was born. No young scholar could have received a warmer welcome, and without him I never would have written this book.

Just as this book was completed, I received the sad news that Oleg Podgorný, director of the Prague Spring, had died suddenly. Oleg was one of the reasons I kept going back to the Czech Republic. His generosity of spirit, goodwill, and sense of humor will be missed deeply.

My own father passed away more than fifteen years ago, but he still serves, along with my mother, as my primary mentor. He sits on my shoulder and tells me, "That won't do," and sometimes "That's terrific." My mother is a person of astonishing creativity and imagination. There is much of her in these pages as well.

To thank one's grandfathers may seem to be off the beaten path, but there is a special reason in this case. My paternal grandfather, Morris Beckerman, bequeathed to me his deep love of music. As he lay dying, a man in his forties, they say he listened endlessly to Schubert's Quintet in C on an old hand-wound Victrola. Charles J. Brim, my maternal grandfather, was a cardiologist, raconteur, biblical scholar, and sometime composer and screenwriter. When I began working on Dvořák's relationship to journalists, I told my mother that I was doing research on a man named James Huneker. There was a long silence on the phone. "Your grandfather was planning to write a book on Huneker." O happy genes that one unwittingly ends up working on one's grandfather's projects!

Also I owe a debt of gratitude to my father-in-law and dear friend Stanley Silverstone, who gave me inspirational advice during the writing of this study, to my mother-in-law, Barbara Silverstone, for her constant support, and to my aunt Miriam Chown for her insights.

The fact that I finished this book probably owes a great deal to my maternal grandmother. Bessie Brim was a hard-nosed Bolshevik who got up every morning at five to clean the house before going to work. When I left a light on, she always said, "Is your uncle Thomas Edison?" Warm love and thanks to Jon, Barbara, Joshua, and Danny.

Finally, I dedicate this book to my wonderful family. To Charlie, who is the most sensitive, creative, and mature teenager I have ever seen. To Bernie, who provides us all with insight, drama, and stand-up comedy. To Anna, who has made us all better, more loving, and more responsible. And to Karen, my life companion, my lover, and my best friend.

San Francisco
January 2002

Selective Chronology

1888	Feb.	Befriended by Tchaikovsky, who visits Prague
1889	Aug.–Nov.	Composes Symphony in G, Op. 88 (No. 8)
1890	Jan.–Oct.	Composes Requiem for Birmingham
1891	Jan.	Begins teaching at the Prague Conservatory as professor of composition
	Mar. 17	Receives honorary doctorate at Charles University in Prague
	Jun. 5–6?	First contact with Jeannette Thurber, who telegraphs from Paris offering him the directorship of the National Conservatory in New York
	Jun. 16	Receives honorary doctorate at Cambridge University
	Jun.–Dec.	Negotiates and signs two-year contract with Thurber to head the National Conservatory
1892	Jun.–Jul.	Composes Te Deum for his first New York concert
	Aug. 3	Begins composing cantata *The American Flag*
	Sep. 15	Leaves for the United States on the S.S. *Saale*
	Sep. 27	Arrives at the Clarendon Hotel in New York
	Oct. 1	Welcomed at the National Conservatory
	Oct. 14?	Attends Czech Circle of New York concert and banquet
	Oct. 21	Inaugural all-Dvořák concert (including his Te Deum and three overtures: *From Nature's Realm, Carnival,* and *Othello,* Opp. 91–93
	Oct.	Columbus Day celebrations, Dvořák's opening concert, begins teaching at the Conservatory
	Oct./Nov.	Receives a copy of Longfellow's *Hiawatha* from Thurber, who suggests that it might be a good subject for an opera; may have met Henry T. Burleigh
	Oct./Nov.	According to James Huneker, goes on a pub crawl with Huneker in lower Manhattan
	Nov. 29–30	Conducts his Requiem in Boston
	Dec.?	Receives the article "Negro Music" from Huneker
	Dec. 19	First sketches for "American" style, possibly based on "Negro Music"

1893   Jan. 8   Completes *The American Flag*

       Jan.–May   Composes the "New World" Symphony

       May 15?   Interviewed by James Creelman about race and music

       May–Jun.   Articles, attacks, and counterattacks in the New York Herald

       May 21   Publication of "Real Value of Negro Melodies" (Dvořák's interview with Creelman) in the *New York Herald*

       May 28   Writes "Antonin Dvorak on Negro Melodies," a letter to the editor (Creelman) of the *New York Herald*

       May 31   Dvořák's children arrive in New York

       Jun. 3   Leaves for Spillville, Iowa

       Jun. 8–23   Composes "American" Quartet, Op. 96

       Jun. 26–

       Aug. 1   Composes String Quintet in E-flat

       Jul. 7   Visited in Spillville by delegation of Czechs from Chicago

       Aug.   Takes part in Chicago World's Fair

       Aug. 12   Conducts Symphony in G, *Slavonic Dances*, and *My Country Overture* in Chicago

       Sep. 1–4   Trips to Omaha and to St. Paul, where he visits the Minnehaha Falls

       Sep. 16   Returns with family to New York City, with a stop at Niagara Falls; first weeks back are difficult for the composer

       Sep. 27–28   Conducts a concert of his works in Worcester, Massachusetts

       Oct. 2   Resumes teaching at the National Conservatory

       Late Nov.–

       Dec. 3   Composes Sonatina for Violin and Piano, containing Minnehaha Falls section

       Late Nov.–

       early Dec.   Prepares for the "New World" Symphony premiere

       Dec.?   Writes first sketches for *Hiawatha* opera (possibly quite a bit earlier)

	Dec. 12	Receives letter from Henry Krehbiel asking for an interview
	Dec. 13	Anton Seidl rehearses the "New World" Symphony
	Dec. 15	Articles about the "New World" Symphony appear in the *New York Herald* and the *New York Daily Tribune*, with material from interviews with Dvořák; the symphony receives its first public performance at a so-called open rehearsal
	Dec. 16	Official premiere of the symphony
1894	Jan. 1	Kneisel Quartet premieres "American" Quartet in Boston
	Jan. 12	Kneisel Quartet premieres Quintet in E-flat and gives first New York performance of "American" Quartet
	Jan. 23	Concert at Madison Square Garden to benefit the *New York Herald* Free Clothing Drive, advertised as "Dvorak Leads for the Fund"; conducts a 120-voice African-American choir, the program including his arrangement of Stephen Foster's "Old Folks at Home"
	Feb. 19–Mar. 1	Composes the Suite for Piano
	Mar. 9	Seidl conducts the "New World" Symphony in Brooklyn; premiere of Victor Herbert's Cello Concerto, which inspires Dvořák's Cello Concerto
	Jan. 5–Mar. 26	Composes Biblical Songs
	Apr. 18	Elected honorary member of the New York Philharmonic Society
	Apr. 28	Signs his second contract with the National Conservatory
	May 30	Arrives back in Europe
	Jun. 6	Welcomed by friends in Vysoká with a procession of Chinese lanterns
	Aug.	Creelman publishes article "Does It Pay to Study Music?" containing an interview with Dvořák, in the *Illustrated American*

	Aug. 7–27	Composes Humoresques for Piano
	Aug. 28	Composes unpublished lullaby
	Oct. 26	Arrives back in New York
	Nov. 1	Resumes teaching at the National Conservatory
	Nov. 8	Begins composing the Cello Concerto (finishes Feb. 9, 1895)
1895	Jan. 10	Honored at a reception hosted by Thurber
	Feb.?	Prepares second group of Hiawatha sketches; his article "Music in America" appears in *Harper's Magazine*
	Mar. 26	Begins A-flat String Quartet, Op. 105 (completed Dec. 30 in Bohemia)
	Apr. 16	Leaves New York
	Apr. 27	Arrives back in Prague
	May 27	Death of Josefina
	Jun.–Sep.	Revises Cello Concerto
	Aug. 17	Resigns his directorship of the National Conservatory
1896	Jan.–Apr.	Composes *The Water Goblin*, *The Noon Witch*, and *The Golden Spinning Wheel*, Opp. 107–9, tone poems based on K. J. Erben's legends
	Mar. 19	First performance of the Cello Concerto
1897	Apr. 3	Death of Brahms
	May–Aug.	Various attempts made to get Dvořák to return to the National Conservatory
1900	Apr.–Nov.	Composes opera *Rusalka*
1901	Jul. 6	Becomes director of the Prague Conservatory
	Fall	Sixtieth-birthday celebrations and concerts
1904	May 1	Death of Dvořák in Prague

PART I

Introduction

In 1892 a strange thing happened. A renowned Bohemian composer and conductor with a fear of both traveling and public performance decided to take up a post as the director of the National Conservatory of Music in New York City, where his duties would include teaching and giving several public concerts. At the time of his appointment, Antonín Dvořák was regarded by many as the second-greatest composer in Europe after Brahms and as a figure who had established himself by forging an unshakable bond between the international "German" style of instrumental music and the sounds of his Czech birthplace. Even more than a century later the question remains: Why would someone with six children who was deeply attached to his own country, who suffered from agoraphobia, and who was often morbidly afraid of travel and illness—travel all the way from Prague to New York?

I

A Composer Goes to America

The most mercenary view of Dvořák's journey holds that he came simply for the money. After all, the $15,000 yearly salary he received was a princely sum in those days, easily the equivalent of a six-figure amount today, with the caveat that very few people pulled down that kind of money in 1893. Such a salary would have been enough to ensure the security of his large family, and his letters from both home and abroad show that financial security was a serious consideration. And why not? Dvořák grew up in lower-middle-class circumstances and suffered great privations, particularly in the early stages of his career, when he sawed away as one of the few violists in the orchestra of the Provisional Theater in Prague. A rumor that he had originally completed training as a butcher's apprentice turned out to be false. However, that did not stop an English journalist from titling his interview with the composer "From Butcher to Baton," and that is the way many people thought of Dvořák in an age that loved its rags-to-riches stories. Certainly the financial security offered by the New York position appealed to him, and also to his wife, who evidently had a fine head for business.

Yet the money was surely only part of the official seduction, expertly arranged by Jeannette Thurber, the wife of a wealthy merchant. There is likely no more determined figure than she in the history of American musical institutions. This formidable organizer and philanthropist played a remarkable role in the cultural history of the country. In 1885 she started the American School of Opera. The school that grew up around it was incorporated in 1891 by an act of Congress as the National Conservatory, an institution that flourished for thirty years. The mandate of the conservatory was remarkably progressive: the most talented Americans, instead of following custom by going abroad to study with the great and near great, might now stay home and study at an excellent educational institution. Thurber's notion of quality was not class-, race-, or gender-bound. The school was to be open to women, people of color, the handicapped, and the poor. Scholarships were available and all were encouraged to apply.

But the school was only one part of her master plan. Thurber was interested in jump-starting an American music movement. Dvořák, who had been so successful in taking Bohemian music into the mainstream, was to her mind the ideal candidate. She spared no expense to land this big Bohemian fish, sending her minions to Europe in order to woo him. Dvořák, himself a determined person, was deeply impressed with her and apparently shared her vision of American music from the time of their earliest contact. As we will see, it did not hurt that she had most of the best music critics in her pocket.

These factors together might not in the end have been enough to move Dvořák out of his Czech comfort zone. We are told by Dvořák's son Otakar that the family actually took a vote to decide whether or not to go to America. Can we imagine what they discussed? One obvious issue that has not often been stressed is that Dvořák, like many Czechs, was truly in love with aspects of American culture. As a young man, Dvořák read Longfellow's *Song of Hiawatha* and fell under its spell. It served as an inspiration for the "New World" Symphony, and Dvořák spent much of his American stay trying to write an opera on the subject. It is even possible that he saw himself as Hiawatha, the hero of the piece, a musical statesman bringing the disparate strains of European music together. Dvořák was one more European irresistibly drawn to a land that was considered by most to be half "civilized" and still half wild, and his desire to spend the first summer of his American stay in distant Iowa is a real testimony to the pull of the landscape, with its prairies, plains, and Indians.

While it is likely that the lure of America was strong, there were also certain artistic pressures in Europe that Dvořák was glad to escape. Although many people thought of him as a composer of "absolute" music, pure and simple—and still think of him this way—Dvořák was ready to move in a different direction. He had just written a series of three programmatic overtures, the last of which was a dramatic tour de force based on *Othello*, begun just after he signed the contract with the National Conservatory. Extra-musical ideas had even crept into his symphonies. His triumphant Symphony in D Minor, now known as No. 7, can be regarded as a battle royal between the national and the cosmopolitan, and he confessed to an English critic that there was a story behind the slow movement of his next symphony, No. 8 in G Major.

This admission posed a problem, since the Viennese musicians who had helped establish Dvořák as a "large market" composer—big names such as Brahms, violinist Joseph Joachim, critic Eduard Hanslick, and conductor Hans Richter—all expected him to follow in the footsteps of Brahms and write works untainted by programs and lurking stories. They may have deemed him a lesser Brahms, to be sure, but a Brahms nevertheless. Dvořák had strong feelings about the older composer, and tremendous respect for him. Brahms was his great mentor, but there was no sign that Dvořák ever wanted to be another Brahms. What he really wanted was to be a kind of Wagner. It is certainly possible that Dvořák came to America in part to get away from expectations and pressures that conflicted so starkly with his own aspirations.

There were other issues as well. Dvořák had become a celebrity, a citizen of the great world, but he had no formal education in academic subjects above an elementary school level.[1] In 1890 he had stood stiffly at Cambridge University as he received an honorary doctorate. The speeches droned on and Dvořák was as pleased as he was nervous, though somewhat bored.

I shall never forget how I felt when they made me a doctor in England: the formalities and the doctors. All the faces so grave and it seemed that none could speak anything but Latin. I listened to my right and to my left and did not know where to turn my ear. And when I discovered that they were talking to me I could have wished myself anywhere else than there and was ashamed that I did not know Latin. But when I look back on it today, I must smile and think to myself that to compose a Stabat Mater is, after all, better than to know Latin.[2]

Although the story has a happy ending, and Dvořák comes up with some felicitous *bons mots*, the sense of being exposed must have been quite real.

Indeed, the year before his fateful journey to the United States, Dvořák had turned fifty years old. The event was marked by celebrations and jubilees similar to the one at Cambridge, and he must have responded in the same way. We may wonder, then, whether Dvořák's journey to New York was one part of a larger midlife crisis. Several years before, probably in the late 1880s, he had begun suffering from anxiety. Although this condition, which required him to have a companion while out and about, was at times disabling, he was not going to give up his life to it. The trip to the New World may thus have been an attempt to begin freshly in a land where he could be himself, or find himself, or even more specifically, a place where he might be cured.

Dvořák's life has always been considered particularly blameless; he's one of the "good guys" of music history—not childish like Mozart, not a Beethovenian sociopath, not a drunk like Mussorgsky or a selfish pig like Wagner. The biographical record mostly supports this verdict, yet Dvořák was no saint at the time he came to New York, he was just a normal middle-aged man. And middle-aged men, like all people, tend to have at least a few secrets. For example, we are told that around 1865 Dvořák fell in love with Josefina Čermáková, an actress in the Provisional Theater and wrote a series of songs with her in mind, but was rejected and eventually married her sister Anna.

Thirty years after composing these youthful songs, known as *The Cypresses*, Dvořák completed his Concerto for Violoncello, which apparently had Josefina as one its subjects. Indeed, after her death in 1895, Dvořák added a cadenza quoting material from a song that was, according to Dvořák biographer Otakar Šourek, one of her favorites. The very layout of this cadenza suggests something particularly intimate. Was she the love of his life, as it sometimes appears? And if so, did he come to the United States to escape a romantic attachment that, consummated, could only bring disaster?

Writing about Dvořák's "New World" Symphony the critic James Huneker said, only half in jest, that Dvořák might have come to America "to rifle us of our native ore." Could Dvořák have come in search of musical material? As a composer, Dvořák was in many ways like Mozart. He had not so much *a* style, but rather a "style of styles." One can find in the first measures of certain Mozart piano sonatas hints of a children's march, a hunt, a serious opera aria, and Bachian counterpoint, all in dizzying succession. In his *Magic Flute*, Mozart does not reside exclusively in the sagacious character of Sarastro, in Tamino the intrepid lover, or in the bird-man Papageno. He is all three at once, and none of them. In the same way, Dvořák had distinguished himself by his ability to create a broad palette of musical styles and gestures. He could sound like Brahms or emulate Bedřich Smetana's "Czechness." Sometimes little bits of Handel creep into his language, or a quick turn to the exotic. When necessary, he could invent an "Old Slavonic" style for his oratorio *Saint Ludmilla*, or draw on all-purpose spooky language in his cantata *The Specter's Bride*. For Dvořák, the attraction of America may well have been that it would be a source of new colors for his musical palette.

There are many other reasons Dvořák might have decided to take such a long voyage to such a faraway land. Maybe he wanted to be in a place where he could be the undisputed musical champion, instead of sometimes being treated as a kind of talking monkey by the more sophisticated Brahms and Joachim. In the end, it might simply have been the spirit of adventure that motivated him.

Dvořák the Reticent

It is not easy to discern the motives of any action by any person, especially since our reasons for doing something are often hidden even to ourselves. But Dvořák is particularly inscrutable, and it is even harder to understand why he made his journey. Dvořák was a reticent person, and although there is nothing wrong with holding back, those who do not explain themselves often find themselves explained by others. As we will see, Dvořák was no Wagner—only occasionally did he declare his position loud and clear. The rest of the time we are left to guess, or to assemble a character out of the available evidence.

For this reason, the Dvořák who most often peers out from biographies is, though an admirable figure, not at first a compelling one. His virtues are honesty and openness, he works devilishly hard, he has a "good Czech heart," and he loves his family. He is musically "gifted" but not an intellectual by any means (though he is not necessarily anyone's fool either). Most important, he is no snob: save for his greatness as a composer, he is the quintessential ordinary man. He has no patience with snootiness, and when he is in America he prefers drinking in the pub with his buddies in Spillville to living the high life in Manhattan.

Critics and audiences, in both the Czech Lands and outside, have come to believe that this is the "real" Dvořák. Because he is simple and therefore appears vulnerable, there is a tendency to wish to protect him. And when a particularly hellish critic struck, in the person of the vituperative Zdeněk Nejedlý, the defenders of the faith rushed to help the innocent and saintly Antonín. And no wonder: though Nejedlý today appears as a mustache-twirling villain, the anti-Dvořák crusade he led lasted for decades and seduced many critics who should have known better. For Nejedlý, Smetana marked the true path of Czech music, and Dvořák was the reactionary side that needed to be stopped. It is Nejedlý, as much as anyone else, who is responsible for a defensive hagiography at the core of Dvořák studies.

There is no doubt that the saintly, innocent Dvořák existed, and there is much evidence to assist us in creating his virtual figure from all the data. Yet how could someone so normal, so uncomplicated, have written such extraordinary music? One way to answer this is to suggest that the connection between music and the real world has been overstated and overrated. We need not live a life of emotional drama in order to write music that suggests a dramatic state, and external boldness of character is no guarantee that we will write exciting and powerful works. The extreme form of this argument is to deny that music expresses anything and to view the composer as a conjurer who creates effects by exploiting contemporary codes of expression.

That view, however, is not the one taken in this book. Rather, I assume that all personality is complex, that motivations are unclear, that all human beings have secrets, and that things are rarely as we think they are. The Dvořák who steps from the following pages is not merely a card-playing homebody but a man who lives a life of conflict and has a rich and sometimes tormented emotional life. He drinks, occasionally too much, and lifts weights to ease the tension. He is a lover, and though he suffers from anxiety, he is never a coward. Though he is modest on the surface, in his breast beats the self-assured heart of a hero, and his life's ambition is to be the great Slavic bard, or, as we will see at the very end, king of the mountain.

It may seem strange at first to search for vestiges of this more "real" Dvořák in the United States, but that is one of the best places to look for him, for two primary reasons. First, Dvořák was *news* at a time and place when many brilliant practitioners of the reportorial arts were active. While it would be unfair to suggest that his every footstep was relentlessly dogged, all his major activities were chronicled, often by several newspapers, and now and again an especially gifted scribe got very close to Dvořák and gives us a view that is at odds with the traditional one. But there is something even more significant. Josef Kovařík, an American-born Czech violist, was Dvořák's almost constant companion while he was in the United States. We will see that Dvořák suffered from agoraphobia, sometimes severe. Kovařík's presence was not a luxury; it was necessary for the composer's survival. During certain periods of time, he was with Dvořák *constantly*. Thus his reminiscences, available in published form and in letters he wrote answering queries from Šourek, give us a unique close-up of Dvořák that was never available while the composer was living in the Czech Lands.[3] Although Kovařík's memory is not perfect—occasionally he telescoped events or got a date wrong—it is clear that these special years meant an enormous amount to him and were to some extent the highlight of his life. Therefore his memories of Dvořák's time in America are especially intimate and carry great weight.

Our search for a flesh-and-blood Dvořák certainly has ramifications for understanding the biographical record. Yet we must always proceed by paradox: we can only look for Dvořák if we have a theory about who he is, but since theories tend to be wrong, we must continually dismantle views with which we have become comfortable when they contradict the evidence. This process of making theories and discarding them is time-consuming and inefficient, but compared to confronting an endless mass of data without any theory whatsoever, it is like using a computer as against counting on toes.

There is a further problem that simply cannot be avoided. In many cases the kinds of evidence for which we are searching concern the very details people have wanted to conceal. Dvořák's anxiety, his romantic life, his drinking—these are not areas and traits anyone has wished to trumpet about, particularly in the past, when the Dvořák–Smetana controversy was raging. For this reason, we must often be content to take small bits of fact and anecdote that have somehow fallen out of the mix and, treating them carefully and skeptically, fashion a new vision concerning various aspects of the composer's life. This process is always open to debate: Is there so little evidence for Dvořák's anxiety because people concealed it well or because it did not exist? Is Dvořák's romantic attachment so difficult to clarify because he had something to hide, or because there is nothing there?

While theories about Dvořák and who he was may ultimately help us understand why the composer came to America, why he chose Hiawatha for a subject, or why he was not present at the first performance of the "New World," dealing with the music requires an even more subtle approach. Dvořák's musical personality, and the way he created it, sheds light on who he was, but, of course, our idea of who he was conditions the way we approach his music. Is there a way in which we can best understand Dvořák's musical language?

Assembling the Musical Languages

As children grow, they learn language, and as composers grow they learn musical languages. The process of acquiring them is both entirely natural and somewhat artificial. A child learns a language as a matter of instinct, simply by listening, speaking, and interacting. Yet the study of language is also highly conscious at certain points, as a student seeks to build vocabulary or grammatical subtlety. A composer may naturally imbibe certain styles and approaches, but careful thought is necessary to integrate them into a larger whole, and much conscious study of musical technique is an inevitable part of the process.

The most celebrated process of learning musical languages is exemplified by the young Mozart's trips around Europe. In these now almost mythical journeys, the boy could play with J. C. Bach's Italianized sound and compare it to that of Karl Stamitz, he could listen to Renaissance-style counterpoint in Italy while conversing with the famous teacher Padre Giovanni Battista Martini, and he could learn to mock the foursquare Parisian style. Over time, Mozart assembled an arsenal of musical dialects that served him throughout his life.

We need look no further than Mozart's late operas to see how critical the notion of musical dialects is in creating a sense of meaning in instrumental works and an illusion of character in opera. The difference between the lowly servant Leporello and the aristocratic Don Ottavio in *Don Giovanni* is measured in dialect, word choice, and speech rhythm, the same way Bottom and Oberon are distinguished in Shakespeare's *A Midsummer Night's Dream.*

Dvořák resembled Mozart in his extraordinary ability to acquire and expand musical languages as he continued to compose. As a child he had learned, and indeed mastered, certain popular dance band styles of his day, and these must have played some role in the way he "heard" the world. But at the core of his professional musicianship was what could be called High Hapsburg style— the dialect created by the German composers who combined rigorous "absolute" principles with the most emotionally suggestive utterances.

The "absolute" approach to instrumental music can be traced to many sources, but my favorite is the seventeenth-century Dutch composer Jan Pieterszoon Sweelinck. Faced with some of the world's most beautiful organs and operating in a Calvinist environment that eschewed the use of instruments in church services, Sweelinck took advantage of the situation by almost single-handedly synthesizing an "absolute" vocabulary for instrumental music, creating some of the earliest nonfunctional music. That is to say, these sounds were not for marching, praying, or dancing, nor were they background for mealtime conversation. This was music for listening! At virtually the same time, Claudio Monteverdi was allowing the notion of "dramatic expression" to push his vocabulary in new directions in both his madrigals and his stage works, such as his opera *Orfeo*. In the new style, or "second practice," certain kinds of dissonance were explicitly associated with states of tension and grief.

These two strands, the attempt to articulate soundmaking that was independent of extramusical reality and the need to develop new languages to parallel new expressive states, had been intertwining as the "mainstream" of Western music since the end of the sixteenth century. According to many musicians, this synthesis had all come to a climax in the works of J. S. Bach and his spiritual heirs Mozart, Haydn, and Beethoven.

For Dvořák the first gods of this rapprochement of expressivity and abstraction were Beethoven and Mozart, followed shortly after by Schumann, Haydn, Mendelssohn, and Schubert. Later still, Dvořák seized on Brahms as the model for this tendency, and without doubt came under the older composer's influence as he began to achieve recognition outside the Czech Lands. In such works as the Symphony No. 6 in D Major, the Trio in F Minor, and *Gypsy Songs* we see the features of this style: a preoccupation with musical form and design; an attempt to elevate the idea of "seriousness" as an expressive category; the notion that the development of musical ideas within a rich tradition is paramount; and, often forgotten, the tendency to use exoticisms such as a "Gypsy" dialect to provide color and contrast.

Dvořák quickly grafted a second style and approach on to High Hapsburgism when he became obsessed with the dramatic power of Wagner and Liszt. He was one of a coterie of Czech musicians who literally stalked Wagner on the streets of Prague in the 1860s when the composer came to conduct. Our image of Dvořák as an older man with a thick beard is so pervasive that it is hard to imagine him as a twenty-two-year-old violist, only just beginning his career as a composer, darting here and there, to get a peek at Wagner.

The results in his music are clear. Several of his early symphonies and chamber works are replete with Wagnerian gestures, quotes, and modeling. His favorite work of that composer, and perhaps his favorite work of all, was *Tannhäuser*. Several of his early string quartets are gigantic pieces, steeped in Wagner. Although Dvořák's biographers speak of Wagnerism as though it was a dreadful disease from which the composer only gradually recovered, it is clear that he *never* recovered from it. Indeed, we will see that the seeds planted in the 1860s took over his life in its final decade.

As Dvořák stood there getting his honorary degree at Cambridge he must have been aware that his presence was due in part to a third dialect he had assimilated, the oratorio style, with its mixture of sincerity, piety, and a sort of contemporary archaism. His models for this style were Handel and Mendelssohn, and it was Dvořák's command of it, so popular with the English, that helped establish and secure his foothold in England. In works such as *The Specter's Bride* and later *Saint Ludmilla*, the composer dipped into the static world of musical pageant and display.

Some of the more stridently modal passages in the oratorio remind us that there is a hidden language in Dvořák as well, but one that is important in creating his style: the Pan-Slavonic. Although the *Slavonic Dances* are usually considered to be "Czech" music, it is not clear that their composer intended them as such. Indeed, Smetana—whether he is viewed as Dvořák's chief collaborator or his competitor in the creation of a Czech style—specifically wrote his own *Czech Dances* as a rebuttal to Dvořák's more cosmoslavitan approach. But it is not merely these works that are evidence of such tendencies. There are two operas, *Vanda* and *Dimitrij*, that draw on Polish and Russian subjects respectively, a fine set of mazurkas, and song collections based on Russian and Slavonic folk songs. Most notable and mysterious are Dvořák's many compositions or movements titled "Dumka." The dumka itself is based on a Ukrainian elegy, but Dvořák's use of it involves the alternation of slow, rhapsodic moments with faster sections. The very richness we find in the *Slavonic Dances*, where the composer mixes a Serbian round dance called the kolo with a Polish polonaise or Slovak *odzemek*, is a hallmark of the composer's style and a microcosm of the Hapsburg Empire's musical diversity.

Yet it is none of these dialects that made Dvořák rich and famous, but another acquired style, what I call "Czechness": a series of musical gestures that, coupled with national symbols and narratives, tell an audience that the music is to be understood in a particular national context. It was the peculiar gift of Dvořák and several of his contemporaries in various countries to convince audiences that their "national style," be it Russian, Norwegian, or Czech, was somehow a unique result of "lived experience" within the geographical and spiritual confines of the nation. In other words, while all other musical styles and dialects were viewed as important, something that any first-rate composer needed to assimilate, there was a sense that only when speaking Czechness was a composer like Dvořák truly speaking "his own language."

Czechness, Nationalism, and Other Illusions

In a famous interview in the *New York Herald*, Dvořák said that he had gone "to the simple, half-forgotten tunes of the Bohemian peasants for hints in my most serious work." While there may be a plausible side to this statement, it is also nonsense, since like all such "national" languages, Czechness à la Dvořák and Smetana was an invented illusion. From the beginning of the century, composers had experimented with creating a sense of nationality in their musical works, and the new access to such elements as a literary program allowed composers to have their works received in a particular context.

Let us take the quintessential example of Czech national style in this regard, the opening of Smetana's famous series of tone poems, *Má vlast*. The first of the poems, "Vyšehrad," opens with a series of four chords. While some listeners might be justified in feeling that this noble musical idea was lifted right out of the Overture to *Tannhäuser*, it becomes something entirely different when Smetana links the gesture programmatically with the image of the great rock Vyšehrad, the ancient seat of Czech royalty, and his audience believes it to be a specifically Czech symbol. By the time the explicit link between sound and nation is reinforced more than half a century later, when Radio Prague used these chords as the symbol of resistance in World War II, no one can convince an audience that they are anything but a purely Czech idea.

It cannot have escaped most citizens in this modern world that someone, somewhere, whether in the realm of politics, advertising, or (God forbid) the academy, is always trying to get control of their brains in order to make them do certain things. This mind control is most successfully accomplished by "encouraging" an audience to make certain kinds of associations rather than others, to group ideas in a particular way in order to come to a specific conclusion.

While ideas about nation are a significant force in our world, their impact on the intellectual climate of Dvořák's time was possibly even greater. Nationalism may be regarded as a series of theories that teach people to make certain connections among the various elements they encounter as they try to make sense of their lives. Obviously, although it is natural for human beings to make sets and groups in their environment, the process is invariably influenced by all kinds of intellectual gravitational pulls. So while a Prague merchant in 1820 might have noticed the wide Vltava River, observed a visitor in regional costume, listened to other Prague citizens speak, looked up at the castle and said, "Ain't it great," fifty years later, the merchant's *grandchild*, perhaps a poet, would have stood in the same place, noting how exquisitely *Czech* was the Vltava, taking pride in "our beautiful *Czech* costumes," rejoicing in the sound of the expressive *Czech* language, and reveling in the historical splendor of the *Czech* castle. A series of theories, political pronouncements, newspaper articles, and demonstrations had convinced our 1870s observer that a set of events, images, sounds, and tastes somehow belonged more together than apart, and that they were the most important way of making distinctions between themselves and members of *other* nationalities.

This way of confronting the world had two ramifications, one spiritual and the other economic. First it was thought that in some mystical way all these elements of the nation fused together to create a whole far greater than the sum of its parts—in short, a national essence. Thus Smetana's synthesis of popular song, aspects of Czech prosody, and historical or local subject matter with elements of Mozartian classicism and Wagnerian music drama gradually was thought to have created a kind of Czechness. The whole process began to resemble a feedback loop, whereby a set of national elements was thought to exude ineffable rays of Czechness, which then shone back on the individual elements themselves, imbuing them with ever more profound aspects of nation.

This illusion was not an idle one, but had significant impact on the dissemination of works distinguished by conspicuous national markings. A two-tiered reception was therefore created, which lasts until today. The local elements—in this case, supposedly Czech—were interpreted by people of that ethnic background as valuable because they spoke directly to them in "their own language," creating special feelings of involvement and patriotic pride. On the other hand, audiences in such places as Germany, Russia, England, and the United States could safely revel in the *exotic* character of the music. In both cases, composers such as Dvořák were able to exploit economic niches waiting to be filled. We should not forget that both the Czech patriot in Prague and the German music teacher in Leipzig bought Dvořák's *Moravian Duets* because they were "good music," but on another level the patriots probably purchased their sets because the music was about "themselves," while the teachers paid their thalers precisely because it was somehow about strangers.

We may take the *Moravian Duets* as a further example of this illusion. These duets, so popular that they virtually launched Dvořák's international career, are based on folk texts taken from the important collection of an ethnographer, František Sušil. Dvořák had access to both texts and melodies, and the original tunes are especially beautiful. What better way to imbue one's work with Czechness than to use the original melodies, or at least create new tunes based on aspects of the older ones! But Dvořák did not do that. He invented a style, combining elements of popular song with his own idiosyncratic vision of what "Moravian music" ought to be. Indeed, Moravian music was to people from Prague what "Czech music" was to the Germans, that is, charming and provincial with all the characteristics of their "primitive" people: simple and disarming, honest, colorful with elemental rhythms. If Dvořák had actually used real Moravian melodies his duets would probably have sunk like a stone. He knew, for all of his supposed naiveté, that music is an illusion. Audiences did not want real Moravian music, whatever that might be, but rather an idea of Moravianness. Dvořák's ability to create such illusions was a great part of his success.

Making American Music

Ironically, the most explicit insight into Dvořák's Czechness comes to us from looking at the way he created his American style. Some of the most revealing confessions concerning Dvořák's attitude toward national style come from a slightly negative context, in fact, an outburst. At some point during his years in the United States, Dvořák evidently became fed up with all the debates about whether his music was "American." Kovařík reports the following tantrum:

> So I am an American composer, am I? I was, I am, and I remain a Czech composer. I have only showed them the path they might take—how they should work. But I'm through with that! From this day forward I will write the way I wrote before.

This comment is filled with implications, even though, like all such comments, it needs to be treated somewhat carefully. In effect, Dvořák is suggesting a couple of things. First, he is as much as admitting that the American style of such works as the "New World" and the Spillville quartets is a mask—that far from simply writing "Dvořák's music," he is self-consciously interposing an "American filter" between his imagination and the final composition. Second, he is implying that this mask could be taken as an object lesson for American composers, and he further implies that he had in mind some recipe for creating national music. The tirade also reveals that he had developed a technique, or formula, for creating *Czech* national music. Finally, the statement raises serious questions: Did Dvořák actually renounce his American style, or were his comments just a rhetorical outburst? Is it possible for a composer to use a certain musical language for just so long and then simply drop it? What does it mean, when all is said and done, to be a "Czech composer"?

In some ways Dvořák treated his activity in the United States as a puzzle and a challenge. From the very first days of his time in this country he was an amazing magnet. He hardly had to do anything—he could practically stand in one place and various musical riches with claims to being "American" were thrust at him. Within weeks of his arrival he had encountered a great variety of things American. Almost immediately, less than two weeks after his ship docked, the celebrations accompanying the four hundredth anniversary of Columbus's voyage began, featuring parades, concerts, and speeches. Some of the marches and performers literally were playing under Dvořák's window. Within a month, Jeannette Thurber had given Dvořák a copy of Longfellow's *Song of Hiawatha* with the suggestion that he write the Great American Opera. In December of 1892 the critic James Huneker brought a journal article that suggested that "Negro melodies" included with the text be used by a "Messiah of American music" to create a new national style. We do not know exactly when, but it was probably during this time, or shortly after, that Dvořák first met Henry Thacker Burleigh, a singer and composer at the conservatory. Over a period of weeks or months, Burleigh sang dozens of songs for the composer, of the kind later called "spirituals." By the spring, Dvořák had also been taken to see Buffalo Bill's Wild West Show, with its band of Oglala Sioux Indians.

With Jeannette Thurber working tirelessly to have Dvořák create a new American style and thus create a new American school of music, and with the combination of this pressure and the stimuli that were being thrust on him, he needed to select elements that would signify this American style. And so, like any good cook, he got out his old musical recipe book and tried to adapt the ingredients to his new locale.

Flipping through the imaginary pages, he would have recalled that in most cases "national music" consisted of a series of marked musical gestures superimposed over a neutral (i.e., German) background. If one wanted to only slightly oversimplify his recipe for making Czech national music, it would look something like this:

1. Create a Czech context, either through subject matter, language, or title.
2. Choose a very few easily recognizable gestures and/or dance tropes (polka, anapest rhythms, use of parallel thirds and sixths).
3. Avoid externalizing craft; for example, stay away from fugues—smacks of German music.
4. Write at least one work that is explicitly and incontrovertibly national in intent.

Just as a single "Czech" gesture can infuse a work with the "Czech spirit," so too can an explicitly national work like the *Hussite Overture* infuse the larger oeuvre with the odor of nation.

We will see how closely Dvořák follows this process in his American works. The prime example is the "New World" Symphony. First, he makes sure his audiences know, by title and program, that the work is to be taken as "American." "New World" is not an incidental title, but a clue, a provocation, an incitement. Again, composers like to control how their works are received. Not only does Dvořák give the work an explicitly national title (after all, in Europe the "New World" meant America), but he also gives several newspaper interviews at the time of the premiere where he makes conspicuous comments about "Negro" music and alludes to passages based on Longfellow.

The musical gestures of the "New World" were part of the same gambit. He chose a few musical devices to represent his view of America. The rhythmic energy of the country was symbolized by a rhythmic figure called the "Scotch snap" with its short initial stress, while the pentatonic (five-note) scale suggested the archaic and primal qualities of America and the landscape. To evoke the physical openness of American space, the composer sometimes stretched out his melodic lines or created a special, languid form of stasis. In place of a more traditional German "symphonic logic" we have programmatic allusions and cyclical recollections. This symphony was to be the one truly nationalist "American" work of his sojourn, and, as it were, it infected the rest from afar.

Connections Anyone? Toward a New Bio-image

So, was Dvořák's American style a construct, something apart from his more real musical speech? Even though most people believe that there is a connection between the intellectual and emotional lives of composers and the music they write, such a thing is impossible to prove. It is easier to demonstrate that *our* ideas about the personality of a composer, what I call the bio-image, may have a profound effect on the way we approach the composer's music.

Listening is not a simple process. Although most of us have no problem reading a book while listening to music in the background, trying to do the opposite is nothing short of impossible. The "real world" of ideas, images, facts and figures, chord names and analytical schemes may not be accessible to us if we are deeply engaged with the musical work. While going back and forth between these worlds models the way many people listen, it is a poor goal for those wishing to penetrate most deeply into the actual present moment of a musical work. If we are always, metaphorically, running off to retrieve information, how deeply can we be involved with the music?

How then should we approach our encounter with a musical work, and what does our approach have to do with our attitude toward a particular composer or composition? It is my belief that the attitude and type of attention we bring to a musical work play an important role in what we end up hearing. This view is of particular moment in nineteenth-century music, which achieves powerful effects through contrast. In other words, Beethoven does not usually create a sense of musical drama by composing twenty minutes of dramatic music, but rather by artfully combining dramatic music with its opposite. The second, legato theme of Beethoven's Fifth Symphony is, more or less, a pastoral image, with a drone in the bass and three repetitions of the phrase. Its role in the symphony, however, is not to call attention to itself or disrupt the general sense of the piece, but rather to reinforce the affective world of the symphony's famous opening through contrast. Inversely, one purpose of the storm in Beethoven's "Pastoral" Symphony is to create a greater sense of harmony and stasis, not to threaten the sense of stability.

Just how do we know any of this? At first we might argue that "the music tells us so"; indeed, we could say that the purely musical evidence is so strong that all sane listeners would be forced to come to the same conclusion no matter what they think of Beethoven. Yet such is not the case. Our bio-image profoundly influences the way we approach a work.

We will see that such a phenomenon has had profound ramifications for the reception of Dvořák's music. Indeed, there are two words most often associated with his music: "lyrical" and "Czech." It is no secret that canonic choices have been made on that basis. The most popular works by Dvořák are the *Slavonic Dances*, the *Carnival Overture*, the Serenade for Strings, and the Largo from the "New World." Just as the idea of Czechness is a feedback loop, so too are the mini-canons we carve out of a composer's oeuvre. Our view of Dvořák causes us to favor certain works, and the repeated encounter with such works confirms our view.

Of course, there are many factors operating here. Musical works are sometimes like species and organisms fighting for living space in a densely populated ecosystem. It is thus possible to argue that Dvořák's popular works were frequently performed not solely on the basis of quality, but because there was an environment niche for them in the ecosystem of nineteenth-century music. Audiences and performers did not need another Brahms or Wagner, but an ethnic lyricist was nice to have around, writing pretty and nonthreatening music.

Whatever the reason posterity has selected various works as representative, it is clear that there are many possible ways to approach Dvořák's oeuvre. If we think him a true Brahmsian, then his real canon should involve works like the Symphonic Variations, the Trio in F Minor, the Sixth and Seventh Symphonies, and the two late quartets. Another canon could be created for Dvořák the Wagnerian, featuring the *Othello Overture*, the "New World" as a kind of mini-*Ring*, the late tone poems after K. J. Erben, and his final operas. Still other mini-canons could be created depending on whether or not we accept the diagnosis of many Dvořák biographers, who decreed that the Master was a simple rustic genius, or who take my revisionist view that he was, at least part of the time, a deeply tormented and reflective composer of intensely dramatic music.

Our search for a new view of Dvořák now takes us to the New World. In Part II of this book, we will see the composer going against his reputation as a classically oriented figure in order to create his most popular work, a hybrid between symphony and symphonic poem. Part III reveals that Dvořák, like no other composer before or since, was deeply influenced by the prodding and at times manipulation of American journalists. Certainly, without such music critics as James Huneker and Henry Krehbiel, and such enterprising reporters as James Creelman, we might never have had a "New World" Symphony, and its reception might have been entirely different. We might not even have had an "American style."

Part IV explores how landscape, whether the wide prairies or Minnehaha Falls, affected Dvořák's musical imagination, and how the composer ingested musical Americanisms in order to create a new sound. Part V seeks to probe some of the secrets, both personal and musical, that animated the composer's creative life.

Stories are largely irresistible, and the ones that are told over and over again are particularly comforting. Dvořák has been both the beneficiary and the victim of such storytelling. The urge to portray him as a modest and uncomplicated Horatio Alger figure has held sway for more than a century. Even if he were simply that and nothing more, it would take a study of the greatest subtlety to explain how a mere "humble Czech character" came to write music of such depth and texture. That Dvořák was modest, straightforward, and uncomplicated is true beyond a doubt—but he was also fully aware of his own worth, deceptive, and complex. That is why he is worth writing about, and more important, why he is no second-tier Master but rather the equal of Wagner, Beethoven, and Brahms.

PART II

Dvořák and Hiawatha

When Dvořák arrived in the United States in September 1892, he brought with him images and dreams of America, many of them embodied in Henry Wadsworth Longfellow's *Song of Hiawatha*. Published in 1855 and based on a series of legends about the Ojibway Indians, *Hiawatha* was a runaway success, quickly becoming one of the most popular works of its time. Dvořák first encountered the poem in the Czech translation of his friend the poet Josef Sládek and fell deeply in love with it. There is ample evidence that *Hiawatha* permeated his imagination throughout the American years, and was the inspiration for many passages in the inner movements of the "New World" Symphony. Yet other compositions—from the Humoresques for Piano to the Sonatina for Violin—were composed under the spell of *Hiawatha*, and some feel that the entire symphony is bathed in the glow of Longfellow's work. Finally, it is tantalizing to contemplate that one of Dvořák's great dreams, unrealized and still somewhat shrouded in mystery, was to create the Great American opera based on *Hiawatha*.

2

Hiawatha and the Largo

Often what we come to know about the genesis of a work is mere coincidence, and that is certainly the case when it comes to the role *Hiawatha* played in the creation of the "New World." Dvořák's sole testimony on the matter appeared in two New York newspapers on December 15, 1893, the day of the work's first performance. The *New York Herald* ran an interview with the composer in which he maintains that the second and third movements are based on the poem, and the rival *New York Daily Tribune* published a lengthy discussion of the symphony by its lead critic, Henry Krehbiel. According to Krehbiel, the second movement is "Dr. Dvorak's proclamation of the mood that he found in the story of Hiawatha's wooing, as set forth in Longfellow's poem," a reference to Chapter 10 of *Hiawatha*. Although there is always the possibility that someone got something wrong (I can imagine Dvořák, with his thick Czech accent, saying "Heeavata vooink"), we can be fairly sure that these comments are accurate.

Yet what kinds of things do such statements tell us? How did the composer use images from *The Song of Hiawatha*? We can get a sense of what might have happened if we look at the two sources a bit more closely.

In the spring of 1893, the *New York Herald* had broken the story about Dvořák's use of "Negro" song to lend an "American" character to his work. Six months later, the *Herald* again had a scoop. An unsigned piece (probably by head critic Albert Steinberg) that appeared in its pages on the day of the "New World" premiere featured the composer's own words:

The second movement is an Adagio. But it is different to the classic works in this form. It is in reality a study or a sketch for a longer work, either a cantata or an opera which I purpose writing, and which will be based upon Longfellow's "Hiawatha." I have long had the idea of some-day utilizing that poem. I first became acquainted with it about thirty years ago through the medium of a Bohemian translation. It appealed very strongly to my imagination at that time, and the impression has only been strengthened by my residence here.

The Scherzo of the symphony was suggested by the scene at the feast in Hiawatha where the Indians dance, and is also an essay I made in the direction of imparting the local color of Indian character to music.[1]

Although the composer never confirmed the veracity of this interview later in his life, he never challenged it either, and it furnished material for Arthur Mees's program notes used for the symphony and for several other reviews, becoming part of the official sanctioned legacy of the work.

Three points in this brief article might strike the reader as curious. The first item to raise eyebrows is Dvořák's statement that he had known *Hiawatha* for over thirty years. Published in 1855, the poem rapidly became a runaway international success, translated into many languages. It was a friend of Dvořák's, the poet Josef Sládek, who published the first Czech translation in 1870. Dvořák may have known the poem earlier through his association with Sládek, so his thirty-year comment may not be the exaggeration it initially seems. Dvořák's enthusiasm for the work was certainly part of a European fascination with America in general and its Indians in particular. As early as 1879, Dvořák might even have encountered some examples of Native American music in the periodical *Dalibor*, and his interest in such music may have been one reason he accepted the offer of a position in America.[2]

A second peculiarity that will immediately strike those familiar with the symphony is the description of the second movement as an adagio; it is, of course, the famous Largo. Why Dvořák might have mixed up these tempo indications will be addressed later.

The third anomaly is the statement that the movement is "different to the classic works in this form. It is in reality a study or sketch for a longer work" to be based on *Hiawatha*. What does the composer mean by suggesting that he deviated from standard form, and what does it have to do with *Hiawatha*?

Let us keep these curious statements in mind as we proceed to the parallel article in the *New York Daily Tribune*, published at exactly the same time, by Henry Krehbiel:

> In the larghetto we are estopped from seeking forms that are native and thrown wholly upon a study of the spirit. It is Dr. Dvorak's proclamation of the mood which he found in the story of Hiawatha's wooing, as set forth in Longfellow's poem.

Krehbiel continued to write about the work in program annotations for several decades, always insisting that this information had been supplied by the composer.[3] Indeed, correspondence between the two reveals not only that Krehbiel wrote to Dvořák almost daily around the time of the symphony's premiere, but also that they saw each other often. Two letters from Krehbiel to Dvořák are particularly important. The first, dated December 12, 1893 (three days before the premiere), refers to Krehbiel's preparation of his December 15 *Tribune* article:

> My Dear Dr. Dvořák,
> I have heard your symphony at rehearsal and read the score. I am delighted with it and intend to print an article to help people to understand and enjoy it on Friday. May I call on you on Wednesday to show you the excerpts I have made from the score?[4]

The second letter is undated but the content makes it clear that it was written on Saturday, December 16:

> Castle Hotel, Saturday
> My Dear Dr. Dvořák,
> I am overwhelmed with your kindness in making the notes on your symphony. It not only relieved me of embarrassment but enabled me also to enlist in a particular degree the interest of about 40 young ladies to whom I talked about the work Thursday night and who heard it yesterday afternoon. I have had no greater happiness from 20 years of labor on behalf of good music than has come to me from the consciousness

that I may have been to some degree instrumental in helping the public to appreciate your compositions, and especially this beautiful symphony. I wish there were some way in which I could show my gratitude for this last act of kindness but till I find out I must content myself by thanking you most cordially and sincerely.

Faithfully your friend and admirer
H. E. Krehbiel

Thus Dvořák not only met with Krehbiel during the week but also surprised him by making personal notes on the symphony. Although these notes have not turned up, the fact that they were written at all supports Krehbiel's claim that it was Dvořák himself who pointed to Hiawatha's wooing as the source of his inspiration. Dvořák confirms as much in a letter to his friend Francesco Berger about seven months later, dated June 12, 1894:

My Dearest Friend Berger,
I am sending you the extract of Mr. H. E. Krehbiel's analysis (musical editor of the New York Tribune) of my Symphony "From the New World" in e minor.[5]

Apparently Dvořák found no fault with Krehbiel's analysis—which, indeed, was essentially his own.[6]

Let us turn to the music of the Largo and see whether any of the references in these two newspaper articles make sense. The first thing we hear is a series of seven ghostly chords that move us from the key of the symphony, E major, to D-flat major. Do these sounds have anything to do with *Hiawatha*? The evidence that they do lies not so much in the newspapers as in Dvořák's American sketchbooks, where he designates his sketch for the movement as "Legenda" and labels these initial chords "Začátek legendy" (beginning of a legend). We know that the concept of legend, or ballad, played a significant role in Dvořák's imagination. From his piano duets titled *Legends* to his love for (and reliance on) the ghoulish ballads of K. J. Erben—a kind of Czech E. T. A. Hoffmann—Dvořák's fascination for magical and heroic things was endless.

Thus the opening chords act as the frame that separates the legend from the rest of the world. The modulation that mysteriously steers us to the key of D-flat major also serves as a musical "Once upon a time."[7]

According to Krehbiel, Dvořák suggested that the now famous main theme was inspired by "Hiawatha's Wooing," Chapter 10 of Longfellow's poem. This chapter, one of the longest at 283 lines, has several parts, and it is not at all clear which he may have used. It opens with Hiawatha dreaming of Minnehaha "Of the lovely Laughing Water / In the land of the Dacotahs." His grandmother, Nokomis, tells him to wed one of his own, to "Bring not here an idle maiden." Hiawatha speaks to her of Minnehaha, and then leaves to find the young maiden by "Striding over moor and meadow, / through interminable forests, / Through uninterrupted silence." We hear that "His heart outran his footsteps," and that he "Heard the Falls of Minnehaha, / Calling to him through the silence."

As this is happening Minnehaha's father, the "ancient Arrow-maker," sits in his wigwam while "At his side, in all her beauty, / Sat the lovely Minnehaha." As the old man sits, he dreams of his youth: "Of the days when with such arrows / He had struck the deer and bison," while his daughter has other dreams: "She was thinking of a hunter, / From another tribe and country, / Young and tall and very handsome."

They hear footsteps approach, and suddenly Hiawatha stands before them. Hiawatha brings a deer as an offering, and as Minnehaha serves the food, Hiawatha tells of his home and his friends. Hiawatha speaks about "the happiness and plenty / In the land of the Ojibways, / In the pleasant land and peaceful." He then asks for Minnehaha's hand in marriage. Her father is proud, and tells Minnehaha to speak. She says only, "I will follow you, my husband!"

Hiawatha and Minnehaha leave the wigwam "through the woodland and the meadow," and they hear the Falls of Minnehaha call to them, "Fare thee well, O Minnehaha!" The ancient Arrow-maker watches them with mixed feelings and bitterly reflects on her departure: "Just when they have learned to help us / When we are old and lean upon them, / Comes a youth with flaunting feathers / . . . And she follows where he leads her / Leaving all things for the stranger!"

The final lines (224–83) describe the pleasant homeward journey of Hiawatha and Minnehaha and feature two thirty-line sections, each beginning with "pleasant was the journey homeward." The first is rich in natural descriptions as the pair travel "Over meadow, over mountain, / Over river, hill, and hollow. / . . . Over wide and rushing rivers / . . . All the stars of night looked at them"; and in the second the birds and the Sun and Moon share their wisdom with the lovers: "Happy are you, Hiawatha, / Having such a wife to love you." In the last two stanzas the moon comes out and whispers to them, "O my children / Day is restless, night is quiet," and in the final lines we are told that Hiawatha has "Brought the moon-light, starlight, firelight, / Brought the sunlight of his people."

So though Krehbiel may have directed us to the correct chapter, pinning down the correct verse and determining what it has to do with the Largo is no easy matter. The least problematic reading takes shape if we take Krehbiel's words literally: "It is Dr. Dvorak's proclamation of the mood which he found in the story of Hiawatha's wooing. / . . ." In other words, Dvořák read the chapter, or imagined the chapter, and a musical thought came into his head, or was called forth by him, an idea suggested by the general events described. If we believe that, it would be foolish to look for a particular moment in the chapter to which the music corresponds. Could this be the case?

Let us consider the nature of the musical material as we find it in the main theme of the Largo (CD 1). Dvořák here draws on one of the most venerable of Western musical traditions: the pastoral language. First appearing toward the end of the sixteenth century, this musical dialect was associated from the outset with two main programmatic series of images, the beauty of nature and the purity of Christmas. Its most notable features are the use of a drone, usually in the bass, over which simple, stepwise diatonic tunes are heard, often with parallel thirds and sixths (CD 2).

It is easy to see how this language became a musical metaphor for idyllic spaces. The static harmony suggests a realm where nothing changes, while the simplicity and consonant sonorousness of the upper voices convey the sense that this timeless realm is one of sweetness. In other words, the pastoral language lacks the very things that stand as musical metaphors for change and flux: short- and long-range dissonance.

Dvořák and virtually all his contemporaries dipped into it regularly; it permeates the works of such composers as Beethoven, Brahms, Berlioz, Schubert, Mahler, and Smetana, and it is the quintessential musical analog to landscape painting. So we might surmise that Dvořák is painting a landscape in this movement. Further, taking all the evidence we have concerning Dvořák's intentions into consideration, it would not be foolish to think that he was painting an American landscape. One of the reasons, of course, that it has been so easy to conflate Dvořák's activities and assume that the "New World" Symphony was written in Spillville, Iowa, is the desire of many people, then and now, to want the work to somehow be based on "reality." In that case, the portrait should be an "authentic" reckoning of the open American spaces. We know differently, of course: since Dvořák wrote the symphony entirely in New York, the only prairie he had seen was that of his imagination, ignited by Longfellow's poem and other influences.

There are two passages in Chapter 10 of the poem that are the most likely to have fired Dvořák's imagination. The first is the place where Hiawatha describes to the Arrow-maker the pleasant and peaceful land of the Ojibway. Remembering that the pastoral world is a zone where nothing changes, such tone painting could well have been inspired by the image of Eden.[8]

The other compelling source is the languid homeward journey of Hiawatha and Minnehaha that occurs at the end of the chapter. Here Longfellow offers us a timeless image of enduring beauty as the lovers travel "very slowly" through the pristine and primeval American spaces.

> *Pleasant was the journey homeward,*
> *Through interminable forests,*
> *Over meadow, over mountain,*
> *Over river, hill, and hollow.*
> *Short it seemed to Hiawatha,*
> *Though they journeyed very slowly,*
> *Though his pace he checked and slackened*
> *To the steps of Laughing Water.*

Yet any interpretation that stresses the idyllic aspects of the music clashes with the reality that over the years many listeners have found the movement nostalgic, dark, and melancholy, or even elegiac. In fact, there is another critical tradition for the movement, more influential than the one derived from the two contemporary newspaper stories. It can be traced to an article, "Antonín Dvořák in America," written by the Czech scholar Kateřina Emingerová in 1919. Supposedly based on materials provided by Dvořák's widow, the study refers to an article in an American newspaper:

> The writer [of the article] acknowledges with gratitude and admiration Dvořák's statement that the second movement was composed under the influence of Longfellow's "Hiawatha" (funeral in the forest).[9]

Otakar Šourek based his discussion of the Largo at least in part on Emingerová's article,[10] and because of the stature of Šourek and his four-volume study of the composer, published over an eighteen-year period from 1916 to 1933, his assessment has served as the source for numerous other biographers, including John Clapham. Clapham's assertion that "the funeral of Minnehaha in the forest, however, inspired the Largo of the symphony" became the source for almost all subsequent Dvořák biographies in English.[11]

The information in Emingerová's article is puzzling, since no American newspaper article says anything about a forest funeral. The closest is a passage in W. H. Henderson's article in the *New York Times* on December 17, 1893, in which he talks about the mood of the Largo and refers to Chapter 20 of *Hiawatha*, "The Famine":

> In the adagio of his symphony he has embodied a great sadness, tinged with desolation. . . . When the star of empire took its blood and sweat and agony and took its way over those mighty western plains agony and bleaching human bones marked its course. Something of this awful buried sorrow of the prairie must have forced itself upon Dr. Dvorak's mind when he saw the plains after reading "The Famine."

Though this article is an unlikely source for Emingerová, it does testify to the impression made by the movement. How does an American pastoral come to have a funereal spirit? Could Krehbiel be wrong about its connection to the wooing?

To answer this question we have to explore the middle section of the movement. Here the key changes from major to minor, and the pastoral tone is replaced by a descending figure repeated several times over tremolos (CD 3). It is not possible to establish any authoritative connection between this figure and the poem. The only (tempting) reference available comes from *The Concert Companion* by Robert Bagar and Louis Biancolli (New York: McGraw-Hill, 1947), but the source is not given: "To his pupil Shelley, Dvořák explained a transitional passage in the Largo, marked Un poco più mosso, as the Indian girl's sobbing as she bids Hiawatha farewell." While there is no moment in *Hiawatha* when a sobbing girl appears, if this quote truly represented Dvořák's words, it is surely a reference to Minnehaha's "sudden cry of anguish" when she calls to Hiawatha with her final breath.

If the first part of the middle section is possibly tied to the tradition of "Lament," the second, with its lugubrious clarinets and "walking" bass part, plunges us into quite another place (CD 4). Is there any way to determine its source?

As we have seen, the documentary evidence for a funeral is not unequivocal, especially considering our inability to determine Emingerová's source. Let us return for a moment to the short passage from Emingerová's article cited above and ponder the parentheses that surround the words "funeral in the forest." Parentheses like these are both frustrating and somehow appealing. At first they imply that the newspaper article identified the source of the movement as the "forest funeral." In that case, Emingerová's view is problematic, because no such article has turned up. But the parentheses can simply mean that she is adding pertinent information to the *Herald* article of December 15 from a special source. What could that source be? Again, we have no proof, but Emingerová states that it was the composer's widow who provided the scrapbook that served as the basis for the article, so possibly such information about the movement came from her.[12]

Others have, albeit loosely, suggested a connection between the movement and something darker. Henry Thacker Burleigh, Dvořák's sometime student and friend, wrote to *Musical America* in 1924 that Dvořák had written the Largo "after he had read the famine scene in Longfellow's *Hiawatha*. It had a great effect on him and he wanted to interpret it musically."[13] Even though Burleigh's reminiscence was recorded years after the fact, it comes from someone who may well have been more intimately associated with Dvořák than Krehbiel ever was.

In trying to figure out how Dvořák might have proceeded in this case, his own words about the difference between this movement and a "normal" adagio are revealing. His remarks imply that it is precisely the gravitational pull of the program that alters the traditional scheme. There is no reason why this "sketch for an opera or cantata" could not have several scenes stitched together. Also, the sketch for the middle section of the movement does not appear with the original sketch for the outer part of the Largo; it is found later in the sketchbook, making it easy for us to conclude that far from being composed in one white heat, the movement had various sources of inspiration.

Yet the most potent argument that can be made about the poetic sources of the middle section is a musical one. Dvořák frequently invoked the funeral march, both as a clear symbol of death in such works as *Holoubek, Rusalka, The Specter's Bride,* and *The Hero's Song* and in a more abstract way in Symphony No. 3, the Piano Quintet in A Major; Symphony No. 8, the String Quartet in G Major, and even the Cello Concerto.

The funeral imagery can be deduced from various features of the section. Most obviously, we have the shift from the more rhapsodic Lament. With almost no preparation (we should bear in mind Dvořák's comment about formal anomalies), a march of some sort appears, coded for all to hear. Another feature that suggests the Dvořákian funeral piece is the tremolo writing in the violins and later in the violas. It has even been pointed out that the theme itself resembles a famous passage in Beethoven's "Marche funèbre" from the "Eroica" Symphony.[14]

If this is, as I believe, a funeral piece, why could it not apply to the sadness of the ancient Arrow-maker?[15] The answer lies in a passage that goes beyond the march in increasing agitation to a depiction of the act of dying itself (CD 5). The chromatic descent, the cessation of the tremolos, and the wrenching, agonizing harmonization as the descent continues are not a musical response to the bitterness of Minnehaha's father but to something far more tragic. Indeed, the passage is almost identical in formula (and in key) to one of the concluding passages of Dvořák's opera *Rusalka,* written in 1901. The Prince has just died and the Water Sprite as Greek Chorus intones the famous "Beda" ("Alas"). We have a chromatic descent followed by a funeral march, based on the motive we hear throughout

Rusalka (CD 6). Such musical gestures have no place in Chapter 10 of *Hiawatha*, but they certainly depict the death and funeral of Minnehaha beginning with these lines from Chapter 20, "The Famine":

> *"Ah!" said she, "the eyes of Pauguk*
> *Glare upon me in the darkness,*
> *I can feel his icy fingers*
> *Clasping mine amid the darkness!*
> *Hiawatha! Hiawatha!"*

Hiawatha hears Minnehaha's "cry of anguish" and the "moaning wailing" of Nokomis; Dvořák heard them as well, and they, I believe, inspired the funeral passage. One further piece of evidence supports this hypothesis. When talking with his student Camille Zeckwer, Dvořák once announced: "What can be more funereal in sound than the low notes of the clarinet?" And it is precisely these low-range clarinets that put forward the dirge after the chromatic descent in CD 5. Undoubtedly, Dvořák had these lines from "The Famine" in mind when he composed the funeral march:

> *Then they buried Minnehaha;*
> *In the snow a grave they made her,*
> *In the forest deep and darksome,*
> *Underneath the moaning hemlocks;*
> *Clothed her in her richest garments,*
> *Wrapped her in her robes of ermine,*
> *Covered her with snow like ermine;*
> *Thus they buried Minnehaha.*

This tragic vision is followed by a passage that could have come right out of Beethoven's "Pastoral" Symphony (CD 7). Krehbiel had this to say about it:

There is a striking passage in the middle of the movement, constructed out of a little staccato melody, announced by the oboe and taken up by one instrument after another until it masters the orchestra, as if it were intended to suggest the gradual awakening of animal life on the prairie scene, and striking use is made of trills, which are exchanged between the instrumental choirs as if they were the voices of night and dawn in converse.

"The gradual awakening of animal life" is certainly in line with the bird-calls we hear in the music. Krehbiel's description squarely fits the second of the passages identified above, the homeward journey at the end of Chapter 10:

> *Pleasant was the journey homeward!*
> *All the birds sang loud and sweetly*
> *Songs of happiness and heart's-ease;*
> *Sang the bluebird, the Owaissa,*
> *"Happy are you Hiawatha,*
> *Having such a wife to love you!"*
> *Sang the Robin, the Opeechee,*
> *"Happy are you, Laughing Water,*
> *Having such a noble husband!"*

Although Krehbiel's use of the expression "as if it were" makes it unclear whether he is speaking for Dvořák or for himself, these images were most likely suggested by the composer. After the considerable amount of time he spent discussing the work with Dvořák in an attempt to be accurate, it would be peculiar for Krehbiel to resort to his own impressionistic reading. Most likely Krehbiel and Dvořák agreed that focusing too much on programmatic details might distract the listener from the musical content of the symphony, and that, indeed, the listener should have only very general images. Support for this view comes from Krehbiel's own words near the beginning of the article: "If there is anything Indian about Dr. Dvorak's symphony it is only the mood inspired by the contemplation of Indian legend and romance, and that is outside the sphere of this discussion."[16]

One main problem arises with the entire scenario as I have presented it. If the main theme of the movement was inspired by the joyous homeward journey of Minnehaha and Hiawatha, why did it sound to so many people as a lament, why does it strike us today as possessing such a quality of nostalgia and sadness, and why doesn't it sound like a journey? Is the theme connected, as is often assumed, with Dvořák's homesickness for Bohemia? To understand this paradox, let us try to imagine a scenario for how Dvořák put the movement together.

The first sketch we have for the main theme is marked "Andante." If we hum the Largo theme at double speed, we can get an idea of how Dvořák must first have conceived it: as the homeward journey of Hiawatha and Minnehaha, or possibly as a tableau suggesting the peace and plenty enjoyed by the Ojibway. Within at most a few weeks, Dvořák decides, in our scenario, to combine this image with music generated in part by pondering the death and funeral of Minnehaha. In the period between March 14, 1893, the date that the fair copy was completed, and the premiere of the symphony in December, the darkness of the middle section exerts a gravitational pull on the entire movement, slowing it down. Though subtle, this change would powerfully influence the effect of the piece on the listener. The change shows itself graphically in the manuscript, where the composer has crossed out "Andante" and replaced it with "Largo."

There is one more element that may have affected the final tempo of the movement, and the impression it makes. The first part of the Largo was doubtless inspired by Dvořák's imaginary vision of the open spaces of America. Imaginary, of course, because when he first conceived the movement, he had never seen the prairie and forests depicted in Hiawatha. For him, as for so many others on the East Coast, such visions were supplied by poets and writers such as Longfellow and James Fenimore Cooper or by showmen like Buffalo Bill. When Dvořák did finally encounter the prairie in the summer of 1893, his response was powerful and surprising. Here is a now famous snippet from a letter he wrote to Emil Kozánek on September 15, 1893, exactly three months before the premiere of the symphony:

It is very strange here. Few people and a great deal of empty space. A farmer's neighbor is often 4 miles off. Especially in the *prairies* there are endless acres of field and meadow and that is all you see (I call it the Sahara). You don't meet a soul (here they ride only on horseback) and you are glad to see the huge herds of cattle in the woods and meadows

which, summer and winter, are out to pasture in the broad fields. . . .
And so it is very "wild" here, and sometimes very sad—sad to despair.[17]

It is possible that over the summer Dvořák's changing conception of the prairie, from something idyllic to something slightly sad, had also colored his view of the Largo; the imaginary landscape through which it passed had become clarified and subdued, and this change could have altered his conception of the movement, resulting in the revised tempo marking. Thus in writing that there was, in the Largo, "possibly also a suggestion of the sweet loneliness of a lovely night on the prairies," Krehbiel may have been representing Dvořák's thoughts *after* the composer seen the prairies and mixed them with the sadness of Minnehaha's death, thereby diverging substantially from his original impulse.

Dvořák's final change, recorded by Kovařík, was abrupt and decisive:

Seidl took up the second movement again in a much slower tempo than imagined by master. . . . On the way home master commented that Seidl has "quite drawn out" the introduction to the first movement, and also the second movement—then he paused in silence—but after a while he added:—"but it is much better in this way!" And when we reached home, he took his own score, prescribed a slower Metronome for the introduction of the first movement—in the second movement he crossed out the "Larghetto" and prescribed "Largo!"

While we may naturally wish the various images that inspired the Largo to compose a genuine narrative, there is no evidence that Dvořák was thinking in these terms. For some reason—perhaps his desire to have the work taken as "American" by his audience—Dvořák opened the doors of his composer's workshop to two reporters on one day in December 1893. Those doors never reopened.

In the end, we should not begrudge a composer who has labored so painstakingly on a work the right to control as precisely as possible the conditions under which the composition is apprehended. The magnificent Largo has its effect. That we can step outside our engagement to consider such things as honeymoons, funeral marches, and the prairie at night only adds to its power.

Postscript: The Largo Gets a Text

The Largo has had quite a career apart from Dvořák, as a gospel song, a bagpiper's dream, a jazz band tune, and a theme in film scores. The person who started all that was William Arms Fisher, a student of Dvořák's. His 1922 vocal arrangement of the English horn melody gained enormous popularity. In a short preface, Fisher wrote that Dvořák told him after his return from Spillville that "he had been reading Longfellow's *Hiawatha*, and that the wide stretching prairies had greatly impressed him."[18]

In a letter Fisher elaborated on how he came to write the words:

> As a musician, I am inclined to look with suspicion on any arrangement based on the work of the great composers. One day, in the summer of 1922, when somebody put in front of me the Largo in a piano arrangement, I played it only for old times' sake. However, as I played, I heard in my mind words coming unbidden: "Goin' home—I'm going home." I wrote them down and took my idea home. Obeying my inner impulse, I elaborated it accordingly.[19]

There is no reason to assume that Dvořák told Fisher the source of his Largo, but the words he chose, with their strange combination of a homeward journey and a funeral, are eerily apt, considering the source of the composer's images:

> *Goin' home, goin' home, I'm a-goin' home;*
> *Quiet like, some still day, I jes' goin' home*
> *It's not far, jes' close by, through an open door*
> *Work all done, care laid by, gwine to fear no more.*
> *Mother's there 'spectin' me, Father's waitin' too,*
> *Lots o' folk gather'd there. All the friends I knew*
> *All the friends I knew. Home, home, I'm goin' home.*

3

The "Local Color of Indian Character" and the Scherzo

Determining the relationship between the Largo and *Hiawatha* is challenging, and even though the composer told us where to look, the field is large. With the Scherzo the situation is almost reversed. When Dvořák told the interviewer from the *New York Herald* that "the Scherzo of the symphony was suggested by the scene at the feast in Hiawatha where the Indians dance," there is only one place he could have meant: Hiawatha's wedding feast, as described in the poem's Chapter 11. Critics have noted the similarities between the music and Longfellow's description of the dance. The problem here is that the movement goes on quite a bit after this. Did Dvořák abandon *Hiawatha* after the dance? To understand just what Dvořák did we must look closely at the dance and what follows it.

The celebration of Hiawatha's wedding, one of the most fascinating parts of the poem, is rich in detail. After a short introduction, the scene is set with a description of raiment, tableware, and victuals, the polished bowls and ivory spoons, the robes of fur, and the buffalo meat. Hiawatha and Minnehaha serve their guests but do not eat. Old Nokomis fills the pipes and calls on Pau-Puk-Keewis to dance "The Beggar's Dance." Pau-Puk-Keewis is brought to life as an athlete and a gambler, a charmer and a dandy. He is dressed in fine soft doeskin, with fringes, quills, beads, and feathers. His face is "Barred with streaks of red and yellow, / Streaks of blue and bright vermilion."

The description of the dance is brief:

> *First he danced a solemn measure,*
> *Very slow in step and gesture,*
> *In and out among the pine-trees,*
> *Through the shadows and the sunshine,*
> *Treading softly like a panther,*
> *Then more swiftly and still swifter,*
> *Whirling, spinning round in circles,*
> *Leaping o'er the guests assembled,*
> *Eddying round and round the wigwam,*
> *Till the leaves went whirling with him,*
> *Till the dust and wind together*
> *Swept in eddies round about him.*
>   *Then along the sandy margin*
> *Of the lake, the Big-Sea-Water,*
> *On he sped with frenzied gestures,*
> *Stamped upon the sand, and tossed it*
> *Wildly in the air around him;*
> *Till the wind became a whirlwind,*
> *Till the sand was blown and sifted*
> *Like great snowdrifts o'er the landscape,*
> *Heaping all the shores with Sand Dunes,*
> *Sand Hills of the Nagow Wudjoo!*

It is easy to understand why investigators such as Clapham and Šourek, exploring the link between the poem and the music, focused on these lines—there appears to be a clear connection between the events in the Scherzo and the unfolding of the dance. Both begin under control, measured, "treading softly." While Longfellow's dance actually accelerates, Dvořák creates an analog through dynamic changes, texture, and syncopation. A hypothetical model of the relationship between the poem and the beginning of the Scherzo is shown below. Of course, it really only works if we recall the four-line introduction to the dance:

> *To the sound of flutes and singing,*
> *To the sound of drums and voices,*

Rose the handsome Pau-Puk-Keewis,
And began his mystic dances.

Surely this is the source for the Beethovenian introduction, with its "drums and voices."

Correspondence between Scherzo and *Hiawatha* (CD 8: melodrama)

To the sounds of flutes and singing, *To the sound of drums and voices,* *Rose the handsome Pau-Puk-Keewis.*	Flutes and drums; introductory.
First he danced a solemn measure . . . *Treading softly like a panther.*	Quiet plucked strings and staccato woodwinds, create a "pantherlike" effect as if something powerful is stalking.
Then more swiftly and still swifter, *Whirling, spinning, round in circles,*	Quick scale passages going up and down create "whirling" effect and sense of acceleration.
Leaping o'er the guests assembled,	"Leaping" up an octave, fortissimo orchestral sound
Eddying round and round the wigwam, *Till the leaves went whirling with him* *. . .*	
Stamped upon the sand, and tossed it *Wildly in the air around him;* *Till the wind became a whirlwind,* *Till the sand was blown and sifted* *Like great snowdrifts o'er the landscape*	Main theme in bass line; chromatic syncopation in the woodwinds suggests something out of control and off kilter, while the final brief passage, with its stark repetition, suggests power and obsession.

This chart provides us with a nice example of the formal difference between literature and music. In Longfellow's poem the dance occurs just once, and it is over and done with in twenty-two lines of text. But Dvořák is writing a scherzo, which uses a fairly set pattern of repetitions. To insinuate that Dvořák wants Pau-Puk-Keewis to do his "mystic dance" five times—for that is the number of times we hear this music in the

Scherzo—is absurd. Indeed, Dvořák gives the general impression of Pau-Puk-Keewis's dance by increasing intensity while decreasing predictability.

The dance itself may also have been inspired by the character of the dancer. Pau-Puk-Keewis is a disruptive force in the land of the Ojibway. In a pastoral realm, everything is predictable. Pau-Puk-Keewis with his charm, his athletic gifts, and his eternal restlessness is the symbol of all those things that threaten the Edenic existence of Hiawatha and his friends. Thus his dance is a challenge, in both its intensity and its fierce determination to break basic rules.

Pau-Puk-Keewis is an illusionist, a magician. Who can say what happened as he danced? Perhaps he sat in one place for the entire time and forced his audience to dream the dance. Like an artist, he controls time and space, forcing the onlookers to understand the world, at least momentarily, from his perspective. We have intimations of this control in the six lines that follow the conclusion of the dance:

> *Thus the merry Pau-Puk-Keewis,*
> *Danced his Beggar's Dance to please them,*
> *And, returning, sat down laughing*
> *There among the guests assembled,*
> *Sat and fanned himself serenely*
> *With his fan of turkey-feathers.*

After the fierce wildness, Pau-Puk-Keewis is neither sweaty nor distressed; he "sits down laughing" and fans himself "serenely." Though his audience may have been swept into the dance, the dancer reveals his own lack of engagement, leaving his identity separate from the activity.

Up to this point, the connection between the poem and Scherzo is hard to dispute, especially in light of the composer's cue, though we might question its significance. Yet we have considered only the opening of the Scherzo! Where does the rest of the movement come from, and does it also reflect the composer's fascination with Native Americans in general and *Hiawatha* in particular? Writing about the Largo in the interview cited above, Dvořák said that it was "different to the classic works in that form." In saying that, he was certainly referring to departures from his "normal" practice mandated by the use of a program. Are there any such departures in the Scherzo?

One of the peculiarities of this movement is the way the pastoral E-major episode just after this opening almost fools the listener into thinking that the Trio, or the second large section of the Scherzo, has arrived. For reference purposes, let us recall the old formal model of Scherzo–Trio–Scherzo, or, broken down further, ABA CDC ABA.

While it is possible in this scheme for B to provide contrast to A, they are much more likely to be closely related. For them to be almost antithetical, as in the "New World," is extremely rare. In order to suggest a reason for this contrast we may return to the very beginning of Chapter 11 where the "plot" of Hiawatha's wedding feast is laid out:

> *You shall hear how Pau-Puk-Keewis,*
> *How the handsome Yenadizze*
> *Danced at Hiawatha's wedding;*
> *How the gentle Chibiabos*
> *He the sweetest of musicians,*
> *Sang his songs of love and longing;*
> *How Iagoo, the great boaster,*
> *He the marvellous story-teller,*
> *Told his tales of strange adventure,*
> *That the feast might be more joyous,*
> *That the time might pass more gayly,*
> *And the guests be more contented.*

So the wedding consists of three events: a dance, a song, and a story. If Dvořák is drawing on the poem as his source, it makes sense to assume that he presented wedding images in succession. Let us look then at the part of the poem that frames the song.

After the dance has ended there is a call for another entertainment:

> *Then they said to Chibiabos,*
> *To the friend of Hiawatha,*
> *To the sweetest of all singers,*
> *To the best of all musicians,*

"Sing to us, O Chibiabos!
Songs of love and songs of longing . . ."

If Hiawatha, with his rational mien, is the Apollonian figure in the epic, and the elusive Pau-Puk-Keewis a mixture of Dionysian sexuality and the quicksilver movements of Hermes, then Chibiabos is the Orpheus of the Ojibway. Just as Orpheus charms the denizens of Hades to reclaim the slain Euridice, Chibiabos uses music to create a semirational universe beyond words. He is sweetness itself, the best friend of Hiawatha and one who with his predictable beauties ensures the continuation of the blissful empire.

The bard begins to sing "in accents sweet and tender" and "in tones of deep emotion." His lyric is one of the most beautiful passages in the poem, mixing the exotic locale of the open prairie with words reminiscent of the Song of Songs:

"Onaway! Awake, beloved!
Thou the wild-flower of the forest!
Thou the wild-bird of the prairie!
Thou with eyes so soft and fawn-like!
  "If thou only lookest at me,
I am happy, I am happy,
As the lilies of the prairie,
When they feel the dew upon them!"

In all, the song of Chibiabos is by turns sensitive, sensuous, reflective, and erotic.

Could the second section of the Scherzo have been inspired by these words? Quite likely. First, and most obvious, the passage immediately follows the dance, and the unusual musical design and the transition to a completely different musical vocabulary suggest that Dvořák was mirroring the moods of the poem.

He may not even have been setting the text, as such, but merely invoking the contrast between the wild dance and a lyrical ballad—the former involving issues of musical process, as it changes from one state to another, the latter being more static. Indeed, in keeping with the lyrics, the E-major passage has all the characteristics of a pastoral love song, with very little tension, harmonic or otherwise. The repeated pattern in the bass line and the constant reiteration of E on the first beat of almost every measure conjure up a world of unchanging consonance, and there is even a hidden "bagpipe" drone in the bassoon part. Yet this is not a simple pastoral but a romance as well, yearning for climax, as the gradually building intensity of the passage suggests.

We can go further and see elements of the text embedded more solidly in the musical setting. Proof that Dvořák adored this poetic passage and a strong suggestion that the E-major section is a setting of the text can be found in Dvořák's American Sketchbook No. 5.[1] Here we have a charming setting of the text for voice alone (CD 9). Once we factor out the differences mandated by the Scherzo's triple meter, the settings have much in common. Both begin with a leap followed by a pentatonic descent and share a variety of rhythmic details. Thus it is not hard at all to hear the text hovering over the E-major section of the symphony (CD 10).

So far I have suggested that Dvořák used a dance and song as models for characteristic passages from the Scherzo. But a third event occurs at the wedding feast: Iagoo's tale, called "The Son of the Evening Star."

If two out of the three parts of the movement are based on images from the poem, we might expect to find something similar in the Trio. Yet before we even bother to link this section with the symphony we ought to remember what almost all the commentators have said: this part, more than any other, sounds distinctively "Czech," almost as if a part of the *Slavonic Dances* found its way into this "New World" work. Here is no pentatonic recollection of African-Americans or Native Americans, but the major tonality and the waltzlike rhythms of the Hapsburg realm (CD 11). We may remember that it was a departure from normal procedure that made us suspect a program in the song of Chibiabos. Is there such a musical clue here?

I believe there is. The second section of the Trio, though it maintains a continental veneer, is filled with piquant modulations and some unusual trills that finally take over (CD 12). When the main material of the Trio returns, it takes over the trills as an accompaniment figure in the violins. Could these strange images have been called forth by the story, the third event at Hiawatha's wedding feast? To test this theory we must look more closely at Iagoo's story.

"The Son of the Evening Star," at 375 lines, is the longest chapter in *Hiawatha*, and with the preceding chapter it forms the centerpiece of the poem as a whole. It begins with the fall of evening and the appearance of the evening star. Then Iagoo declaims:

> *"Behold it!*
> *See the sacred Star of Evening!*
> *You shall hear a tale of wonder,*
> *Hear the story of Osseo,*
> *Son of the Evening Star, Osseo!"*

The story tells of a hunter who lived with ten beautiful daughters in the Northland. All of them married young and handsome warriors, with the exception of the youngest, Oweenee, who wed an old man named Osseo ("Broken with age and weak with coughing, / Always coughing like a squirrel.") Though old and infirm, his spirit was beautiful because he had descended from the Evening Star.

The handsome young husbands, some of whom had been rejected by Oweenee, mock the old man. One day, while on the way to a great feast (the wedding itself?), Osseo looks up to the sky and says, "Pity, pity me my father." The other couples laugh at him. But as they walk they come to an uprooted tree. Osseo walks into one end of it and comes out the other as a young man, his youth restored. At the same time, Oweenee is turned into an old woman.

During the feast, Osseo sits silently, "looking dreamily and sadly." He hears a voice telling him the spells that have bound him are broken. Suddenly the lodge begins to rise, and as it does, it is transformed, turning to silver and crimson. The couples who have mocked Osseo are turned into birds. Oweenee, however, remains an old woman until Osseo gives "another cry of anguish" and her beauty returns.

Osseo's father appears in a radiant halo and tells him to hang a birdcage on the doorway of his wigwam. He warns Osseo about the evil musician who had turned him into an old man. By and by a son is born to Oweenee and Osseo. They make a toy bow and arrow for him and allow him to shoot at the birds. Finally he hits one, and it changes into a beautiful young woman with the arrow in her breast. When her blood spills on the ground, all spells are broken. The birds resume their mortal shape, only now they are little people, like pygmies. On summer evenings they can still be seen flitting about the woodlands.

Iagoo finishes his story with an injunction to his listeners: "Let them learn the fate of jesters." The chapter ends with another song by Chibiabos, about a maiden's lamentation for her Algonquin lover.

There is one part of the poem, beginning at line 135, that is a possible source for the Trio. A voice is heard from afar, "Coming from the starry distance, / Coming from the empty vastness, / Low, and musical, and tender"; it announces that all old spells are broken. The voice goes on:

"Taste the food that stands before you;
It is blessed and enchanted,
It has many virtues in it,
It will change you to a spirit.
All your bowls and all your kettles
Shall be wood and clay no longer;
But the bowls be changed to wampum,
And the kettles shall be silver;
They shall shine like shells of scarlet,
Like the fire shall gleam and glimmer.
*   "And the women shall no longer*
Bear the dreary doom of labor,
But be changed to birds and glisten
With the beauty of the starlight,
Painted with the dusky splendors
Of the skies and clouds of evening!"
What Osseo heard as whispers,
What as words he comprehended,
Was but music to the others,
Music as of birds afar off,
Of the whippoorwill afar off,

Of the lonely Wawonaissa
Singing in the darksome forest.

Though Dvořák could easily have modeled the radiant C-major opening of the Trio on the passage above, it is more likely that he used the spell-casting sequence as his source. The rising line, C–E–G, would then refer to the rising action described below, while the plodding rhythm would be an attempt to render Longfellow's metrical scheme:

And they felt it rising, rising,
Slowly through the air ascending,
From the darkness of the tree-tops
Forth into the dewy starlight,
Till it passed the topmost branches;
And behold! the wooden dishes
All were changed to shells of scarlet!
And behold! the earthen kettles
All were changed to bowls of silver!

The musical sequences with their trills probably refer to the magical act whereby the mocking couples are turned into creatures of the air (CD 13):

All the sisters and their husbands,
Changed to birds of various plumage.
Some were jays and some were magpies,
Others thrushes, others blackbirds;
And they hopped, and sang, and twittered,
Perked and fluttered all their feathers,
Strutted in their shining plumage . . .

The last peculiar trills probably represent both the sound of the birds and the action described in the last line of the section (CD 12 again):

And their tails like fans unfolded.

The entire musical passage fits the poem quite well (CD 14: melodrama). It must also have been great fun for the composer to write. After all, he was a noted bird fancier, keeping a famous flock of pigeons at his summer house in Vysoká; he once proclaimed: "Do you hear them? How they sing! *They* are the real masters." There are many birdsong passages in his music. In one of the sketches for his contemplated *Hiawatha* opera, we find a passage marked "birds," and it is well known that the "American" Quartet absorbed the sound of a bird, possibly the scarlet tanager. The somber opening bars of the Eighth Symphony are interrupted by bird calls in the flutes, and the Cello Concerto has various birdlike passages in the slow movement. Dvořák once remarked to someone that the sound of his pigeons would make it into the "New World" Symphony.[2]

Though the relationship between the poem and the music becomes less clear as the movement goes on, Dvořák surely depended on the poem for several of the fundamental musical ideas. There are, however, at least three questions about the Scherzo that remain unanswered. The first is suggested by the title of this chapter. Where should we look for the "Indian color" that Dvořák promises us in the *Herald* interview? This question is important, considering Dvořák's changing comments on the role of Indian music in the New World, and particularly his perplexing comment, seized upon by many of his detractors, that "Negro" and "Indian" music were "practically the same." His supporters, then and now, respond that he was talking solely about the use of pentatonic gestures in both musics. We will see later whether he treated both worlds as if they were the same.

There is another question as well. Considering the composer's reliance on the poem, how do we characterize the movement? If it contains within it the seeds of the dance, the song, and the story, is it a piece of program music, and are its narrative elements of any consequence for us?

There are several adequate responses to this question. Like so many of his contemporaries, Dvořák not only drew on but often depended for inspiration on poems, plots, stories, and legends. Becoming involved in a world—whether it was the world of Longfellow, or later of the Czech K. J. Erben—was simply one of the ways Dvořák generated what we might call "primary" musical images.

Also, Dvořák must here have been engaged by the challenge of dealing with three methods of communication. In the same frame, as it were, he had to paint musically the motion of the dance, the lyrical passion of an exotic love song, and a mystery story of magic, and try to transform their essential qualities into sound.

But we should recall Dvořák's sense that he was writing a symphony as an object lesson for American composers. As I suggest in the Introduction, part of his role in the United States was to provide a how-to manual for creating a National American School. To do that he needed, in addition to anything else, certain elements that would be incontrovertibly certifiable as "local." Longfellow's poem fulfilled the requirement in two ways. First, by alluding to the poem in a general way in newspaper interviews and program notes, Dvořák could advertise the symphony's American bona fides. Second and more important, he could convince his most critical audience—himself—that the national sources of the work give it an essential truth.

A final question remains: What about the two parts of the Scherzo movement that have not yet been dealt with, the transition to the Trio and the Coda? Are they part of this scheme, and need we find images for them in the poem? Seen in the context of Longfellow, the "spooky" variant of the theme from the first movement could very well have something to do with the casting of spells that immediately precedes the elevation of the lodge.

The Coda could simply be a musical response, having nothing to do with any poetic material, or it could refer to that most dangerous creature Pau-Puk-Keewis, who, though fanning himself disengagedly following his choreographic display, nonetheless contains sparks that at any time could turn into a conflagration.

The larger question of whether we need to link all the images in the symphony and relate them to *Hiawatha* is the subject of the next chapter.

4

A Nose for *Hiawatha*

We may never know what rather suddenly made the reticent Dvořák divulge more about the "New World" Symphony's programmatic sources in one week than he would for the rest of his life. Whether it was the tremendous excitement of the premiere, his close and pleasant relationship with Krehbiel and perhaps Steinberg from the *Herald*, or some desire to ensure that the work was understood, the composer invited interested readers into his workshop—though for only a single day.

In the two previous chapters I have conservatively weighed the evidence we have concerning the Largo and the Scherzo to discover which parts of *Hiawatha* likely caught Dvořák's interest. Yet what of the outer movements? In the past few years several commentators, finding it peculiar that Dvořák would use material from the poem only in the inner ones, have argued more broadly for the existence of a Hiawatha symphony.[1]

The three reasons cited most frequently to support this position are the curious fact that the symphony is always quoting itself, a belief that programmatic connections cannot be "switched on and off," and a sense that certain details in the first and last movement make sense only when we realize a program is lurking somewhere.[2] Thus, it has been argued that the main theme of the first movement is typically "masculine" and heroic, and that it may be linked to the name "Hi-a-wa-tha"; that the lament of the slow introduction may be associated with the Prologue of Longfellow's poem, invoking a graveyard; and that the final movement likely represents the chapter titled "The Famine," which includes the funeral of Minnehaha.

As appealing as these scenarios and arguments may be, they are unlikely. I will try to show why, and then consider other approaches to the issue.

Here are three possible procedures Dvořák might have followed, along with some speculations about his intentions.

1. Dvořák decides to write a symphony based entirely on Longfellow's *Hiawatha*. Every or almost every theme, gesture, and, especially, thematic recollection refers directly to the poem.
2. Dvořák begins composing his symphony with no known extramusical stimulus other than the gauntlet thrown down by James Huneker and the pseudonymous "Johann Tonsor," about whom more later. He decides, either at the outset or along the way, that the second and third movements will be based on *Hiawatha*, and no other movements are related to the poem.
3. Dvořák commences writing the symphony, and as he composes, begins reading *Hiawatha* in conjunction with the inner movements. He continues using it for various parts of the Finale.

For none of these procedures is the evidence incontrovertible. The first one has consistency on its side, yet anyone who advocates it has to explain why Dvořák specifically mentions the inner movements if the whole symphony is based on the poem. Why dissemble in such a fashion, particularly with the trusting Krehbiel? Why call attention to something only to suppress it, particularly if you have gone to the trouble of embedding the hero's name in the main themes? While in subsequent years a few scant references to the inner movements slipped out, no one around at the time of the composition ever assumed any broader *Hiawatha* scenario, and none has ever leaked out or been mentioned—until now. Perhaps the composer was somewhat embarrassed by his reliance on the poem and was determined, for reasons that are unclear, to have the work received in the context of a broad, "absolute" symphonic tradition, while at the same time drawing some attention to *Hiawatha*. It should also be noted that Dvořák was sometimes a man of secrets.

If we want to rely on documentary evidence to determine Dvořák's compositional procedure, we surely will be disappointed. Only one piece of musical evidence could shed light on some of the questions regarding the first movement, and it is ambiguous. There is a setting of the word "Hiawatha" in Dvořák's hand in conjunction with the opera project (CD 15).

At first, this sketch looks like good news for advocates of the Hiawatha symphony. After all, the composer is considering a Hiawatha leitmotiv, the motive has four notes to match the syllables, and the dotted rhythm is in place for the first two. On the other hand, the whole shape of the theme differs greatly from the first-movement motive, suggesting something more powerful and subtle. Besides, the main theme of the first movement also makes an appearance in the transition between the Scherzo and the Trio. If, as I firmly believe, this movement is based solely on events from the wedding and involves three other characters—Pau-Puk-Keewis, Chibiabos and Osseo (with Hiawatha simply as a bystander)—the presence of the first-movement theme has to do with cyclical coherence rather than any reference to Hiawatha himself. If the theme represents anything, then, it is America itself, with its energy and bustle.

Another problem with the Hiawatha symphony hypothesis is the notion that the whole work becomes more coherent if we account for "all the details." Although in the case of one of the symphonic poems Dvořák may have thought that way, there is no evidence that he slavishly followed texts.

Indeed, Dvořák employed several strategies in the middle movements. Sometimes a narrative serves, as in the dance embedded in the Scherzo, but in other places, such as the Largo, a more impressionist approach is taken. Critics have tended to consider the various leitmotivic reminiscences as programmatically significant, but we should note that the work cites itself only in a cumulative way: the first movement quotes no other movement, the second and third quote the first, and the fourth quotes all of them. The whole scenario might be more convincing if, for example, parts of the fourth movement appeared in the first or second. While it might be possible to infer various *Hiawatha* episodes *backward*, we would then be implying that only *after* he had based the second and third movements on the poem did he realize that he had subliminally been considering the first movement as part of this scheme all along. But this interpretation is too clever by half.

Also, we must recognize that the "cyclical reminiscences" are precisely what Dvořák or any composer might use if he were stitching discrete episodes together. In other words, it is entirely plausible that Dvořák uses these cyclical reminiscences to give coherence to a formal approach that has at almost every level been "contaminated" by the pull of program.

This is all to say that while a "Hiawatha Symphony" reading is possible, it is not supported by logic or evidence at this point and remains unlikely. A reading of the symphony that argues for secrets everywhere, with funeral marches and laments hiding around every bush, is perfectly consistent with my reading of the composer; I only wish I could believe it.

We ultimately realize that our interpretation of the outer movements is very much affected by a consideration of just who Dvořák was. As much as anything, our inability to bring him into focus makes answering these *Hiawatha* questions so difficult. Are we looking at the Dvořák of *The Water Goblin*, where the composer actually wrote the words of Erben's poem under the music? In that case, we would expect specific scenarios, similar to those that have been outlined for the first part of the Scherzo. Or is this the Dvořák of the Seventh or Eighth Symphony, who deals with a much vaguer programmaticism? In that case, a reading that takes Dvořák at his word—that sees the Largo as "in reality a study or a sketch for a longer work"—will less likely necessitate that we are talking about a continuous narrative. These questions all become magnified when we turn to the Finale.

The Finale

This movement poses interesting problems. Since all the evidence suggests that Dvořák wrote the movements of the "New World" successively, it is possible that Dvořák became engaged with Longfellow's poem only after he composed the first movement. Obviously, such an argument could not possibly hold for the Finale. Indeed, it is difficult for us to imagine that the composer would immerse himself in the world of the poem for the middle movements and suddenly cast it aside. So if one of the outer movements is more likely to be under the spell of *Hiawatha*, it is the Finale.

Let us proceed by juxtaposing my reading of the movement with one that combines interpretations by musicologists James Hepokoski and

Robert Winter.[3] Readers may judge for themselves whether any of these readings has any business being associated with the symphony, but the process of coming to grips with various hints ultimately tells us much about the music, and especially how we think about it. In this process, we must ask ourselves what scholars frequently do: How do you operate when you have no evidence? Or, rather, how do you proceed when your evidence is minimal?—for after all, we do have the poem and the symphony, at the very least.

Obviously, though, in the absence of any hints, we tend to fall back on the "general quality" of the music, a procedure that is both wildly speculative and the same time entirely appropriate.

Although we cannot say what a particular piece of music means, we can understand that it has a range of characteristics that, in a given context, allow it to be read more easily some ways rather than others. In any communication there are always missing pieces. All we need is enough clues to allow us to construct a whole.

In the case of the Finale we have music that, according to tradition, lends itself to being associated with some kind of strong emotion, such as anger or grief. The first measures create a sense of anticipation and malaise as the opening figure is incessantly repeated and accelerated, while the use of horns and trumpets to introduce the main theme is suggestive of military imagery, perhaps implying a battle (CD 16).

It is a peculiarity of music that while we can never say what it is, we can rather often be sure of what it isn't. Thus the chances of this theme being associated with "Downward through the evening twilight" (*Hiawatha*, Chapter 3), "Two good friends had Hiawatha" (Chapter 6), or "By the shore of Gitche Gumee" (Chapter 22) is remote.

In their evaluation of the Finale, both Hepokoski and Winter focus on "The Famine," Chapter 20 of the poem. They hear the associations between the opening ideas and the raging of the disease, and both hear the transitional theme in terms of Hiawatha's maddened rush into the forest (CD 17).

They consider the second theme to be another incarnation of Minnehaha, or Hiawatha's love for her (CD 18).

The development is described as an intensification of the famine, while the recapitulation is Minnehaha dying or dead. Other elements involve

Hiawatha's timeless swoon, his sudden turn back to reality, the "end of a legend," and a series of reminiscences including the funeral of Minnehaha, where the theme is presented as a funeral march (CD 19).

These recollections and conclusions end, in Winter's version, with the parting words of Hiawatha and his declaration that soon he will follow in Minnehaha's footsteps. Hepokoski is particularly deft and nicely poetic in discovering thematic connections—for example, when he argues that the fleeting reminiscence of the opening of the third movement represents "echoes of the wedding-dance scherzo now dropping like tears"(CD 20).[4]

Certain aspects of this compound reading are attractive. First, it focuses on the key romantic relationship of the poem in its most dramatic form. We will see that Dvořák showed a parallel interest in a *Hiawatha* opera libretto and displayed his own romantic yearnings; in light of these manifestations, the love between Minnehaha and Hiawatha is an ideal subject for the composer. Though the scenario offered cannot account for *all* the events and reminiscences of the movement, it does account for many. Further, as noted earlier, Dvořák would in a matter of years be following a text as slavishly as it is maintained here he is following Longfellow's.

Despite all these arguments, there are several reasons for rejecting this reading. While the "funeral march" in the second movement could be taken as a lament related to the sadness of the old Arrow-maker, the passage preceding its second appearance depicts the act of dying. If Dvořák, true to his avowal that the Largo is "a study or sketch for a longer work," combined two scenes in the movement, it is highly unlikely that he would use the same scene again to inspire the Finale. The only other possibility would be to assume a scenario in the Largo where, as the deliriously happy pair walk away, the Arrow-maker is imagining his daughter's death—a hypothesis that requires too great a leap of the imagination.

Another element to consider could go either way. If Dvořák had written virtually all the main dramatic parts of the work and stuck them into the symphony, would he really have whiled away so many hours sketching his *Hiawatha* opera? It could be argued that this was precisely the reason he wanted to write the opera—that he'd already written the music!—but it is difficult to imagine an opera filled with the now famous strains of the symphony. In what may be the only case of a symphonic theme to be used in the opera, the love song of Chibiabos, we see how artfully the passage was changed into something similar yet different. There are no hints in the sketches that any other themes were to be treated that way.

Then there are some peculiar musical details, particularly the transition that has been heard as "the maddened Hiawatha." Too, there are humorous effects in the movement: a strange little bassoon dance and the "Yankee Doodle" music in the development, hardly in keeping with the mood of "The Famine."

With all this in mind, I propose another scenario, which, to be sure, has its own strengths and weaknesses. The final movement of the symphony starts with an intense growl. While such emotional weight can be found at various parts of several chapters, including most notably "The Famine," only one chapter actually *begins* the way the movement sounds, Chapter 17, "The Hunting of Pau-Puk-Keewis." (The opening lines of "The Famine" refer to the "long and dreary" winter). These lines surely would call forth music of battle, war, and rage.

We can assume that Dvořák was quite familiar with this chapter, for according to the scenario for his *Hiawatha* opera, the second act was to have closed with just this section of the poem.[5] The events of Chapter 17 are set up by the preceding one in which Pau-Puk-Keewis does the unforgivable—he kills Hiawatha's favorite pets, his mountain chickens:

> And he killed them as he lay there,
> Slaughtered them by tens and twenties,
> Threw their bodies down the headland,
> Threw them on the beach below him,
> Till at length Kayoshk, the sea-gull,
> Perched upon a crag above them,
> Shouted: "It is Pau-Puk-Keewis!
> He is slaying us by hundreds!
> Send a message to our brother,
> Tidings send to Hiawatha!"

Hiawatha becomes enraged. (We can also imagine Dvořák, the great pigeon fancier, sharing that feeling.) The opening of Chapter 17 unfolds amid images of pulsing anger. It is possible to hear these images in the music, especially the correlation between measures 6–10 and Hiawatha's buzzing and muttering like a hornet:

> *Full of wrath was Hiawatha*
> *When he came into the village,*
> *Found the people in confusion,*
> *Heard of all the misdemeanors,*
> *All the malice and the mischief*
> *Of the cunning Pau-Puk-Keewis.*
> *Hard his breath came through his nostrils,*
> *Through his teeth he buzzed and muttered*
> *Words of anger and resentment . . .*

Then comes the main theme, approached as it were from a musical colon:

> *"I will slay this Pau-Puk-Keewis,*
> *Slay this mischief-maker!" said he.*
> *"Not so long and wide the world is,*
> *Not so rude and rough the way is,*
> *That my wrath shall not attain him,*
> *That my vengeance shall not reach him!"* (CD 21)

Once again the musical material could almost be a funeral march, and as we already know, it does become one at the end. We must be careful, since the dangerous thing about this analytical process is that these connections start to become inevitable. Yet, as physicist Richard Feynman once said: "The important thing is not to fool yourself. And you're the easiest one to fool." Though the music fits this text perfectly, in fact, it also fits the words uttered in "The Famine," since this type of music is usually associated with rage and the potential for violence:

> *"Behold me!*
> *I am Famine, Bukadawin!"*
> *And the other said: "Behold me!*
> *I am Fever, Ahkosewin!"*

There is one more aspect to the theme: Dvořák had surely composed something like it already. For whatever resemblance it has to any African-American song, and however much it may have been inspired by passages from the poem, it belongs to Dvořák's "Hussite mode." One of the great symbols of the Czech nation, musically speaking, is the fifteenth-century song "Ye Who Are God's Warriors," sung by the Hussite warriors who were carrying the banner for the Czech "heretic" Jan Hus. Smetana used it both at the conclusion of his opera *Libuše* and as the basis for the final two movements, "Tabor" and "Blanik," from *Má vlast*, where it is associated with militant resistance to foreign domination. Dvořák himself made use of the tune, juxtaposed with an even older *St. Wenceslaus* melody in his *Hussite Overture* (a piece, incidentally, loathed by Brahms for its nationalist fervor). Another famous use of the tune occurs at the beginning of the Symphony No. 7, which, according to Dvořák's notes, was written in association with a patriotic demonstration; and still another resemblance may be found in the fanfare "motto" theme of the Eighth Symphony finale. That lowered seventh so characteristic of Burleigh's singing had been in Dvořák's imagination for a long time, and the emotional quality associated with it was almost invariably warlike.

If my reading of the connection between the theme and Hiawatha is correct, the middle section of the main theme might be derived from the text between Hiawatha's two oaths:

> *Then in swift pursuit departed,*
> *Hiawatha and the hunters*
> *On the trail of Pau-Puk-Keewis . . .*

while the return of the theme might signal his second outcry:

> *And aloud cried Hiawatha,*
> *From the summit of the mountains:*
> *"Not so long and wide the world is,*
> *Not so rude and rough the way is*
> *But my wrath shall overtake you,*
> *And my vengeance shall attain you!"*

Of course, the texts we associate with the piece of music may determine how we ultimately perceive it. Thus, the sharp change from a warlike dirge to the bouncing rhythms of the transition does not fit so well with the images others have offered from Chapter 20 of a maddened Hiawatha, but it goes rather nicely with the escaping Pau-Puk-Keewis. We can hear him scampering and running "like an antelope," and we can identify the streamlet among all the water imagery.

> *Over rock and over river,*
> *Through bush, and brake, and forest,*
> *Ran the cunning Pau-Puk-Keewis;*
> *Like an antelope he bounded*
> *Till he came unto a streamlet*
> *In the middle of the forest,*
> *To a streamlet still and tranquil.* (CD 22)

Since this is music and not narrative, the passage is repeated, and we can hear more water, and perhaps the beaver rising up to the surface.

> *From the bottom rose the beaver,*
> *Looked with two great eyes of wonder*
> *Eyes that seemed to ask a question,*
> *At the stranger, Pau-Puk-Keewis.*

In his most wheedling tones, with all his considerable charm, Pau-Puk-Keewis implores the beaver to transform him:

> *On the dam stood Pau-Puk-Keewis*
> *O'er his ankles flowed that streamlet,*
> *Flowed the bright and silvery water,*
> *And he spake unto the beaver,*
> *With a smile he spake in this wise:*
> . . .
> *"Cool and pleasant is the water;*
> *Let me dive into the water,*
> *Let me rest there in your lodges. . . ."* (CD 23)

One criticism of this scenario is simple: Why would Dvořák waste a great love theme on Pau-Puk-Keewis? If I am correct, he was fascinated by that character. As we saw in relation to the Scherzo, Pau-Puk-Keewis is the Antichrist, the disrupter of the Ojibway pastoral, an undisciplined natural force, the virtual antipode of Hiawatha. Perhaps his wheedling and his ability to transform himself were to provide the most powerful dramatic scenes in the opera.

Here we are led once again to ask fundamental questions about the composer. Is Dvořák someone who simply responds to a text, in which case the plea of Pau-Puk-Keewis could easily receive what sounds to us like a "love" theme, or does he reserve themes for only certain specific situations (i.e., love themes only for romantic love)? We cannot resolve this matter to everyone's satisfaction, but critics will look in vain for any consistency in Dvořák's music. In *The Devil and Kate*, written after his return to Bohemia, the Princess we hardly know gets the most heartrending music in the opera, while the most memorable theme in *Jacobin* is reserved for a rehearsal of an amateur serenade. In the case of the "New World" Finale, Dvořák needed a contrasting theme and chose one of great seductive beauty. We must keep in mind that as far as he was concerned, with nosy and perhaps wrongheaded musicologists a safe century away, there was no danger that his gorgeous second theme would be associated with a speech made to a beaver. Certainly, the tune and text have several features in common, including a wheedling quality, while the accompanying clarinet riff suggests something more flighty and quicksilver than a love theme.

Other parts of the movement echo the events of this chapter though quite a few lines later. Hiawatha catches Pau-Puk-Keewis and kills him. But his soul escapes and is turned into a bird. Dvořák first writes the part of the bird and then depicts Hiawatha in hot pursuit:

Saw the wings of Pau-Puk-Keewis
Flapping far up in the ether
. . .
And behind it, as the rain comes,
Came the steps of Hiawatha. (CD 24)

The music that follows, which builds in a manner usually associated with a tempest, may relate to the place in the poem where Pau-Puk-Keewis takes refuge in the caves of the Old Man of the Mountain. Hiawatha, in close pursuit, insists that he be let in:

"Open! I am Hiawatha!"
But the Old Man of the Mountain
Opened not, and made no answer
From the silent crags of sandstone,

   •   •   •

   Then he raised his hands to heaven,
Called imploring on the tempest,
Called Waywassimo, the lightning,
And the thunder, Annemeekee;
And they came with night and darkness,
Sweeping down the Big-Sea-Water
From the distant Thunder Mountains;
And the trembling Pau-Puk-Keewis
Heard the footsteps of the thunder,
Saw the red eyes of the lightning,
Was afraid, and crouched and trembled.
   Then Waywassimo, the lightning,
Smote the doorways of the caverns,
With his war-club smote the doorways,
Smote the jutting crags of sandstone,
And the thunder, Annemeekee,
Shouted down into the caverns,
Saying, "Where is Pau-Puk-Keewis!"
And the crags fell, and beneath them
Dead among the rocky ruins
Lay the cunning Pau-Puk-Keewis,
Lay the handsome Yenadizze,
Slain in his own human figure. (CD 25)

The next passage, with the strange dance in the bassoon, can refer to

"Ended all his mischief making," while the following climax may represent the moment when "the noble Hiawatha" took the soul of Pau-Puk-Keewis and turned it into an eagle soaring over the land.

It is no easier to tie the Coda to Pau-Puk-Keewis than it is to "The Famine." If we take the Scherzo theme as a reminder of the wedding, then what follows is certainly the funeral march of Minnehaha. On the other hand, since some have argued for leitmotivic activity from the very beginning of the symphony, why not hear the dance reminiscence (CD 20) simply in relation to the end of Chapter 17, with Pau-Puk-Keewis's ghostly dance?

> *And the name of Pau-Puk-Keewis*
> *Lingers still among the people,*
> *Lingers still among the singers,*
> *And among the story-tellers;*
> *And in Winter, when the snow-flakes*
> *Whirl in eddies round the lodges,*
> *When the wind in gusty tumult*
> *O'er the smoke-flue pipes and whistles,*
> *"There," they cry, "comes Pau-Puk-Keewis;*
> *He is dancing through the village,*
> *He is gathering in his harvest!"*

In the end, there are two reasons that the different scenarios fit the music so well. First, and most obviously, music has always been vulnerable to "stories" associated with it. But there is something more: Dvořák was so steeped in the images, rhythms, and spirit of *Hiawatha* during his time in the United States that it might not even have mattered where he dipped into it. For this mixture of the morbid, the exotic, the violent, and the romantic appears everywhere in its pages, from the rape of Wehnona to the battle between Hiawatha and his father, and from the prologue in the graveyard to the farewell when Hiawatha departs in his birch canoe, "In the glory of the sunset / In the purple mists of evening." Yet I have come to believe that this movement was inspired by Hiawatha's rage, Pau-Puk-Keewis's flight, the storm, and the killing of the great dancer. The similarities are too marked, and the fit between the passage and the music is astounding.

Postscript

Where does this leave us? It is clear that the music of the "New World" Symphony *means* something, but we can never say precisely what. As a matter of fact, the closer we try to get, the more knuckleheaded our attempts become, since the meaning of the symphony is in no way equivalent to the meaning of Longfellow's poem, which was, at most, an "inspiration." It is like one of those "three-dimensional" images that come to us only when we are in some altered state of visual consciousness and that cannot even be explained to someone who has not been there as well.

We should not feel too bad, though, if we cannot say in all cases which bits of poetry inspired which musical passages. One of Dvořák's students, Harry Patterson Hopkins, went to stay with Dvořák for several months in Bohemia, spending time with the composer in Prague and Vysoká. "One of my principal aims," he writes, "was to gain knowledge concerning the 'New World' Symphony." [6] Every day he went for long walks in the woods with Dvořák, and raised many questions about the symphony. He found out nothing.

5

Dvořák's *Hiawatha* Opera

The American years, with such compositions as the Humoresques for Piano, *Biblical Songs*, the Suite for Piano, and the chamber works, are framed by two giant "bookend" works: the "New World" and the Cello Concerto. But the largest work of all was meant to be somewhere in the middle. That it was never written is by turns amusing and confounding, and in the end sad. The symphony and the concerto were meant to be joined by an epic opera on the subject of Longfellow's *Hiawatha*.

Like the use of *Hiawatha* material in the "New World" Symphony, the story of Dvořák's contemplated *Hiawatha* opera is not new—in fact, most of what we know about it is available in Czech sources, although not always in great detail. The Hiawatha opera episode is critical, for the poem is a leitmotiv that runs almost entirely through the composer's stay in America. In the words of one of the most imaginative of the Czech critics, Antonín Sychra, "The key to understanding the intellectual and ethical sense of Dvořák's American activity and works is above all the undying interest with which he again and again returned to Longfellow's *Song of Hiawatha*."[1]

The most extensive material about Dvořák's *Hiawatha* opera comes from two writers, both of whom have transcribed some of the sketches. The first is Otakar Šourek, whose four-volume biography traces the composer's relationship to the poem and outlines his attempts to write the opera. More depth, and some of the best writing about the composer, can be found in Antonín Sychra's *Estetika Dvořákovy symfonické tvorby* (The Aesthetics of Dvořák's symphonic works), in which the author provides reproductions of several sketches and raises the issue of the composer's American style.[2]

Despite these summaries, which have been available for several decades, more recent writing about Dvořák's *Hiawatha* opera has tended to minimize the significance and value of this project. Dvořák biographer John Clapham treats Dvořák's *Hiawatha* sketches lightly, saying simply, "On arriving in New York he became seriously interested in composing an opera on this subject, but he did not get beyond a few preliminary sketches." Although Clapham gives a brief summary of the sketch material, he concludes that by the time the composer found an adequate libretto, he was "deciding to leave America, and consequently he abandoned the idea of writing an opera on this subject."[3] The truth involves a great deal more than Dvořák's lack of interest.

Dvořák arrived in the United States at the end of September 1892. Josef Jan Kovařík, Dvořák's American-born Czech secretary, remembers: "Shortly after the Master's arrival in New York Mrs. Thurber recommended that the Master read Longfellow's poem *Hiawatha* and added that she thought it would make an excellent subject for an opera. I obtained the book, and the Master became totally absorbed by it." This story is completely in keeping with Thurber's desire to have Dvořák spark an American musical movement, with its roots in both African-American and Native American culture.

While it is possible that this version accords with the facts, it may actually have been Dvořák who suggested the work, since, as we know, he had encountered it in a Czech translation as early as the 1870s. Jeannette Thurber's recollection supports the latter version: "In one of his letters to me he says, 'As you know, I am a great admirer of Longfellow's *Hiawatha*, and I get so attached to it that I cannot resist the attempt to write an opera on this subject, which would be very good fitted for that purpose.' "[4] She also claimed that she obtained permission from both the publishers and Alice Longfellow to use the poem.

Before he considered any operatic project, however, Dvořák had other plans for the poem. Although Thurber never believed that images from *Hiawatha* appeared in the symphony "From the New World" ("That was one of his operatic projects," she said when asked about it), [5] the composer left no doubt about the relationship.

It is significant that even as he was composing the symphony, Dvořák had not decided whether the project would be an opera or something more modest, at least according to Francis Neilson, an actor and director who was in close contact with many of the important figures in the musical life of New York at the turn of the century. He offers yet another view of Dvořák's relationship to this subject.

> Seidl told me Dvorak was looking for a cantata on an American subject and was greatly attracted by the poem *Hiawatha*. When I consulted Dvorak about the matter, he told me that he would like to have a book [libretto] based on Longfellow's poem. I worked at this for a long time but. . . I became convinced that the subject was far too big for a cantata; that it contained all the elements of music drama. I told this to Dvorak, but he shook his head and said something about it being too much trouble. He preferred a simple cantata, and asked if I could recommend someone else to do the job but, though I mentioned the names of one or two men the matter never got any further. Huneker, who was always [Dvořák's] interpreter, used to joke about Dvorak getting the Indian and Negro mixed. This was after the production of the Symphony From the New World, for some of the themes in it were those he had in mind for the cantata on Hiawatha.[6]

At least two items here are pertinent if we take the report at face value. First, the opera project was not a certainty even after the premiere of the symphony; and second, we gain another piece of evidence that themes from the "New World" were to be used in another context.

The evidence is contradictory at this point. According to her recollections, Jeannette Thurber played a significant role in the process:

> We discussed the possible librettists and I took him to see Buffalo Bill's Indians dance as a suggestion for the ballet. It is really to be regretted that this operatic project came to naught. Hiawatha would have been sung in English. When I first met Dr. Dvorak in London he told me that he had wanted to meet me as he considered I had made music a possibility in America by having opera sung in the vernacular.[7]

By the summer of 1894, the reporter James Creelman, possibly on a tip from Thurber, was able to boast that the *opera* project was about to get into full swing: "He is now preparing to write a grand opera, the story to be supplied by Longfellow's 'Hiawatha.' The story will be sung in English and the pupils of the National Conservatory will have a chance to show the results of their training."[8]

Kovařík never mentions any cantata project at all and dates the first sketches for the opera to November 1893, that is, a month before the premiere of the "New World." He also offers at least one candidate for the libretto:

> After sending his works to Simrock the Master took up for some time the libretto for the opera "Hiawatha."[9] I don't know with certainty who wrote the libretto, but I think it was written by Mr. Edwin Emerson Jr. (the last two letters mean "junior")—who later helped the Master with his article "Music in America" which appeared in Harpers Magazine in February of 1895. Mr. Emerson visited the Master often during the time he was engaged with the libretto, and that's why I think he was the source of the libretto. While the Master was involved with the libretto he made notes in his sketchbook.

Since there is nothing in the sketchbooks that specifically mentions an opera, as opposed to a cantata, and since this libretto has never been found, Emerson, or whoever wrote the libretto, certainly could have been working on the text for a cantata.

The first group of *Hiawatha* sketches does not answer the question either way. In the third American Sketchbook, pp. 23–25, we find two themes for Minnehaha, one in B minor, one in G Major, birdsongs, and motives labeled "Animal," "Dance—wedding—merriment," and so forth (see Fig. 16). Many of these sketches are in what we have called the "American mode," that is, they favor pentatonic scales and the sharp first-beat accent that is often called the "Scotch snap." There is even a motive titled "Hiawatha seeks and reflects." Just below the last identified sketches, marked "birds" and "beasts," is an allegro in G minor that might be an "Indian dance," so it is possible that the Hiawatha motives continue. Indeed, it is difficult to know which, if any, of the unmarked ideas might have been intended for the opera, and whether there is *Hiawatha* material on any of the previous or subsequent pages.

According to Kovařík, Dvořák abandoned the project because "at the end the jury which was supposed to judge the libretto, found it inadequate!" And, he adds, "Hiawatha was done for!"

The libretto's treatment at the hands of the jury is one of the most peculiar aspects of the matter. Nothing further has come to light. Why did the libretto have to be presented to a committee? Did it have something to do with Creelman's assertion that the work was to be preformed by students at the conservatory? Was it business as usual for Thurber's wishes—for we assume she was strongly behind the project—to be ignored? Probably a panel of judges was taken from the conservatory's own committee on librettos, which included the following as listed in documents of the National Conservatory: Dr. Antonín Dvořák; Mr. Thomas Bailey Aldrich, Boston; Mr. Elwyn A. Barron, Chicago; Mr. C. A. Bratter, New York; Mr. Henry A. Clapp, Boston; Mr. Eugene Field, Chicago; Mr. George P. Goodale, Detroit; Col. Thomas Wentworth Higginson, Boston; Mr. M. G. Seckendorff, Washington; Mr. Edmund C. Stedman, New York; Mr. Benjamin Edward Woolf, Boston; and Mr. William Winter, New York.

It is surprising to find so many Boston people on the jury, especially since at just this time yet another journalistic battle was raging between Henry Krehbiel of the *New York Daily Tribune* and Philip Hale of the *Boston Journal* concerning the idea of an American music. As Krehbiel put it, "the sarcastic and scintillant Mr. Philip Hale . . . makes merry of the terms and thinks it wondrous amusing that anything should be called American that has attributes or elements that are also found among the peoples of the Old World." Dvořák's relationship with the Boston musical establishment had become particularly sour after he became involved in a series of newspaper stories claiming that the future of American music lay in the use of the Negro melodies. The dean of Boston composers, the eminent John Knowles Paine, aptly summarized the position in Boston: ". . . the time is past when composers are to be classed according to geographical limits. It is not a question of nationality, but of individuality, and individuality of style is not the result of limitation—whether of folk songs, Negro melodies, the tunes of the heathen Chinese or of Digger Indians, but of personal character and inborn originality." After proceeding in this manner for a few paragraphs he opened the big guns: "Dr.

Dvořák is probably unacquainted with what has been accomplished in the higher forms of music by composers in America. In my estimation, it is a preposterous idea to say that in [the] future American music will rest upon such an alien foundation as the melodies of a yet largely undeveloped race."[10]

While some of the Boston members of the libretto committee may originally have been more welcoming to Dvořák's approach to the creation of an American music, the polemics during his first year might have changed things. The flap in May over Dvořák's use of "Negro" melodies to build an American music was followed seven months later by the exchanges between Krehbiel and Hale.

The Boston–New York antipathy that had developed is at least one possible explanation for the committee's rejection of the libretto. Another is that notwithstanding Dvořák's enthusiasm about *The Song of Hiawatha*, many poets found its rhythms numbing and its subject trite, and like many a runaway popular success it drew the ire of professionals. But so far there is no real explanation for the mysterious rejection of the libretto.

There is an additional, and equally puzzling question: If the subject was of the utmost interest for the composer, why didn't he write the work anyway, despite the disapproval of the committee? An answer is suggested in Kovařík's memoirs, although the source of the projected libretto raises other additional questions:

> I guess that at the time the Master would have composed "Hiawatha" in spite of the inappropriate libretto, but Mrs. Thurber said to the Master that she would procure another, and wrote at that time to Vienna, to whom I don't remember, the name eludes me, and asked someone to write a libretto based on Longfellow's poem "Hiawatha."

By this time the opera had been announced, and it was rumored to be almost complete. This is a sample from the Czech journal *Dalibor*:

> And now we will have a real American opera, and prouder than ever the American Eagle will be under its nationality. This will be the fate of Hiawatha in all its magnificent flood of melody, as soon as Dvořák completes the final notes of his opera. It seems that he had wished to

compose this opera for quite a long time. Even as a boy he pored over Longfellow's verses with delight and felt their music. Many Americans have felt that Hiawatha was capable of the development which Dvorak will confer upon it.[11]

But as we know from the sketches, the opera was far from finished; it did not even have a libretto. Almost all the evidence about the later fate of the matter comes from Kovařík:

> And when he finally finished the Cello concerto—he spent a long time on the score—he still made changes here and there. Even when he had finally given me the score to copy, every now and then he required occasional corrections and I had to make many changes in the rewritten parts. But at just that time the requested Vienna "Hiawatha" opera libretto arrived, and Mrs. Thurber had immediately had it translated into English.

We may be forgiven if the idea of importing a *Hiawatha* libretto from Vienna sounds unbelievably wacky to us today, and yet Dvořák took the matter in stride. Kovařík continues:

> The Master became absorbed by the awaited libretto, he forgot about the cello concerto—he again took up "Hiawatha" and then reread the poem and so I didn't have to redo the concerto. Finally one day the Master came back from the conservatory and brought the English translation of the "Hiawatha" libretto. The Master became absorbed with the libretto, read it several times, and began to make sketches in his sketchbook.

The second group of sketches, according to Kovařík, was done after the Cello Concerto was finished, but we really have no idea when Dvořák started them. The labeled sketches begin on p. 34 of the sketchbook and go to the end. First we find a Hiawatha motive, an andante, that recalls the second theme of the Cello Concerto, various smaller sketches, and a curious passage at the bottom of p. 34 simply marked "voice," which is very clearly in the American pentatonic style. The next page features a choral piece, and some themes below that appear to be in the "Hussite" mode of the "New World" Finale. The next two pages have no specific Hiawatha markings, but the final page is the gem of them all, something that looks almost like a small scene from the opera (see Fig. 17).

This single-line sketch begins with a march in Dvořák's "Indian" style, looking very much as if it was intended for brass, particularly the part on the second system that suggests echoing brass fanfares. A middle section in B-flat minor adds an accompaniment pattern and is interrupted by recollections of the opening fanfare. This introduces an aria that in key and tone matches the fanfares. This charming setting of "Onaway" from Hiawatha's wedding is very close in many ways to the E-major section of the "New World" Scherzo, which was likely inspired by the same text. The notation implies a flexible, arioso style, and features some striking modulations to return to B-flat major at the aria's end.

In this unfinished form it is hard to judge what the final product might have been like. Yet I believe that this would have been a marvelous aria, perhaps even a rival to the famous aria to the moon in Dvořák's *Rusalka*. The sketch will have to suffice to suggest what might have been. (CD 26 is a fanciful realization of the sketch.)

Kovařík's memoirs speak of Dvořák's deep commitment to the *Hiawatha* opera:

He constantly spoke about "Hiawatha" but as long as the jury assembled by Mrs. Thurber had not approved the libretto he couldn't get down to work. As soon as he returned from the conservatory he always got out the libretto, sat down at the piano, and patiently waited for the decision of the jury. The jury finally rendered their verdict—on the jury were two leading American poets and the other three were theater directors—the libretto was considered to be better than the first, but unsuccessful. In short, the jury said it was unacceptable.

Kovařík says that Thurber wrote to Vienna once again for yet another libretto—"And so Mrs. Thurber who had already taken Hiawatha into her heart, sent immediately to Vienna to get a new libretto"—but by this time he may well have become confused by the whole scenario. It cannot be emphasized enough how devastating the jury's decision must have been for Dvořák. Not only had he expended much creative energy on the project, but the judgment must have felt to him like a slap in the face from his own colleagues.

Current Dvořák biography treats the *Hiawatha* opera as a curiosity that essentially died because the composer lost interest in it. Yet here is Thurber describing how eager the composer was to work on the project:

> He was deeply interested in his project for a *New World* opera. One day [probably some time in late 1893/94] he wrote me: 'But I am longing for the libretto of *Hiawatha*. Where is it? If I cannot have it very soon—much is lost.' "[12]

From the sketches and the documents, we can conclude that the composer was passionately interested in completing the work but was foiled by the libretto committee—not once, but twice. The whole tale is still a great mystery. Although I have suggested a "Boston Conspiracy," it is equally possible that someone influential at the National Conservatory, such as James Huneker, convinced the committee that a *Hiawatha* opera by Dvořák would be a travesty. But if we can trust Kovařík's dating, Dvořák thought seriously about a dramatic work based on *Hiawatha* from shortly after his arrival in 1892 to at least 1895, when he wrote the *Hiawatha* sketches after completing the Cello Concerto.

Although Dvořák never composed his *Hiawatha* opera, two later projects may have borne some relation to it. The most famous musical treatment of the poem is *Hiawatha's Wedding Feast* by the English composer Samuel Coleridge Taylor, who held Dvořák in great esteem and who may have known about Dvořák's *Hiawatha* project. Ironically, an article in the *Boston Transcript* of October 6, 1906, reveals that Dvořák's friend the conductor Anton Seidl left an unfinished *Hiawatha* opera at his death. Though it differed in concept from Dvořák's work, it shares with it the distinction not only of being unfinished but of having the same librettist, the actor Francis Neilson, as Dvořák's first *Hiawatha* project.

What Was *Hiawatha* to Dvořák?

Why are composers attracted to certain subjects? In Dvořák's case, what is it that sustained his interest in Longfellow's poem for more than thirty years?

First, and most obvious, the subject was exotic, not merely for a Czech, but for any city dweller. The scenes and images would have deeply impressed Europeans sitting in their domesticated landscapes, and notions of wild warriors barely beyond the horizon must have been intoxicating to Dvořák, his imagination already vibrating with images from the ancient legends of Czech balladry. And the sense of scope and open space, provided both by Longfellow's epic style and the nature of his descriptions, would have appealed to the composer and his fellow Czechs, since it was a stark contrast to their settled environs.

Dvořák, only newly arrived on American shores, realized that *Hiawatha* was the very thing he had been searching for in so many ways: a potent substance that would strike average Americans as somehow belonging to them. In his own words, he wished to "get into touch with the common humanity of the country."[13] He must also have been attracted to the themes of the poem itself. When Longfellow wrote in his Introduction, "Ye who love the haunts of nature / Love the sunshine of the meadow," followed it with "Ye who love a nation's legends, / Love the ballads of a people," and then connected this to the lines "Ye whose hearts are fresh and simple / Who have faith in God and Nature," Dvořák must have felt that the poet had penetrated to his very core, for these loves—of nation, ballads, God, and nature—were central to Dvořák's world view.

There could also have been more personal things at work. Perhaps Dvořák identified with Hiawatha, a great warrior and a successful statesman. Though known internationally as the Czech Brahms, Dvořák secretly yearned to be the Slavic Wagner. A massive epic such as *Hiawatha* would have been tempting to any Wagnerian, with its magic spells, violent confrontations, and mixture of love and death. Also, he obviously was taken with the character of Pau-Puk-Keewis, the conjurer who is both engaged with and distant from his own work.

Finally, both the sketches and the documentary evidence about the "New World" Symphony make it clear that Dvořák was deeply taken by the love story between Hiawatha and Minnehaha. The two inner movements, the only ones for which we have any documentary evidence, draw on passages revealing the love between the two characters. The Largo includes both the wooing—with its pleasant journey homeward—and the funeral of Minnehaha, while the Scherzo depicts the wedding. The opera sketches contain several themes for Minnehaha and a special setting of the love song from the wedding, "Onaway, awake beloved!"

Clearly, for the opera project to have fallen apart despite the commitment of the composer there must have been some who felt that a *Hiawatha* opera would have been a terrible mistake, that it might have become the same kind of laughingstock as the poem, that is, a bit of operatic doggerel. Perhaps they simply found Dvořák's "racialized" Americanism abhorrent. We will probably never know, just as we can have no real idea of what his opera might have been like. There is an immense chasm between an "almost finished" artistic creation and a "finished" one. Terrible ideas (imagine someone describing the "Ring" project to you in 1850) can come off as monumental works, while terrific projects (Schubert's *Zauberharfe*) can barely stand a revival. A work never created is a matter for our fantasy alone, and in this case a great fantasy.

The last word concerning the failure of the *Hiawatha* opera to materialize should be left to Kovařík. Not only does he describe most eloquently Dvořák's feeling after the last episode in the debacle, but as the only person likely to have heard Dvořák's pianistic renditions of the material, he offers his own view of what the work might have been:

> This second disappointment with Hiawatha the Master took very hard—and it is a pity that Hiawatha would never be realized—I say a pity not only because as an American-born citizen, I regret that the Master never wrote an opera on an American subject, but I also regret it because the Master looked forward to the work immensely. During his entire time in America he had Hiawatha on his mind, he was completely absorbed by it, always spoke about it, he thought about it, and he surely would have worked on it with special love, huge interest and incentive, and therefore would have made an extraordinary magnificent work. Therefore alas.

PART III

Dvořák Among
the Journalists

In August 1996 the *San Jose Mercury News* ran a series, "Dark Alliance," in which the claim was made that the Central Intelligence Agency protected Nicaraguan rebels who brought crack cocaine into South Central Los Angeles in the early 1980s. After all these charges were proved false, the executive editor of the newspaper declined comment, saying through a spokeswoman simply that he "would prefer to report the news instead of being part of it." How different were things a century ago when a new breed of imaginative and aggressive "yellow" journalists tried to do exactly the opposite! The fact that Dvořák's visit to the United States occurred during the great age of yellow journalism is not merely a curious coincidence but had profound repercussions for both the composer and posterity.

Although Czechs in Europe were certainly interested in Dvořák, journalism had recently gone off in a different direction in the United States. In particular, the ambitions of such newspaper moguls as Joseph Pulitzer, William Bennett, and William Randolph Hearst led to the growth of a whole industry dedicated to disseminating the sensational and the lurid. That Dvořák got caught in this whirlwind was to be expected, but the extent to which it affected his activity has not been well understood. Toward the end of his life, Dvořák very much regretted that, as he put it, he "could not speak." Yet while in the United States, he had a corps of reporters fawning over him, cajoling him, and writing him up in dozens of articles, interviews, pamphlets, and reviews. The composer was news, and to be news in the "Golden Age of Journalism" was to have the greatest opportunity to speak, though the speech was filtered through the personalities and agendas of the journalists. We will see, indeed, that some of these reporters were probably in the pay of other figures, such as Jeannette Thurber.

At first Dvořák was an innocent, asking a reporter after an interview in Boston, "Now you won't say that I said things that I didn't, will you?" After six months in the United States, Dvořák knew the ropes better. In a letter to his friend Kozánek written at the beginning of April 1893, he writes: "The papers here are terribly fond of gossip that not even Cleveland escapes—and so they wrote a variety of things about me and it was all what they call: *sensational gossip*, nothing more." Little did he know what America would have in store for him little more than a month later!

Not only was it the great age of the Star Reporter, but it was a magnificent time in the history of American music criticism—with figures such as Henry Krehbiel, James Huneker, Philip Hale, and many others achieving international reputations for their wit, knowledge, and discernment. When the "New World" was first performed, there were significant reviews and discussions in more than a dozen places, with the leading lights of the critics' brigade contributing articles. Even more noteworthy, however, is that Dvořák may be the only composer whose activity in a given time and place was so deeply affected by contact with journalists. Without Krehbiel, Huneker, and James Creelman, we would likely never have had the "New World" Symphony or the American style at all, or we would certainly know far less about them. We will see, in the next three chapters, how this journalistic influence came about.

6

Two Who Made the "New World"

The Man Who Made the "New World"

The most brilliant and perplexing journalist encountered by Dvořák during his American years was undoubtedly James Gibbons Huneker. In his thirties he was already one of the leading American music critics. He spoke French and German fluently, taught piano at the National Conservatory, and later wrote more than a dozen books about music, literature, and philosophy, including a famous best-seller on Chopin. Despite his considerable charm and his abiding interest in Dvořák and his music, he has ended up playing the role of the "heavy" both in scholarly Dvořák studies and in popular treatments of the composer, such as Josef Škvorecký's novel *Dvorak in Love* and Zdeněk Mahler's recent "fact-tion" docudrama "Dvořák in America." But there is cause to dispute the negative image of Huneker, and I can offer new evidence that his contribution to Dvořák's American style in general and the "New World" Symphony in particular was formidable, perhaps even without parallel. Indeed, we will see that the only figure who may have played a greater role was a mysterious writer from Louisville, Kentucky, who wrote under the name Johann Tonsor.

James Huneker was an amazing polyglot and a devotee of "greatness." The titles of two of his books, *Melomaniacs, Iconoclasts, Visionaries*, and *Egoists*, give us an idea of his ambition and his cleverness. In his writing, he often prided himself on being slightly naughty and always strove to attain what he described as "the happy mean between swashbuckling criticism and the pompous academic attitude. " H. L. Mencken left an indelible record of Huneker as *prestissimo* raconteur and monologist:

What a stew indeed! Berlioz and the question of the clangtint [tonal quality] of the viola, the psychological causes of the suicide of Tchaikovksy, why Nietzsche had to leave Sils Maria between days in 1887, the echoes of Flaubert in Joseph Conrad (then newly dawned), the precise topography of the warts of Liszt, George Bernard Shaw's heroic but vain struggles to throw off Presbyterianism . . .[1]

The list of Huneker's subjects, which continues at great length, also includes "what to drink when playing Chopin . . . the defects in the structure of *Sister Carrie* . . . the origin of the theory that all oboe players are crazy . . . [and] the sheer physical impossibility of getting Dvorak drunk."[2] We will see that Huneker based the last comment on his own experience.

Huneker was probably the first journalist Dvořák met in New York, though Dvořák may not have seen the writer in his most prominent role. Huneker, in his own words, "taught piano classes twice weekly for ten years, and in addition was the press representative of the Conservatory and secretary to the Secretary, Mr. Stanton, and after he died, I was a secretary to Mrs. Thurber, my chief duty being a daily visit at her residence, where I sat for an hour and admired her good looks."[3] Though Dvořák was Huneker's nominal boss as director of the National Conservatory, in reality they were more like colleagues. They must have spent a good deal of time together, at least during the first year the composer was in the United States. We may remember that according to actor and writer Francis Neilson, Huneker served as an interpreter during discussions about a project to compose a *Hiawatha* opera in the Fall of 1893.[4]

Huneker's place as an *enfant terrible* (with an emphasis on *terrible*) in Dvořák studies was ensured by a reminiscence about the composer published in a volume of memoirs called *Steeplejack*. According to Huneker, Thurber—who was doubtless aware of Dvořák's preference for companionship when out and about—asked him to escort the composer around town. He relates first off that the composer was nicknamed "Old Borax." (This makes sense only if you say the phrase quickly with the accent on the first syllable of the second word in a near rhyme with "Dvořák.") Although it is hard to assess from the distance of a century, the nickname suggests how exotic people found him, while it expresses a certain affection for his toughness. Of course, it also reminds us how hard it was for people to pronounce his name. Huneker writes:

He was a fervent Roman Catholic, and I hunted a Bohemian church for him as he began his day with an early Mass. Rather too jauntily I invited him to taste the American drink called a whisky cocktail. He nodded his head, that of an angry-looking bulldog with a beard. He scared one at first with his fierce Slavonic eyes, but was as mild a mannered man as ever scuttled a pupil's counterpoint. I always spoke of him as a boned pirate. But I made a mistake in believing that American strong waters would upset his Czech nerves. We began at Goerwitz, then described a huge circle, through the great thirst belt of central New York. At each place Doc Borax took a cocktail. Now, alcohol I abhor, so I stuck to my guns, the usual three-voiced invention, hops, malt, and spring water. We spoke in German and I was happy to meet a man whose accent and grammar were worse than my own. Yet we got along swimmingly—an appropriate enough image, for the weather was wet, though not squally.[5]

The part about Huneker as a mild drinker is surely meant as irony. He was a noted beer swiller—Mencken speculates that Huneker had quaffed his "tenth (or was it twentieth) *Seidel* [mug] of Pilsner" during their evening chat. Later an ailing Huneker wrote Mencken "My father always warned me not to bet my kidneys against the brewery, but I did. I've lost."[6]

The next part of his recollection deals with Dvořák's compositions and their effect on American music. Here Huneker reveals a certain degree of condescension and more than a touch of racism. His overall verdict about Dvořák is by turns complimentary and dismissive:

Dvorak had a fresh, vigorous talent, was a born Impressionist, and possessed a happy colour sense in his orchestration. His early music was the best; he was an imitator of Schubert and Wagner, and never used quotation marks. But the American theory of native music never appealed to me. He did, and dexterously, use some negro, or alleged negro, tunes in his "New World Symphony," and in one of his string quartets; but if we are to have true American music it will not stem from "darky" roots, especially as the most original music of that kind thus far written is by Stephen Foster, a white man. The influence of Dvorak's American music has been evil; ragtime is the popular pabulum now. I need hardly add the negro is not the original race of our country. And ragtime is only rhythmic motion, not music.[7]

The tale of Dvořák continues, according to Huneker, as the two continue to drink their way through Manhattan:

But Borax! I left him swallowing his nineteenth cocktail. "Master," I said, rather thickly, "don't you thing it's time we ate something?" He gazed at me through those awful whiskers which met his tumbled hair half-way: "Eat. No. I no eat. We go to a Houston Street restaurant. You go, hein [in]? We drink the Slivovitch. It warms you after so much beer." I didn't go that evening to the East Houston Street Bohemian café with Dr. Antonin Dvorak. I never went with him. Such a man is as dangerous to a moderate drinker as a false beacon is to a shipwrecked sailor. And he could drink as much spirits as I could the amber brew. No, I assured Mrs. Thurber that I was through with piloting him. When I met Old Borax again at Sokel Hall, the Bohemian resort in the East Side, I deliberately dodged him.[8]

It is not clear just what Huneker hoped to achieve with this reminiscence. He may simply have been trying to write a clever chapter for his book, using Dvořák as the jumping-off point for his fantasy. In any case, it is easy to recognize that tone of damning with faint praise, that fascinating way some have of diminishing people by including them as part of a humorous vignette. To say that Dvořák was either an imitator of Schubert or a genius who drank to excess might be acceptable, but to combine the two verges on character assassination. Why would an eminent critic like Huneker do such a thing, and how did their relationship go from friendly to strained? They had been good friends, and Huneker was clearly interested in playing a role in Dvořák's creative process. Kovařík recalls a significant episode:

After the completion of the AMERICAN FLAG, a longer period elapsed before Master started a new work. It was usual with him to start work on a new composition immediately after he had completed the preceding one. This time, nevertheless, he took a little longer in preparing—and the reason was as follows . . . Mr. James Gibbons Hunneker [*sic*], piano teacher at the National Conservatory, and also music reviewer for the music weekly MUSICAL COURIER, brought on a certain day a cutting from some monthly for Master to see, an essay on Negro songs, with a few "typical" Negro tunes reproduced. During his next visit, Mr. HUNNEKER asked for Master's opinion—did he think it possible to start a "national American" music founded on Negro melodies?—upon which master told Mr. HUNNEKER, that he "believed this to be possible!" On the following day, the New York HERALD brought a long article—unsigned—assessing that Master declared, that American music should and must be built on the foundation of the Negro songs, and that he himself was going to write the first work of this kind.[9]

At first, it appears that the evidence is worthless because Kovařík telescoped several events (as he did elsewhere in his writings). After all, if Huneker visited him with song samples, it must have been sometime in the late fall of 1892 or the winter of 1893, since *The American Flag* was completed in the beginning of January. On the other hand, the article referred to in the *Herald* did not come out until May of 1893. Unless we can imagine that Huneker went five months between visits, we must conclude that Kovařík simply mixed up Huneker and famed yellow journalist James Creelman, author of articles on Dvořák's views of race and music.

Yet the following self-reference is taken from Huneker's review of the "New World":

The writer was the first to suggest to the composer the employment of characteristic negro melodies for symphony or suite, citing John Brockhoven's charmingly conceived "Suite Creole." This was a year ago. Dr. Dvořák listened attentively and evidently was predisposed to favor the idea. Who knows but that the Bohemian came to America to boldly rifle us of our native ore! At all events he accepted some specimen themes and also a book on the characteristic songs of the American birds.[10]

This excerpt generally corroborates Kovařík's account of the same meeting between Huneker and Dvořák and fixes the time of Huneker's visit as late December or January. Yet if Huneker did bring Dvořák an article with "specimen themes," what article was it, and how can we be sure it had a significant impact on the composer's activities?

"Negro Music"

The subject of African-American music was attracting more and more attention in the periodicals of the day, and there are several publications within a few years of Dvořák's arrival that featured music examples. Considering that Huneker mentions Brockhoven's *Suite Creole*, the first serious candidates would be two articles by George W. Cable on Creole music called "The Dance in Place Congo" and "Creole Slave Songs,"published in *The Century Magazine* in February and April 1886. Both these articles included many examples, some of which may have served as the basis for the now vanished work by Brockhoven mentioned by Huneker in his review. But there are no plantation melodies in this collection, and because it is hard to imagine Huneker trotting around town with clippings from six year-old journals under his arm, it is not a likely candidate.

One of the more interesting journals in the country, then in its first year, was *Music*, published in Chicago and edited by W. E. Matthews, a writer, pedagogue, and critic. In December 1892, *Music* published an article titled "Negro Music" written by one Johann Tonsor of Louisville, Kentucky (a complete facsimile of this article appears in the appendix). Not only is the date much closer to the visit than that of the *Century* article—indeed, it is perfect—but the content matches both descriptions in that both Kovařík and Huneker refer specifically to "Negro" songs.

Yet how could a few pages in a journal have made such a profound impression on two such different individuals—Dvořák, who was deeply religious and notoriously reticent, and Huneker, the most garrulous atheist in New York? To understand what appealed to Dvořák, we need only read the very beginning of the text:

To one who has passed his childhood in the South, no music in the world is so tenderly pathetic, so wildly, uncouthly melancholy, so fraught with an overpowering *heimweh*, as that of the negroes.

Even if Dvořák was not up to reading the English perfectly, it is certain that the one German word, which means "homesickness," would certainly have caught his eye. Dvořák was excited by the United States, but he was undeniably, even famously, homesick for his own country. Writing like this must have been a revelation to the composer: here he could make his work American and yet still express his longing for home. If he was moved by the article's first sentence, the next two might have hit even deeper, considering Dvořák's fascination with myth and legend and his passion for the forgotten past:

> When he hears one of these quaint old airs, he needs but to close his eyes and the potent spell of the music revivifies the past. Old memories, that he had deemed forgotten, rise as if obedient to the voice of enchantment.

Dvořák was somewhat sentimental, and doubtless noticed the beginning, but what could have attracted Huneker to the piece? Both he and Dvořák must have been intrigued by the challenge at the end:

> When our American musical Messiah sees fit to be born he will then find ready to his hand a mass of lyrical dramatic themes with which to construct a distinctively American music.

From what Kovařík tells us, *that* was what Huneker really came to ask: "HUNNEKER [*sic*] asked for Master's opinion—did he think it possible to start a 'national American' music founded on Negro melodies?"

The text in between the opening and the final peroration gives some particulars about the contexts of various songs and provides some serious technical discussion of the songs:

> Genuine negro music is invariably in a peculiar minor, which differs from the civilized scale in two particulars; the sixth note of the gamut is omitted and the seventh is half a tone lower. . . .When the blacks came into contact with the major scale of the whites, they adopted it, preserving still the syncopated rhythm and the omission of one note of the scale (the seventh in the major). . . .There is the same omission of the seventh in Scotch music.

If some of this sounds familiar, complete with its contemporary notions of what "civilized" means, it is perhaps because Dvořák's discussion of this music in the *New York Herald* a few months later is based on it almost completely.[11]

Most interesting is the connection between the tunes included in the article and Dvořák's sketches from around the same time, just before the composition of the "New World" begins in earnest. For example, there are some similarities between the first melody, in the appendix (CD 90); Dvořák's first surviving American sketch, from December 19, 1892; and the opening of the "New World" (CD 27).

Not only are the sketch and the song both in G minor, but the fall of a third from D to B-flat is a prominent feature of the two selections. The harmony Dvořák eventually chose for his sketch, the famous variations of the slow movement of his Quintet in E-flat, is eerily implied in the first example in the article. This sketch from December 19 may have been Dvořák's first attempt to put America into music, metaphorically but also literally, for according to Kovařík, the sketch was a study for a new national anthem to the words of "America."

There are several more striking connections. The only really conspicuous quotation in Dvořák's American works is the recollection of "Swing Low, Sweet Chariot" in the first movement of the "New World." It has always been assumed Dvořák heard this tune sung by Henry Thacker "Harry" Burleigh, a student at the conservatory, who later composed popular arrangements of spirituals, and that his first significant encounter with African-American music was through Burleigh. In this context, Dvořák scholars commonly assert that the "New World" Symphony was at least in part inspired by tunes, including "Swing Low," that Dvořák heard sung to him by Burleigh *before* he began composing the symphony. But the presence of the tune as an example in the article may already have had a powerful effect on the impressionable composer, and his contact with Burleigh may well have *followed* his reading of the article.

There are other musical figures that ring familiar. Part of the first tune in "Negro Music" metamorphosed into the scherzo theme from the Quintet in E-flat (CD 28), and the end of the third tune prefigures the second theme of the first movement of the "New World." We might note that even the key of G minor is preserved in the "New World" (CD 29).

Finally, the end of "I would not live always" (which, significantly, Dvořák also received from Krehbiel a year later) is identical to the opening of the symphony (CD 30).

That "Negro Music" is indeed the article in question has been confirmed by the recent discovery of a copy in the Dvořák archive in Prague.[12] It is difficult to imagine how this obscure article could have gotten among Dvořák's possessions unless he had brought it with him. But there is more: written upside down in the margin of one page are the words "I love you Daddy" (*Mám tě moc rád, tati*), almost certainly in the hand of Dvořák's youngest son, Antonín, or "Toník." This inscription (see facsimile, page 231) not only proves that Dvořák read the article but provides us with a charming image of domesticity. We can imagine Dvořák avidly scanning the article, absorbed, and as he reads, his young son, perhaps for fun or to get some attention, writes the words in the margin.

The implications of this discovery suggest that it is time to revise both the history of the "New World" Symphony and the genesis of Dvořák's American style. It has always been assumed that it was inevitable for Dvořák to compose a symphony as his first major work in the United States. A further assumption has been that the use of African-American melodies was the natural course to have been taken, given the presence and preferences of such people as Thurber, Krehbiel, and Burleigh. Now, though, it is possible, and even likely, that the seeds for a symphony based on "Negro" music came as a result of a single visit by Huneker in December 1892.

On the basis of this new evidence we can create a possible scenario. Huneker comes to visit Dvořák at the beginning of December in 1892. He brings with him a copy of *Music*, hot off the press, containing Johann Tonsor's article on Negro music. He tells Dvořák about Brockhoven's *Creole Suite* and wonders if Dvořák might consider doing something similar with the melodies he has brought. A week later—or more probably, several months later—Huneker visits again and Dvořák tells him what he is doing and what he has done. Possibly through Jeannette Thurber this news gets to the swashbuckling James Creelman, who in May and June of 1892 publishes an interview with Dvořák on the "Real Value of Negro Melodies"—and the chase is on.

But Why American?

Huneker's role in the creation of the "New World" and the American style goes a long way toward explaining his later views on the symphony. Although his review of the "New World" symphony is not as positive as the unequivocal raves of Steinberg, Henderson, and Krehbiel, it is complimentary and insightful, if a bit provocative. He refers to Dvořák as a "wonderful man," and to the "New World" as "exceedingly beautiful," though he mentions that he prefers the composer's two previous symphonies (a preference shared by many Dvořák scholars).

Even though Huneker is aware that Dvořák has "saturated himself with the so-called negro music of the South and has evolved thematic material that preserves some of the spirit and color of the original, while lending itself readily to symphonic treatment," he nonetheless believes that the effect is broader: "The most abiding impression of the new work is its extreme musical character and the utter absence of striving after local flavor, either in the character of the themes or their treatment."

What really bothers Huneker is the claim that the work is "American," and a mocking tone about that issue lies at the core of his review. Huneker is having none of it: "The American symphony, like the American novel, has yet to be written. And when it is, it will have been composed by an American. This is said with all due deference to the commanding genius of Dr. Dvorak." He ends his review of the "New World" with this final peroration:

> Dvorak's is an American symphony: is it? Themes from negro melodies; composed by a Bohemian; conducted by a Hungarian and played by Germans in a hall built by a Scotchman. About one third of the audience were Americans and so were the critics. All the rest of it was anything but American—and that is just as it can be.

Such chiding was nothing new for Huneker, since he had been voicing or endorsing such views in the pages of the *Courier* for months, in fact since Dvořák's theories had appeared in the *Herald*. On July 19, 1893, the journal printed an article by Alexander McArthur, who, we are told, was formerly a secretary to the composer Anton Rubinstein. This attack, "to which we heartily subscribe our assent," in the words of the *Courier* and therefore Huneker, begins by quoting Dvořák's dictum "The future music of America—its national music—must be based on Negro melodies." The article begins simply, "In serious music there is no such thing as the National," and toward the end trumpets, "Music is beyond and above all nationalities."

Henry Krehbiel, speaking for Jeannette Thurber and possibly for Dvořák, penned a pair of persuasive articles in the *New York Daily Tribune* on December 15 and 17. Arguing for the American quality of the "New World," he wrote, "All that it is necessary to admit is the one thing for which he has compelled recognition—that there are musical elements in America that lend themselves to beautiful treatment in the higher forms of art."[13]

Huneker's main review of the "New World," which appeared less than a week later—on December 20—was for him relatively restrained. Soon, though, he was busily attacking Krehbiel in an editorial, arguing that Southern blacks were not the only Americans: "Here is where we beg to differ with Mr. Krehbiel. Why should a section of this country represent it in toto?"[14] And besides, he goes on, "A sort of musical 'brogue' is negro music, and all attempts to dignify it as a language are futile." He is respectful when mentioning Dvořák: "Dr. Dvorak is Slavic, and it is quite natural that he should be attracted to this vein of tunes. It is not American, however, and curiously enough neither is his E minor symphony. It is more Celtic and Slavic than even negro." His peroration is two-edged. The first part strikes a combative pose: "We are a composite race, no part has yet voiced our multifarious nationalities; even Walt Whitman's 'Cosmic yawp' failed to more than catalogue the enormous potentialities of the nation." The article concludes in a more judicious tone: "Let us master the materials before evolving a new school. Evolution moves in majestic grooves. You can't hatch out a poet or a composer over night. Dr. Dvorak's attempt is praiseworthy, and the result lovely, musical; but why American?"

In the January 1894 edition of the *Courier*, an unsigned review of the "New World" performance in Boston, surely by Philip Hale, praises the quality of the symphony while viciously poking fun at the "American" bona fides of the work:

According to the New York "Herald" the said Mr. Dvorak began to study native music after his arrival in New York. Unfortunately for the future historian we are not told how he studied it, or whether he disguised himself in his exploration so that the music would not become suspicious, frightened, and then escape. It would be a pleasure to read of his wanderings in the jungles of the Bowery and in the deserts of Central Park. It would be interesting to know precisely his first thought on seeing the Harlem goat, an animal now rare. The composer is a modest man, and he has not even hinted at his perilous trips on the Elevated Railway or the Belt Line.[15]

After continuing in this vein he then exclaims: "But, bless your soul, Dvorak has written delightful music, music that can be enjoyed by men and women, and children of any or every land, and without indulging himself in Americanisms." By "Americanisms" one assumes that Hale meant any musical device that conspicuously calls attention to its non-European derivation, from a tom-tom to a plantation song.

A week later, Hale is back in the *Courier* with a fascinating review of Dvořák's "American" Quartet and a savage attack on Krehbiel. Once again Hale sneers at any and all who believe that this is national music: "There are others who suspect or are sure they see a negro in Dr. Dvorak's woodpile. But the negroes on Dvorak's plantation have a singular habit of whistling Scotch, Scandinavian and Bohemian tunes."[16]

One would think that this kind of writing is what put Huneker in the doghouse with Dvořák and his biographers, since he clearly endorsed Hale's fiery prose, but that is another story entirely, and certainly forms the strangest aspect of Huneker's relationship to the composer. Once again the source is Kovařík:

Mr. Hunneker [*sic*] was very likely most unpleasantly affected by Master's elusive answers to all his queries. But it had been precisely these "elusive answers" which at the time marred the intentions of the journal "Musical Courier" and of its editor—to wit, they were after "propaganda"—they wished to be the first to tell the whole musical world that master wrote a new "American Symphony" built on the basis of Negro and North American Indian songs, and that—if it were not for the journal "Musical Courier" and its principal editor who did all he could to win master's interest for these songs—America would be waiting still in vain for a work of similar scope. This "plan" was undermined—therefore the journal took care to manufacture propaganda of a different kind! After the first performance of the Symphony, the journal "Musical Courier" came out with an infamous story. Its contents were approximately the following: The Symphony was not "American"—it was not written in America at all—it was an earlier work—performed in Hamburg years ago, and all that was borne out by Mr. Stoegickt, the first clarinetist of the New York Philharmonic who—to prove his point—folded up his music during the first rehearsal of the Symphony and played the clarinet part entirely "by heart!"

The whole story was a fabrication on the part of Mr. Hunneker. . . . [17]

Kovařík goes on at some length to argue that since rehearsals were closed, there was no way in which Huneker could have witnessed such an act. Kovařík speculates that the editors of the *Courier* were hoping for a letter of rebuttal from Dvořák, and goes on to say that Mrs. Thurber counseled Dvořák not to respond.

Finally Kovařík describes a letter to Dvořák in which Stoegickt denies all claims made by the journal and offers to write a denial, and even includes details of the clarinetist's visit to Dvořák. The composer told him to drop the matter. Kovařík closes his account thus:

The journal *Musical Courier* never got any reply, and the disappointed editors still thought they might force Master to do something by repeating their "story"—they reprinted it in two more issues, and receiving no reply whatsoever, left off.[18]

This is the deep dark coda to the legend of the evil Huneker, retold by the biographers, including Šourek and Jarmil Burghauser, who always regarded Huneker as a malicious figure, a characterization taken over by just about everyone else.

What was Huneker's role in the matter? Certainly, as Kovařík implies, the critic may have felt jilted—he expected an exclusive and got Dvořák's famous reticence instead. But things were not quite as Kovařík suggests.

Huneker did not start the rumor, although he might not have been entirely innocent in the matter. Here is what happened. On February 8 the following note appeared in *The Musical Courier* under the heading "Something Startling":

> From the "New Dramatic News" for February 3 we clip the following startling item: The very latest news in musical circles reveals the fact that the "New American Symphony," written especially by Antonin Dvorak to tickle the Yankee ear, is in reality an old work rejuvenated and served up to the benighted West. This is related by an old man who plays in the orchestra. At rehearsal he recognized the symphony as a work he had played fourteen years ago in Hamburg, and closing the music he played his part from memory from beginning to end. This piece of information will undoubtedly set some tongues a wagging, and ought to make the composer of the "New American Symphony" do a good deal of thinking.

The only other mention of the affair that could be found in the pages of the *Courier* at any time is the following unsigned editorial from February 8, doubtless by Huneker:

> Several prominent musicians scout the idea that Dr. Dvorak should have utilized an early symphony for his so-called American Symphony. That he may have taken the groundwork of an earlier work and pressed into service some of its thematic material is equally untenable, for the work was made up entirely of melodic ideas based on or suggested by negro music and even Indian music. But we would like to hear what Dr. Dvorak or Mr. Anton Seidl have to say on the subject, or even from that clarinet player whose memory was so tenacious, a word would not be remiss.[19]

Well, Huneker is being a bit naughty by asking publicly what Dvořák (or Seidl!) thinks of the matter, but his response is crystal-clear. He is the *least* likely of anyone to give credence to such a rumor, since he probably still wants some recognition as the one who introduced "Negro melodies" to Dvořák.

Beyond these accounts, we have nothing but a slim reference, in an article on Harry Burleigh in *Musical America* twenty-two years later, to "a

Hamburg clarinet player" who "claimed that it [the "New World"] was an early work, composed by Dvorak in Europe and retouched for American consumption."[20] Unless more information comes to light, we might even suspect the clarinet player Stoegickt. Perhaps it was he, in a moment of weakness, who said something like "Oh, I've seen this. We played it years ago." Certainly his abject apologies to Dvořák and the absence of any of the incriminating material might be consistent with such a scenario. In any case, we have no evidence whatsoever to suggest that Huneker was behind it.

The great Dvořák scholar Jarmil Burghauser believed that the poison pen portrait of the composer in Huneker's *Steeplejack* was a crude and vicious caricature based on events that never occurred. Burghauser assumed that Huneker was pathologically jealous of Dvořák, an inflated mediocrity coming into contact with a real genius.

Yet we know of other reasons why Huneker left such a damning picture of Dvořák. If we acknowledge the outsized role Huneker probably played in the creation of Dvořák's American style, we might compare his attitude to that of Dr. Frankenstein. After all, he only brought some melodies for Dvořák to incorporate into his works; he had no idea that music based on them would become known as the American style par excellence, despite the intention of the article's author. He must have been appalled, as his comments in the spring of 1894 show. Considering that over the years this racially "tainted" music continued its popularity, Huneker's affront must have grown year by year (witness his comment on ragtime, above). Indeed he grew to hate the "New World," feeling that it was shallow and insincere. If, as the actor Francis Neilson suggested, he was also involved with the *Hiawatha* opera project, it must have confounded him to find Dvořák considering the same kinds of "Negro" themes he had used in the "New World" to depict the world of the Indians. Further, he must have genuinely hated the discussions associated with any purported school of American national music, feeling it was pious cant. This is especially true given two of his maxims: "I don't believe in schools, movements, or schematologies, or any one method of seeing and writing" and "Be cosmopolitan."

It was clear that if the *Herald* and, especially, the *Daily Tribune* were going to take the idea of American music as a rallying cry, praising

Dvořák's role in the struggle, the *Courier*, under Huneker, would take the opposing side. Despite our natural tendency to identify with Dvořák, we might note that it is the *opposition* that is most progressive, viewing issues of nation with a skepticism and subtlety we might applaud even today. Yet the *reasons* for their view are so caught up with intellectual preciousness and downright racism that it is difficult for us to embrace fully the views of Huneker, Hale, and the *Courier* no matter how cleverly they are presented.

The situation is not without irony: Huneker wished to be the hero of the day, Dvořák's great guide to American music, and he ended up as the villain of the piece. Although he played a major role in the genesis of the "New World" Symphony, not a word about his contribution has been written before now—Krehbiel, Thurber, and Harry Burleigh have usually gotten the credit.

Yet Huneker hardly needs our pity. He was not a simple man, and it is difficult after a century to understand his motives. If he was less likely than the flamboyant James Creelman, whom we will meet in the following chapter, to wish to alter the course of human events, he still wanted to inscribe himself within them in an idiosyncratic manner. If he could not be acknowledged as the catalyst for Dvořák's American style, perhaps he would become the devil's advocate in the matter and make his reputation there, hence his stylized reminiscence of Dvořák.

A telling insight into Huneker's journalistic side comes from the epigram for his autobiography, *Steeplejack*. The title of the volume refers to one who erects towers, a kind of counterpart to Ibsen's *Master Builder*. Yet Huneker's version is based on the dark philosophy of the nineteenth-century German nihilist Max Stirner, whose philosophy is quoted in *Steeplejack*:

And now when the Great Noon had come Steeplejack touched the tip of the spire where instead of a cross he found a vane which swung as the wind listeth. Thereat he marvelled and rejoiced. "Behold!" he cried, "thou glowing symbol of the New Man. A weathercock and a mighty twirling. This then shall be the sign set in the sky for Immoralists: A cool brain and a wicked heart. Nothing is true. All is permitted, for all is necessary."[21]

Like most cynics, though, Huneker sells himself short. He had far more than a cool brain and a wicked heart, and it is likely that without him there would have been no "New World" Symphony, and perhaps no American style for Dvořák. That surely is something.

Postscript: The Woman Who Made the "New World"

There remain only two small questions to ask. Just who was Johann Tonsor (whose 1892 article in *Music* appears in the Appendix), and how did someone with a German name get to become an expert in the African-American music of Kentucky? Solving these questions would, I thought, have been fairly simple, and indeed, after a few telephone calls I was happily hooked up with Mr. Pen Bogert of the Filson Club of Louisville, a repository of local lore. I explained the issues involved, and asked if he wouldn't mind tracking down Johann Tonsor. He said he would be pleased to do so.

A day passed, and then another, and I was beginning to think he had forgotten me when finally a message arrived: there was no Johann Tonsor listed in Louisville, or anywhere else. Could he please check again, I asked. He did, and reported that there were not only no Johann Tonsors at that time, but there were indeed, no Tonsors whatsoever in Kentucky from 1840 to 1920. Unless we were to imagine a character living hermitlike in the woods (such as the Bohemian-born "American Beethoven" Anton Philip "Papa" Heinrich, a refugee from 1820s Boston) and evading the census takers, we were dealing with a pseudonym. After entertaining the brief, heady, and not altogether impossible notion that the whole thing had been concocted by Huneker, Bogert and I put our heads together and thought some more.

We had to find someone who knew enough about the music to write such a piece, a person with training, intellect, and a certain dramatic flair. Bogert informed me that the most outstanding local expert on African-American music at the time was a woman named Mildred Hill, a collector and writer on the subject who had written a chapter on music in Louisville. She was in a position to know all the things that "Tonsor" knew, and she was certainly in contact with many of the same people as Dvořák was, as a passage from an article in the July 10, 1898, *Louisville Commercial* makes clear:

At the recent music teachers' national convention, held in New York, Mr. Krehbiel, the eminent critic, gave a lecture on the "Folksongs of America," in which he was assisted by his wife, and I am told by one who was present that Miss Mildred Hill was often quoted. Miss Hill is an authority on this subject, having given much time to the collection of old negro songs, which if not collected and preserved will soon be lost to us forever. It is popular to sneer at the negro folksongs, but those who do so do not know them. . . . Dvorak considered the negro melodies of sufficient interest to use them for the themes of his New World Symphony.

Indeed, there was probably close contact between Hill and Krehbiel around the time of the symphony's premiere. On December 26, 1893, a week after the performance, Krehbiel sent Dvořák several melodies accompanied by a note reading: "I have just received three more singular negro songs from Kentucky. I send the melodies for you to examine and would be more than delighted if you care to suggest a harmonization."[22] One of the melodies is "I Would Not Live Alway," a wonderful tune that was printed, albeit a trifle differently, a year earlier in Tonsor's article. Written just above the tune are the words "From Boyle Co. Ky. Heard 55 years ago." Here is what Krehbiel says in his *Afro-American Folksongs*, published in 1914: "Miss Mildred J. Hill, of Louisville, who gathered for me some of the most striking songs in my collection from the singing of an old woman who had been a slave in Boyle County, Ky."

The fact that both name Boyle County as the source of their melodies is significant, since no one else mentions it as an important collecting site—Hill clearly believed that there was no more fertile collecting area than that of Central Kentucky. Finally, in an essay on American folk music, Hill expresses herself very much like "Tonsor" on the subject of how to employ folk idioms in the high style:

The great composers of to-day are constantly using folk music of their respective countries as a basis for their compositions. Dr. Dvorak, the head of the American Conservatory, is attempting to do it for us, but he is a foreigner, and it must remain for an American composer to do this properly.[23]

There is also another detail in Tonsor's article that Hill mentions in her essay, which opens with an extended discussion of black music. She writes, "Another branch of folk music which is already lost is that of the roustabouts on the Mississippi and Ohio River steamboats. These negroes were with the whites constantly, but kept to themselves in a peculiar degree, and, therefore, their music was untainted."[24] Tonsor mentions "the dusky figures of the roustabouts" and includes one of their songs.

Hill's interest in Dvořák, incidentally, continued. There is a listing in the Dvořák Museum for a "Hill Mildred," which includes a letter to Dvořák dated March 2, 1895, and several musical examples. After confessing that she undertook "a trip of nearly three hundred miles to hear Mr. Seidl direct your New World Symphony in Cincinnati" she adds that it "takes a real southern person to really understand your work in that symphony," echoing Tonsor's "To one who has passed his childhood in the South . . . " The enclosed examples turn out to be African-American street cries from Louisville that she hopes will be of interest to Dvořák (see Fig. 18).

There is little doubt that Mildred Hill has something to do with Johann Tonsor, thereby raising a host of questions. Why did Mildred Hill write under a pseudonym? We do not know very much about her. Perhaps she was shy, or knew that she had a greater chance of being taken seriously with an authoritative-sounding German name—a peculiar one at that for a lifelong Southerner. She was certainly acquainted with things German, since she discussed German musicians at enormous length in her history of music in Louisville. The German background could explain both the pseudonym and the use of such words as *heimweh* and *volkslieder* in the article. Whatever the case, without the collecting zeal, the industry, and the eloquence of one Mildred Hill, the "New World" Symphony might never have been born.

There is one other possibility for the authorship of the article. Hill had a circle of woman friends with whom she spent a good deal of time. Adele Brandeis, writing in the May 7, 1962, *Louisville Courier-Journal* in an article titled "Reminder of a Brilliant Career," remembers Hill:

She, my mother, the Misses Virginia and Charlotte Meldrum, Mrs. William Belknap and Mrs. Morris Belknap regularly lunched together

and sometimes played the piano. They called themselves the F.C.'s.
What that stood for we never knew, perhaps Friendly Circle. But we, an
irreverent younger generation, maintained it was "Foolish Cuties."

Later in the article she mentions the interest in astronomy she shared
with Mildred and noted that they "called ourselves the F.R.S.S.G.'s—Fel-
lows of the Royal Society of Star Gazers." This letter-play suggests that
Tonsor is an acronym, and possibly even that the article was jointly written with Mildred's circle of friends. My best guess to this point is "**T**he
Oldest **N**egro **S**ong **O**n **R**ecord" or some such thing.

Just as Huneker's story has its ironies, so does the Tonsor episode. Here
was Krehbiel trying to interest Dvořák in the "authentic" Negro melodies
from Kentucky in December 1893, and the composer had already
encountered them a full year earlier in "Negro Music," and probably made
them the basis for the "New World" Symphony. Here Tonsor-Hill had
thrown down the gauntlet for a "Messiah of American music" to create a
national style. Dvořák had taken the challenge, written the symphony, and
was found wanting by the challenger, who, no doubt ignorant of her role
in the affair, wrote: "it must remain for an American composer to do this
properly."

Considering Dvořák's ill-advised comment—made in Boston—that
women did not really have the mental power for composition, it is utterly
fitting that ultimately the intellectual formulation of a woman, or possibly a group of women, should have inspired the "New World" Symphony.[25] In this regard we might recall that it was women—Jeannette
Thurber and her emissary Adele Margolis—who got Dvořák to the
United States in the first place, and another woman, Amy Beach, who
wrote the great response to his symphony, with her own "Gaelic" Symphony. And finally the greatest irony: Mildred Hill was the only person
with whom Dvořák came into contact during his visit to the United States
who wrote music that would eventually become far more famous than his
own. Quite likely based on some of the street cries she was collecting, she
was the composer of "Happy Birthday."

7

The Real Value of
Yellow Journalism

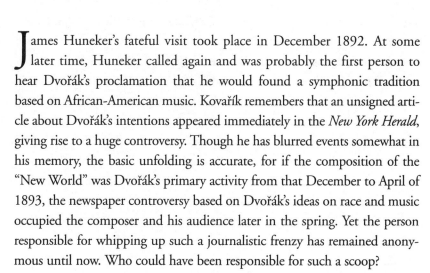

James Huneker's fateful visit took place in December 1892. At some later time, Huneker called again and was probably the first person to hear Dvořák's proclamation that he would found a symphonic tradition based on African-American music. Kovařík remembers that an unsigned article about Dvořák's intentions appeared immediately in the *New York Herald*, giving rise to a huge controversy. Though he has blurred events somewhat in his memory, the basic unfolding is accurate, for if the composition of the "New World" was Dvořák's primary activity from that December to April of 1893, the newspaper controversy based on Dvořák's ideas on race and music occupied the composer and his audience later in the spring. Yet the person responsible for whipping up such a journalistic frenzy has remained anonymous until now. Who could have been responsible for such a scoop?

In the summer of 1894 an article titled "Dvorak's Negro Symphony" appeared in the *Pall Mall Budget* of London under the byline of James Creelman. Among other things it contained the following extravagant claim:

> How well I remember the rainy day in New York when the Bohemian composer told me, between whiffs of cigar smoke, that a new school of music might be founded on the so-called negro melodies! . . . Within two weeks I had set forth this picture before the public in a series of articles, and a storm arose.[1]

A stunning pronouncement. Could it be true? The articles in question had been unsigned, and Creelman was not a music critic of any kind. Yet part of his statement would have rung true to even the greatest skeptic, for in May and June 1893 the usually reticent Dvořák had unburdened himself and advanced the surprising thesis that the future of American music lay in the study and cultivation of so-called Negro melodies. Who was James Creelman, and is there any way to substantiate his role in the matter? To do so we must look first at the events of that spring in some detail, and then at Creelman's background and his relationship to the composer.

The first salvo was fired on May 21, 1893, when a long article titled "Real Value of Negro Melodies" appeared in the *New York Herald*. Part interview, part manifesto, and part advertisement for the National Conservatory in New York, it featured dynamic pronouncements that might have been expected from Wagner or Liszt. The subheadlines screamed out "Dr. Dvorak Finds in Them the Basis for an American School of Music." Dvořák declared passionately, "In the Negro melodies of America I discover all that is needed for a great and noble school of music." The article continues by announcing that the National Conservatory was actively seeking "colored students" and agitating for more government support for the institution. It includes letters by Jeannette Thurber and by Fanny Payne Walker, the latter a heart-rending application for a scholarship from a poor orphaned singer. The article concludes with the announcement of prizes to be awarded by the Conservatory.[2]

The reaction was swift, so swift that it has an orchestrated feel to it. The following day a condensed version was printed in the Paris edition of the *Herald*, and within a week reporters had solicited opinions from Berlin, Vienna, Paris, and Boston interviewing more than a dozen composers and performers, including Anton Bruckner, John Knowles Paine, Hans Richter, Joseph Joachim, and Anton Rubinstein. The reactions ranged from curious to totally dismissive. The greatest hostility came from Boston and perhaps Vienna (the second and third headlines in the article from Vienna read "What Eminent Viennese Composers Think of Dvorak's Negro-Melody Idea" and "A Cold Water Douche").

Yet the commotion was far from over. A week later, the composer amplified his viewpoint in an article titled "Antonin Dvorak on Negro Melodies."[3] His contribution came in the form of a letter to the editor in which he said that the article a week earlier had made a "great impression" on him. He went on: "It is my opinion that I find a sure foundation in the negro melodies for a new national school of music. . . .The new American school of music must strike its roots deeply into its own soil." We can recognize here an echo of the sentiments expressed in "Negro Music" by "Tonsor"! A final article, on June 4, contains various letters to the editor about Dvořák's ideas, mostly critical.[4]

In order to understand how James Creelman could have pulled off such a coup, we must look briefly at his biography. Born in Canada on November 12, 1859, Creelman became a cub reporter for the *Herald* at the age of seventeen.[5] In the next few years, as part of his work, he ascended a balloon in Montreal, was shot at by one of the Hatfields while covering the Hatfield and McCoy feud, got arrested by British marines for his part in a scheme to challenge the quality of English security by placing an imitation torpedo on a warship, and paddled up the Missouri River to inteview Sitting Bull. In 1889, Creelman became the *Herald*'s special correspondent in Europe, editing the *London Herald* in 1889–90 and the *Paris Herald* the following two years. During that time he wangled a highly coveted audience with Pope Leo XIII, debriefed the explorer Henry Stanley about his rescue of Emin Pacha, and went to Russia to investigate pogroms against the Jews, where he also managed to interview Tolstoy about his views on marriage as outlined in *The Kreutzer Sonata*. Upon returning to New York he briefly became the editor of the *Evening Telegram*, the *Herald*'s sister paper. He probably left the *Herald* sometime in 1893 after a dispute with its editor, James Gordon Bennett, Jr. After that he managed the London edition of *Cosmopolitan* magazine, and, in the summer of 1894 became a contributor to the *Illustrated American*; he returned to New York as a contributing editor to Pulitzer's *New York World* in 1894.

Thus, as the editor of the *New York Evening Telegram* in May 1893, Creelman was in a perfect position to encounter Dvořák. Moreover, he was one of the most experienced interviewers of his time, having interviewed at least eight American presidents and Otto von Bismarck. He died while on his way to interview the Kaiser.

Even more significant in this case were Creelman's views on the role of the journalist. He clearly felt that a reporter should communicate directly and personally with the reader: "The frequent introduction of the author's personality is a necessary means of reminding the reader that he is receiving the testimony of an eyewitness."[6] As he worked for Pulitzer's *New York*

World and later Hearst's *New York Journal*, he was among the first in his profession to propose an activist "yellow" journalism, which he later wrote about as "that form of American journalistic energy which is not content merely to print a daily record of history, but seeks to take part in events as an active and sometimes *decisive agent*" (italics mine). [7]

This yellow journalism could take many forms, ranging from sinister to merely batty. For example, Creelman wrote that he and Arthur Brisbane, a reporter for the *Sun* and later the *World*, went to France to cover the heavyweight title fight between Charlie Mitchell and John L. Sullivan. Visiting Mitchell in his dressing room before the fight, Brisbane said something that annoyed the fighter, who took a swing at him. Brisbane punched him back, giving him a pretty decent shot, which certainly did not help the fighter, who lost to Sullivan.[8]

In later years, reporters like Brisbane, Sylvester Scovel, Richard Harding Davis, and Creelman became involved in intrigues that had them presenting peace plans to Cuban insurgents (Scovel) and breaking a woman out of a Cuban jail. Even though there is no evidence whatsoever that Hearst had a hand in blowing up the *Maine* (a favorite belief of conspiracy theorists), Creelman liked to boast, "Things that cannot be referred to even now have been attempted."[9] So how did such ideas play out in relationship to Dvořák and his "New World" Symphony?

At first thought, Creelman's claim to have been involved with a "series of articles" dealing with Dvořák and American music is perplexing, There are no such articles in the *New York Evening Telegram*. Yet though scholars refer to only one "article" in the *Herald*, "Real Value of Negro Melodies," and a letter to the editor the following week, there were in reality seven articles published about the subject in the *New York Herald* between May 21 and June 18, and three news briefs: May 21, "Real Value of Negro Melodies" (article); May 28, "Antonin Dvorak on Negro Melodies" (mostly Dvořák's letter to the editor); May 28, "Dvorak's Theory of Negro Music" (comments from leading European musicians, from the European edition); May 28, "Dvorak's American School of Music" (news brief); May 29, "Negro Melodies in America" (Reyer);[10] May 29, "Dvorak Awakens the Musical World" (news brief); June 4, "Criticisms on Dvorak's Theory" (comments from American musicians); June 15, "American Music" (news brief); June 15, "America's Musical Future" (reprint of article datelined

Fig. 1. Dvořák, in an engraving by T. Johnson, published in Century Magazine, *1892.*

Fig. 2. Jeannette Thurber, philanthropist, who financed Dvořák's sojourns in the United States.

Fig. 3. Josef Kovařík, Dvořák's amanuensis. Courtesy of the Museum of Czech Music.

Fig. 4. Mildred Hill ("Johann Tonsor"), author of the article "Negro Music" and composer of "Happy Birthday."

Fig. 5. James G. Huneker, critic and essayist for the New York Recorder *at the time of Dvořák's visit, in a later photograph.*

Fig. 6. Henry Thacker Burleigh, singer and composer, who sang African-American songs for Dvořák, in a photograph from about 1892.

Fig. 7. James Creelman, journalist for the New York Herald, *in 1893.* Courtesy of John Creelman.

Fig. 8. Main Street of Spillville, Iowa, where Dvořák spent the summer of 1893.

Fig. 9. St. Wenceslaus Church, Spillville, Iowa.

Fig. 10. The Turkey River, Spillville, Iowa.

Fig. 11. Minnehaha Falls, St. Paul, Minnesota, which Dvořák visited in 1893.

Fig. 12. Photographic postcard of Dvořák, marked Spillville, Iowa, 1893.

Fig. 13. Photograph of Dvořák with family and friends taken by Josef Sládek, poet and translator of Longfellow's Hiawatha, *in 1894. Dvořák is second from left. Anna Dvořáková is above him to the right, and Josefina is to her right, next to Count Kounic, the bearded man in the middle.* Courtesy of the Museum of Czech Music.

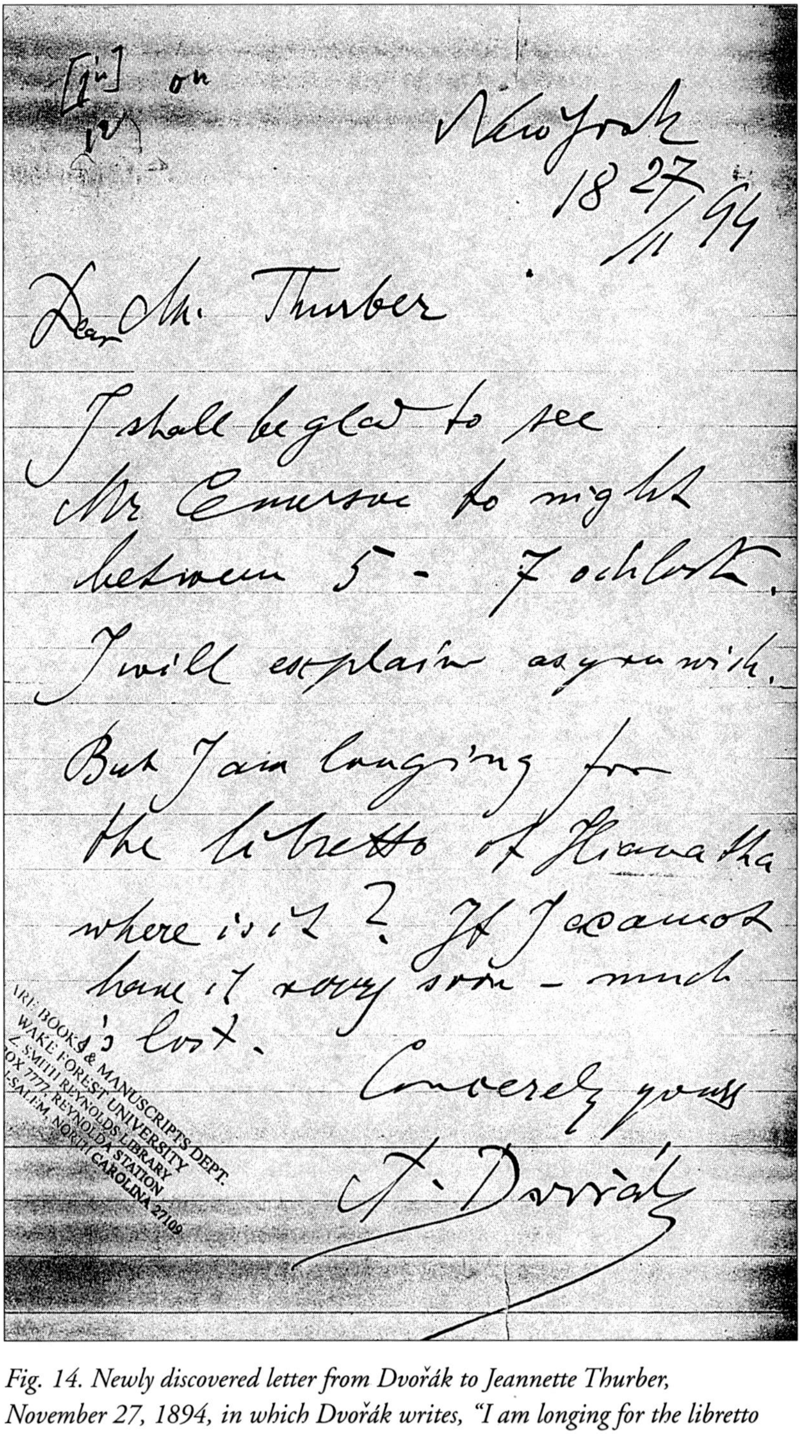

Fig. 14. Newly discovered letter from Dvořák to Jeannette Thurber,
November 27, 1894, in which Dvořák writes, "I am longing for the libretto
of Hiawatha, where is it? If I cannot have it very soon—much is lost."
Courtesy of the Rare Books and Manuscripts Department, Wake Forest University.

Fig. 15. Cartoon of Dvořák teaching at the National Conservatory.

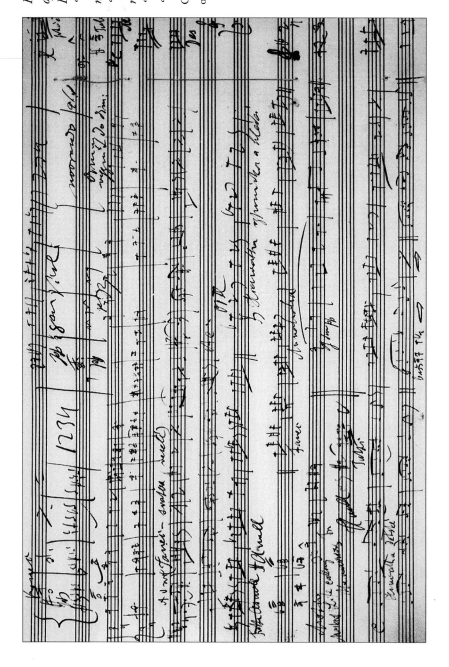

Fig. 16. First group of Hiawatha sketches: Line 5 of the music, "Dance—wedding merriment"; line 7, "Hiawatha seeks and reflects"; line 9, "Life calling," "Minnehaha theme." Courtesy of the Museum of Czech Music.

Fig. 17. Second group of Hiawatha sketches: March and Aria, "Onaway! Awake, beloved!" Courtesy of the Museum of Czech Music.

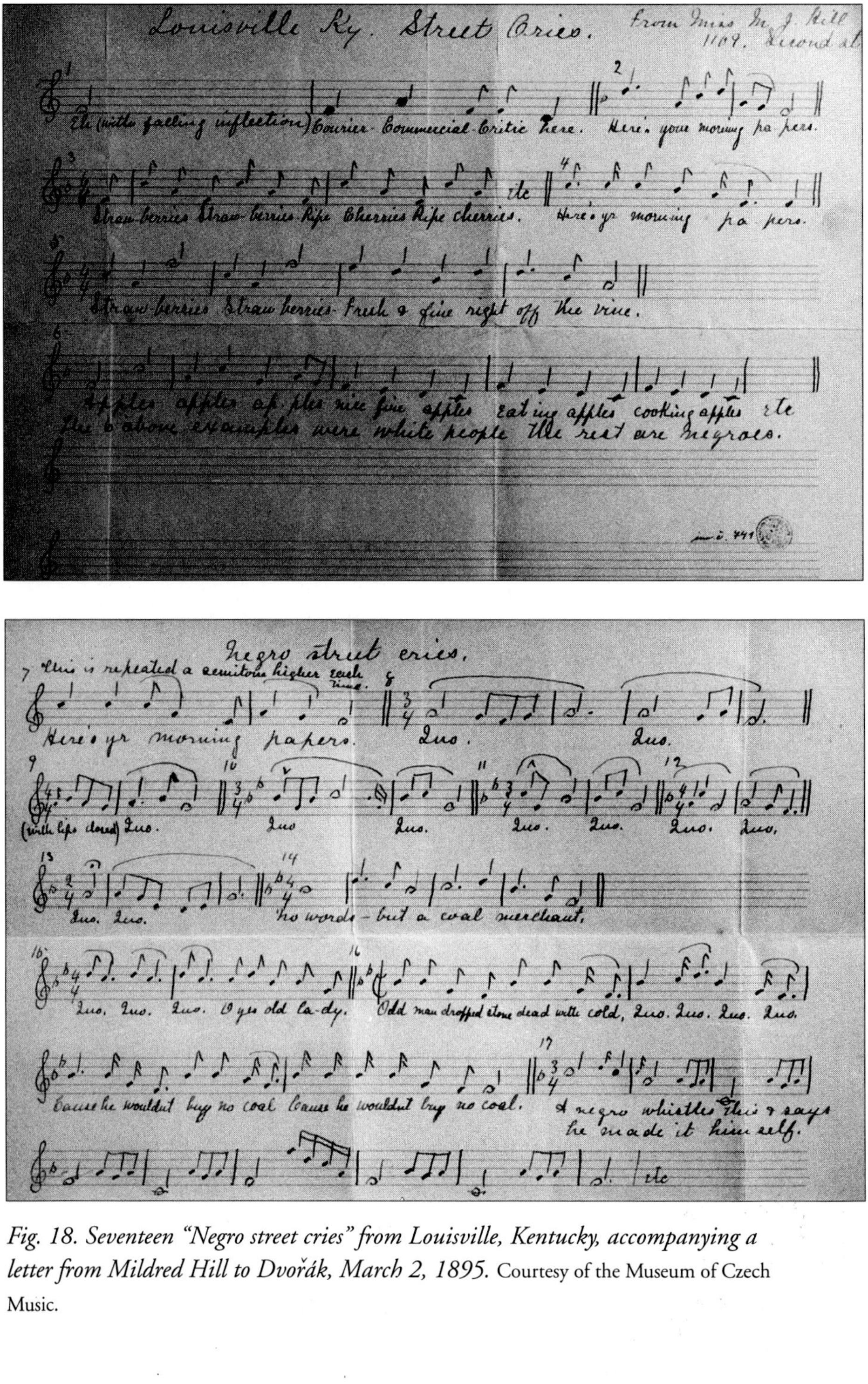

Fig. 18. Seventeen "Negro street cries" from Louisville, Kentucky, accompanying a letter from Mildred Hill to Dvořák, March 2, 1895. Courtesy of the Museum of Czech Music.

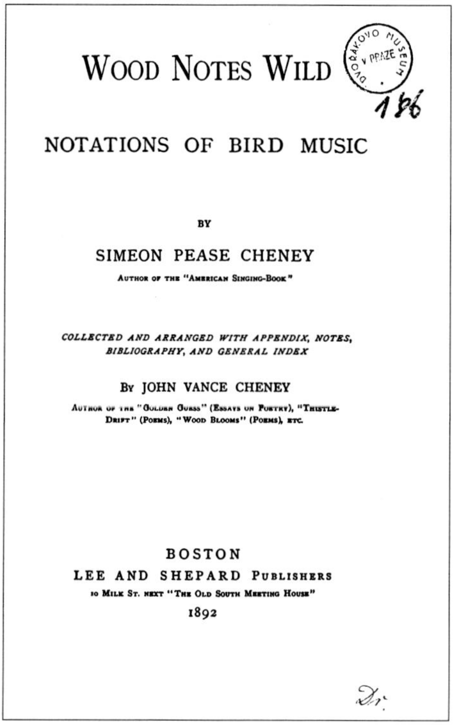

WOOD NOTES WILD

NOTATIONS OF BIRD MUSIC

BY

SIMEON PEASE CHENEY

AUTHOR OF THE "AMERICAN SINGING-BOOK"

COLLECTED AND ARRANGED WITH APPENDIX, NOTES,
BIBLIOGRAPHY, AND GENERAL INDEX

BY JOHN VANCE CHENEY

AUTHOR OF THE "GOLDEN GUESS" (ESSAYS ON POETRY), "THISTLE-
DRIFT" (POEMS), "WOOD BLOOMS" (POEMS), ETC.

BOSTON
LEE AND SHEPARD PUBLISHERS
10 MILK ST. NEXT "THE OLD SOUTH MEETING HOUSE"
1892

Fig. 19. Wood Notes Wild, *given to Dvořák by James Huneker, from which the composer took several snippets of birdsong.* Courtesy of the Museum of Czech Music.

Fig. 20. "Music of Hungary," anonymous poem, dedicated to Dvořák, showing where the composer has in every case crossed out "Hungary" and written in "Bohemia." Courtesy of the Museum of Czech Music.

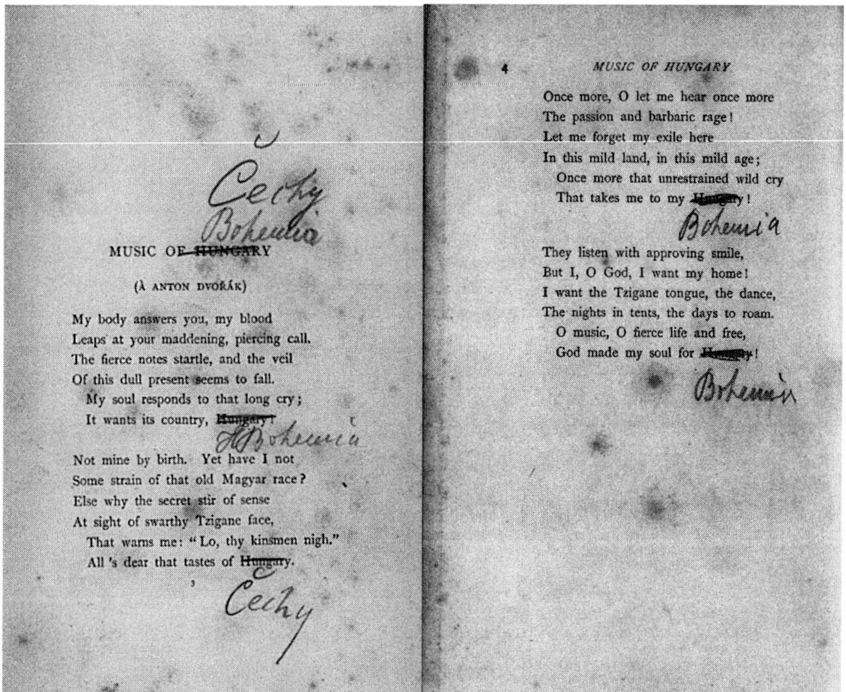

MUSIC OF ~~HUNGARY~~

(À ANTON DVOŘÁK)

My body answers you, my blood
Leaps at your maddening, piercing call.
The fierce notes startle, and the veil
Of this dull present seems to fall.
My soul responds to that long cry;
It wants its country, ~~Hungary~~!

Not mine by birth. Yet have I not
Some strain of that old Magyar race?
Else why the secret stir of sense
At sight of swarthy Tzigane face,
That warns me: "Lo, thy kinsmen nigh."
All 's dear that tastes of ~~Hungary~~.

4   MUSIC OF HUNGARY

Once more, O let me hear once more
The passion and barbaric rage!
Let me forget my exile here
In this mild land, in this mild age;
Once more that unrestrained wild cry
That takes me to my ~~Hungary~~!

They listen with approving smile,
But I, O God, I want my home!
I want the Tzigane tongue, the dance,
The nights in tents, the days to roam.
O music, O fierce life and free,
God made my soul for ~~Hungary~~!

Fig. 21. Henry E. Krehbiel,
music critic for the New York
Daily Tribune.

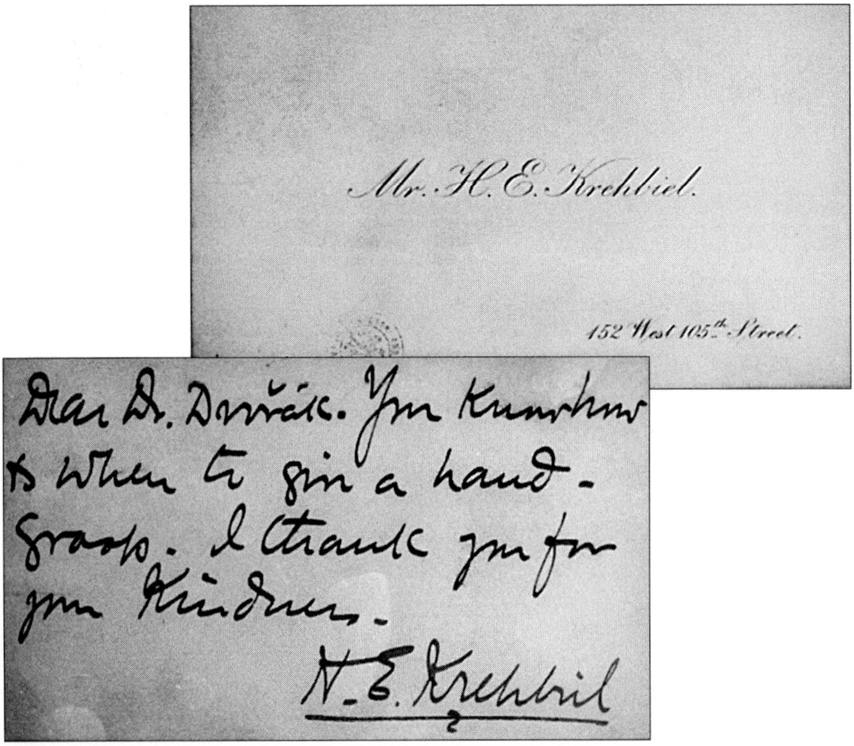

Fig. 22. Krehbiel's visiting card, with a note written on the back: "Dear Dr. Dvořák.
You know how and when to give a handgrasp. I thank you for your kindness.
H. E. Krehbiel." Courtesy of the Museum of Czech Music.

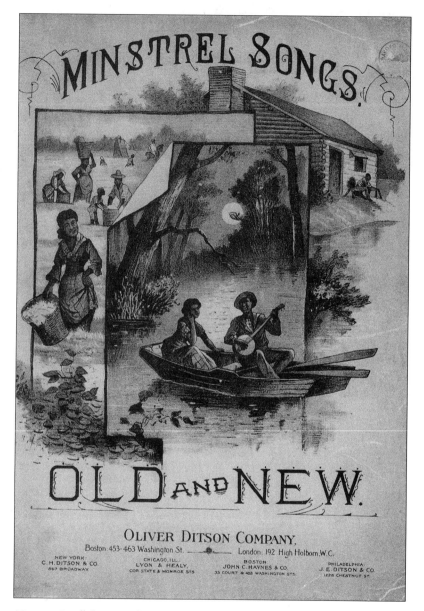

Fig. 23. Dvořák's copy of Minstrel Songs Old and New, *discovered in Prague.*
Courtesy of the Museum of Czech Music.

Fig. 24. First page of Minstrel Songs, *containing Stephen Foster's "Old Folks at Home," which Dvořák arranged for orchestra. Kovařík sent the volume to Prague with a note at the bottom of the page explaining that Dvořák had left it in the United States.* Courtesy of the Museum of Czech Music.

Fig. 25. Page 2 of "Nicodemus Johnson," with Dvořák's blue pencil marks. The rhythm of the composer's Humoresque in G-flat Major may have been drawn from this song. Courtesy of the Museum of Czech Music.

Vienna, from the European edition); June 18, "Negro Song Writers" (a discussion with the songwriting team of Braham and Harrigan, Victor Herbert, and an anonymous person about Dvořák's proclamation).[11]

Creelman at this time, in addition to his work with the *Telegram*, was a regular contributor of features to the *New York Herald*, and was ideally poised to have interviewed Dvořák and gotten the results quickly into print. So when he claims to have set forth "a series of articles" before the public, he is surely referring to some of these.

Creelman's assertion that he was in close contact with Dvořák can be substantiated. The article in the *Budget* includes a photograph of Dvořák taken in New York by W. M. Spiess. In the upper left-hand corner Dvořák wrote: "To my friend James Creelman."[12] Just below are the first four bars of "Old Folks at Home," under which Dvořák signed his name and entered the date, January 22, 1894.

It is also possible to show that Creelman had an abiding interest in Dvořák and his symphony "From the New World." In an undated character sketch of her husband, Alice Creelman referred to the "Creelman Symphony," presumably since he was always talking about the work and directing everyone's attention to it.[13] James Creelman continued his interest in Dvořák, his music, and the American musical scene. In a signed article in *The Illustrated American* of August 4, 1894, with the provocative title "Does It Pay to Study Music?" Creelman wrote forcefully about the need to support the National Conservatory and quoted Dvořák at length: " 'I would not stay in America for one month unless I believed that I was engaged in a great national work,' said Dvorak the last time I saw him. 'I am not a young man, and every day of my life must bear some fruit. I have no right to waste the influence of my name.' "[14] I will suggest at the conclusion of this inquiry that Creelman wrote, but left unsigned, at least one more article about Dvořák.

Before marshaling further evidence in support of Creelman's claim, we need to explain one aspect of his *Budget* article that does not add up in the least. Here is Creelman writing about the genesis of the "New World" Symphony:

At last the strain of the controversy became too great, and in sheer desperation the great Bohemian announced that he would write a symphony suggested from beginning to end by negro melodies. He dashed off a few bars in his note-book—which through the courtesy of the composer, we reproduce, and started out on a long summer vacation at Spillville, Iowa. Here, among a few Bohemian emigrants, surrounded by the mighty plains and filled with a sense of the vastness and solitude of the West, he poured out his soul in harmony.

This is a howler by anyone's definition. It is well known that the "New World" Symphony was written almost entirely in New York City just *before* the series of articles appeared in the *Herald*. Certainly the writer of any of these articles should have known that, especially since the second of the four headlines accompanying Dvořák's letter to the editor on May 28 (about Negro melodies) reads, "The Bohemian Composer Employs Their Themes and Sentiment in a New Symphony." The article makes it clear that the symphony is complete.[15]

How then are we to deal with what is either an almost unforgivably ignorant mistake or an outright lie? Before we can answer this question, we must run through the evidence for Creelman's authorship.

The most telling proof that Creelman wrote "Real Value of Negro Melodies" can be found by exploring five references in the article that deal with matters other than Dvořák, thus giving us some insight into the preferences and experiences of the writer.

1. "Americans vaunt their hospitals, and yet I have seen the most extensive and most perfectly equipped bacteriological institute in the world maintained by a few Russians without a word of boasting."
2. "Rubinstein told me that Wagner was a poor musician because he lacked the power of musical invention. . . . "[!]
3. "Many of the negro melodies—most of them, I believe—are the creations of negroes born and reared in America. That is the peculiar aspect of the problem. The negro does not produce music of that kind elsewhere. I have heard the black singers in Hayti for hours at the bamboula dances, and, as a rule, their songs are not unlike the monotonous and crude chantings of the Sioux tribes."
4. A quote from Francis Bacon: "Who taught the raven in a drought to throw pebbles into a hollow tree so that the water might rise so that she might come to it? Who taught the bee to sail. . . . "

5. "Take those simple themes and weave them into splendid and harmonious forms. Glorify them: give them breadth. So the Dutch painter talks to his pupils. Do not try to imagine the angel in heaven, but try to paint that wrinkled peasant woman at your side, that the angel in her may be seen by ordinary eyes."

Of all the reporters in New York City in the 1890s, Creelman was certainly the only one who was known to have visited Russian hospitals, interviewed Rubinstein, and spent time in Haiti. Further, he was a special admirer of Sir Francis Bacon, whom he referred to in his memoirs as "the greatest philosopher since Plato." Finally, Creelman's signed article in the *Pall Mall Budget* ends with the following lines, a direct parallel to no. 5 above:

It is better to go to the common people for themes, for only that can survive which expresses their natures. The modern painter who expresses the idea of prayer by a haloed woman with folded hands and kneeling attitude, falls far below him who paints a grey-haired woman about to eat a crust of bread raising her reverent, thankful eyes toward Heaven.

Both passages are vintage Creelman, who together with his wife, Alice Buell Creelman, was a serious art collector—for a time they may even have owned Constable's famous *Salisbury Cathedral*. He was even a composer of sorts.[16] Doubtless he is the author of "Real Value of Negro Melodies."

We can draw several larger conclusions from this determination. First, it is probable that only someone with Creelman's ability as an interviewer could have elicited such an unusually detailed and candid response from the composer. Second, and along the same lines: by establishing the author of the piece we must realize that "Real Value" is an *article* by James Creelman that includes an interview with Dvořák, not merely an *interview* with Dvořák, and still less, an article *by* Dvořák. Knowing now what we do about Creelman, we might want to be a trifle cautious about how we attribute this material to Dvořák. We know how journalists, then and now, can transform material to suit their own views, and even though Dvořák never complained, we will never know precisely what he said, and what precisely Creelman did with it. Furthermore, Creelman's interviewing technique is quite idiosyncratic, as the following exchange describing his method reveals:

> *Do you take notes during your interviews?*
> Never. I am always thoroughly conversant with the subject under discussion, and deeply interested in what my companion will say, so it is an easy matter to remember all the notable and striking things and those are all the public cares to read.
> *Do you then go to your room and write out the conversation?*
> I never write a line with a pen or pencil. I always dictate to a stenographer or typewriter.[17]

Unless Creelman possessed an eerie ability for total recall, this technique is not likely to produce a completely accurate transcript of the event.

The entire episode of May and June 1893 was probably orchestrated by Creelman, as this kind of undertaking was a specialty of his.[18] He definitely wrote the first article and was surely involved in the second, and probably subsequent ones as well. He must have used his experience as an international correspondent to quickly reach *Herald* outposts in Boston and Paris and dispatchers in Vienna and Berlin.[19] We may remember he had edited both the London and Paris editions of the *Herald*, and his contacts must have helped to get such quick responses from various composers and musicians. In fact, knowing what we do about Creelman, he was the only personality around who could have galvanized such a tumultuous response so quickly. This kind of orchestrated journalistic event became a specialty of his during his years with Hearst. Thus we should consider that a good bit of the commotion surrounding the premiere of the symphony "From the New World" in December was due to the excitement generated by Creelman. Indeed, stirring up news fit in neatly with Creelman's mandate as a journalist.

As an aside, it is now possible to argue that at least one of the articles written at the time of the premiere of the "New World" Symphony is also by Creelman. On December 17, 1893, the *Herald* published a piece on page 5 titled "Dvorak's Symphony a Historic Event." This article has Creelman's fingerprints all over it, though it does not, of course, carry his byline. The article includes the same sketch from the symphony that Creelman would later publish in the *Budget*, claims that the symphony was written *after* the *Herald* articles, and mounts the same spirited defense of the National Conservatory that we find in "Real Value" and, especially, in Creelman's signed article in *The Illustrated American*. Other statements in the article are Creelmanesque, especially the following poke referring to the controversy over Dvořák's opinions: "Hardly had this appeared in the *Herald* when the so-called music critics in this country wagged their heads and said that Dvorak was all wrong." It does not stand to reason that such a statement was written by a music critic, nor does this article have the stamp of the professional critic. (This is especially clear when we compare the article to another one published in the *Herald* on the same day, "Dr. Dvorak's Great Symphony," probably by Albert Steinberg.) The article ends by suggesting that there is a "conspiracy of silence" about acknowledging Jeannette Thurber's role in the whole process, a Creelman staple— the two of them were close, and the reporter was likely a paid publicist for Thurber.[20]

Even though the writing in "Dvorak Leads for the Fund," of January 24, 1894, is a trifle too technical to be Creelman's, and the article "Hear 'The Old Folks at Home,'" which appeared the day before, sounds a bit too naive, the journalist was certainly involved with another of Dvořák's notable American activities: the *Herald* clothing drive.

A little-known aspect of Dvořák's time in the United States is his relationship to the changing economic realities. The year 1893 was a difficult one for the American economy. Railroad stocks collapsed, and many banks failed.[21] The New York City area was hit particularly hard. In the words of the *Herald*:

> The results of the great industrial panic can hardly be exaggerated. Poverty on a scale never known before in this country has been forced upon multitudes of people hitherto strangers to want. Gently bred men are sleeping in wretched lodging houses. Young girls, driven to desperation by their necessities, are becoming an easy prey to shame. What chance has a ragged man in broken shoes and a worn out hat to get a position as a bookkeeper? . . . Feed a man and you make him comfortable. But clothe him decently and you restore his hope and self-respect.

Creelman, no doubt in cahoots with Thurber, came up with a scheme to raise needed money for clothing and at the same time bring attention to the National Conservatory. To this end, a wonderful concert was planned and executed. There is a letter to the editor in Dvořák's hand about the *Herald*'s Free Clothing Drive, dated December 17, 1893, among the Creelman papers at Ohio State University.[22] Although Creelman may simply have taken the letter as a souvenir, it is far more likely that Dvořák either gave him the letter at the time of the "New World" Symphony's premiere or that Creelman received *all* letters addressed to the editor that dealt with the clothing drive.

The letter, clearly edited by a native English speaker (probably Creelman), announces Dvořák's intention to hold a benefit concert at Madison Square Garden on January 23, 1894. In the words of the *New York Herald* on the following day:

> Each soloist, with one exception, belonged to the colored race. This idea was due to Mrs. Thurber. She threw open the doors of her excellently equipped musical educational establishment to pupils of ability, no matter what their race, color or creed. Bodies had been liberated, but the gates of the artistic world were still locked.

Vintage Creelman. And what a concert it was! Harry Burleigh sang, and so did Sissieretta Jones ("the Black Patti"), accompanied by the chorus and orchestra of the National Conservatory, conducted by Dvořák. Dvořák's own arrangement of "Old Folks at Home" received its first performance.

It was at just this time, actually one day earlier, that Dvořák inscribed a photograph "to my friend James Creelman." From all this it follows that Creelman was a major player in organizing the clothing drive for the *Herald*, and that he wrote many of the articles for the event. This kind of publicizing, one of Creelman's great gifts, was to come to a much more visible spectacle when the reporter orchestrated the notorious "homecoming" of Evangeline Cisneros, who had been freed from a Cuban jail by another Hearst reporter, who had been hired to "kidnap" her.

The only question remaining in the relationship between Creelman and Dvořák involves the "New World" Symphony. Did Creelman lie about the genesis of the symphony, and if so why? Could he actually be telling the truth? In his *Herald* article of December 17, 1893, Creelman claims that Dvořák, after writing his letter to the editor on May 28, offered a further communication to the newspaper announcing that "he would write a symphony based upon American negro and Indian melodies to prove that his position was sound and sincere." If, indeed, there was such an announcement, it could only have appeared between May 28 and June 3, when Dvořák left for Spillville, since it is unlikely the composer would have cabled the *Herald* from the road. Creelman turns out to have been correct; there was another announcement concerning Dvořák's symphony: in a news brief that appeared on Monday, May 29, it was announced once again that the composer had *finished* the work![23]

The only way Creelman could have thought that the symphony was actually written in Spillville would have been if he wrote the first article in the series and somehow missed all the rest, especially the article containing Dvořák's letter to the editor on May 28. While it is remotely possible that Dvořák himself might have confused the issue—Creelman is not the only person who stated that large chunks of the symphony were written in Spillville—and it is even more remotely possible that Creelman, in a burst of pathological megalomania, could have convinced himself that he really *was* the instigator of the symphony, it is much more likely that Creelman was indulging in his taste for hyperbole, in one stroke both claiming responsibility for the entire symphony and symbolically setting its composition in the heartland of America.

There is no better illustration of this yellow journalism in action than an etching that shows Creelman leading a successful charge up a hill during the Spanish-American War. Yet the most telling episode came later, after Creelman had been injured, supposedly when he stupidly taunted the Spanish by waving a flag. The reporter was taken to a roadside hospital, where he lay in agony for hours. Suddenly Hearst appeared at his side wearing a revolver in his belt. "But now he was living the ultimate dream—after the battle of El Caney, interviewing a wounded hero, who was one of the Journal's own. With painstaking care Hearst wrote down word for word Creelman's story, which was interrupted only by twinges of pain. When the task was complete, Hearst solemnly stated to Creelman: 'I'm sorry you're hurt.' Then, with his face radiant with enthusiasm, he announced: 'But wasn't it a splendid fight? We must beat every paper in the world.' "[24]

While such shenanigans do not make Creelman the most reliable witness in the world, they do not in the least disqualify him from having written the articles in the *Herald*, especially considering the overwhelming evidence in his favor—indeed, they make it more likely that they were by him.

James Creelman's long association with the *New York Herald* came to an end sometime in 1893. At least part of the reason involved his desire to have a byline—a draft of a letter sent to Bennett around the time of the premiere of Dvořák's symphony states that "Bennett's most recent communication leaves me free to take up a purely literary career and to write over my own name." It is tempting to think that one of the Dvořák articles decided Creelman's fate and sent him off to a career as one of the leading war correspondents of his time and the ultimate Hearst reporter. For those of us who rather arrogantly assume that the subject of our work is the most famous person at the time, I should note that Creelman does not even mention Dvořák in his book, *On the Great Highway*, leaving the stage to the likes of Tolstoy and Teddy Roosevelt.[25]

Creelman's false claim that the "New World" was composed as a response to the articles in the *Herald* remains troubling and mysterious to the end: he loved the work deeply yet managed to distort its genesis. Why? Perhaps he felt, in his yellow journalist's zeal, that the symphony would be taken more seriously if it was presented as the result of a colorful controversy, with its composition set amid the prairie grasses. It is possible that the information was passed to him by James Huneker after one of the visits mentioned by Kovařík, and it simply got muddled in the retelling. Maybe Creelman was just too lazy to get all the facts. Rather than trying to explain his actions, we can leave the last word to the man himself: "The author has attempted to give the original color and atmosphere of some of the great events of his own time, and leaves the duty of moralizing to his indulgent patrons."[26]

8

Dvořák, Krehbiel, and the "New World"

The fires generated by James Creelman's published interview with Dvořák flashed sparks until mid-June. By then, though, Dvořák was happily on his way to a glorious summer stay in Spillville, where, among other things, he touched up his symphony, giving rise to the potent myth that the symphony was composed in Iowa. In the middle of November 1893, Anton Seidl, conductor of the New York Philharmonic, asked Dvořák if he could present his newly composed symphony to the American public. Dvořák agreed, and the date was set for the following month. This forthcoming premiere of a symphony already somewhat notorious from the brouhaha in May caused a scramble among local journalists to get comments from the Great Man. If we are to believe Kovařík, James Huneker was rebuffed in his request, taking revenge on the composer in various places, including, most notably, his memoirs, where we encounter "Doc Borax" the boozer. Perhaps in the busy days before the first performance, Dvořák met once again with James Creelman. Certainly the acerbic Albert Steinberg of the *Herald* came to call, and he was able to publish a brief but fascinating interview with Dvořák on the day of the first performance.[1] But the real plum went to Henry Krehbiel. For if Huneker was there, as it were, at the conception, and Creelman was the Star of Bethlehem, surely Henry Krehbiel was at least two of the Three Kings who brought news of the great event to the American public.

On December 15, 1893, a mammoth article by Krehbiel appeared in the *New York Daily Tribune*.[2] Over 2500 words long, and complete with analysis, observations, and musical examples, the piece offered a comprehensive discussion of the "New World," that was to have its premiere that evening. Krehbiel's article had wide resonance: not only was it reprinted the next day in the *Cincinnati Gazette Inquirer*, but on December 20 it was again presented in full as part of a larger discussion of the new work in *The Musical Courier* opposite the lengthy, somewhat combative essay by James Huneker noted in the preceding chapter. Although Krehbiel's article has a claim to fame as probably the most exhaustive analytical essay on music ever to appear in an American newspaper, there is something even more distinctive about it: the piece was compiled on the basis of special notes that the composer made for the critic.[3]

It says a great deal about Dvořák that, at least for a while, he could maintain friendships with flashy types like James Huneker and James Creelman, but it is no surprise at all that he hit it off with Henry Krehbiel. While Krehbiel's advocacy of "American" music reveals at least a tinge of the outsized ambition that was the legacy of the two Jameses, the methods he used were more sober, and his long-term investment in the whole program of national-music building marked him off from the vast number of critics hoping to make news by sensationalizing whatever happened to be hot at the time.

Dvořák and Krehbiel

Krehbiel was born in Ann Arbor, Michigan, in 1854 and studied law before turning to journalism. He worked first for the *Cincinnati Gazette* and then spent more than forty years as the critic for the *New York Daily Tribune*.[4] He was not merely a journalist, though, but someone of wide-ranging interests. He lectured regularly on folk music and showed an intense interest in Greek music theory, Wagner, and the music of the American Indians. He read widely and was responsible for putting Thayer's *Life of Beethoven* into finished form. He wrote several books and was a key figure in the musical life of his age. When he died in 1923, an obituary by Richard Aldrich in *Music and Letters* referred to him simply as "the leading music critic of America."[5]

Krehbiel once categorized most of those who write about music as either "pedants" or "rhapsodists." The former, he felt, "are concerned with forms and rules, with externals, to the forgetting of that which is inexpressibly nobler and higher." Yet they cause few problems, "because they are not interesting; strictly speaking, they do not write for the public at all, but only for their professional colleagues." Krehbiel's real enemies are the "rhapsodists," who "take advantage of the fact that the language of music is indeterminate and evanescent to talk about the art in such a way as to present themselves as persons of exquisite sensibilities rather than to direct attention to the real nature and beauty of music itself." [6] These words ring as true today as they did one hundred years ago.

Krehbiel also devoted himself to education, publishing a music appreciation book, *How to Listen to Music*, in 1896. In the last section of the volume, "Musician, Critic, and Public," he aptly discusses the relationship between critic, audience, and performer/composer. The conclusion of the chapter is worth quoting in full, not only for the philosophical questions it raises but also because it is almost impossible to resist comparing Krehbiel's approach with that of many contemporary music critics:

> The critic should be the mediator between the musician and the public. For all new works he should do what the symphonists of the Liszt school attempt to do by means of programmes; he should excite curiosity, arouse interest, and pave the way to popular comprehension. But for the old he should not fail to encourage reverence and admiration. To do both these things he must know his duty to the past, the present, and the future, and adjust each duty to the other. Such adjustment is only possible if he knows the music of the past and present, and is quick to perceive the bent and outcome of novel strivings. He should be catholic in taste, outspoken in judgment, unalterable in allegiance of his ideals, unswervable in integrity.[7]

The blend of fiery advocacy and a conservative bent reflected in these remarks goes a long way toward explaining the affinity Krehbiel felt for Dvořák. We do not know when they first met, but an article by Krehbiel greeted the composer upon his arrival in the New World. Published in the *Century Illustrated Monthly Magazine* in September 1892, the article introduces Dvořák to American audiences with a flourish that makes Krebhiel's position clear:

In Dvorak and his works is to be found a twofold encouragement for
the group of native musicians whose accomplishments of late have
seemed to herald the rise of a school of American composers. . . .There
is measureless comfort in the prospect which the example of Dvorak has
opened up. It promises freshness and forcefulness of melodic, harmonic, and rhythmic contents, and newness and variety in the vehicles
of utterance.[8]

For Krehbiel, the promise of Dvořák lay in his deep-seated belief that
musical composition, in order to be profound, had to embrace national
spirit:

> Like tragedy in its highest conception, music is of all times and all peo-
> ples; but the more the world comes to realize how deep and intimate are
> the springs from which the emotional element of music flows, the more
> fully will it recognize that originality and power in the composer rest
> upon the use of dialects and idioms which are national or racial in ori-
> gin and structure.[9]

Krehbiel had both specific ambitions for American music and an affinity for Slavic composers; clearly, he saw Dvořák not merely as a European
representative, but more specifically as a Slav. It was on the elemental vitality of this group that Krehbiel pinned his hopes for a bright new future
for American music:

> The answer [to the cry for new directions in musical development] has
> come from the Slavonic school, which is youthful enough to have pre-
> served the barbaric virtue of truthfulness and is fearless in the face of
> convention. . . . Its characteristics are rhythmic energy and harmonic
> daring.[10]

As we have seen, Krehbiel and Dvořák were in frequent contact around
the time of the "New World" premiere. Krehbiel wanted to have a close
look at the score, and surviving letters from him show that he visited
Dvořák in his home around that time, and that Dvořák made notes about
the symphony for him.[11] That Dvořák would do this for Krehbiel, and

for him alone, suggests that they had an especially warm and trusting relationship.

Krehbiel's enthusiasm, erudition, and admiration must have flattered the composer, who was ordinarily reluctant to talk about his music.[12] Dvořák for his part probably felt that Krehbiel understood him as well as anyone could, and he gave the critic the most intimate access to his creative process. No one else, not even Jeannette Thurber, knew as much about the symphony as did Krehbiel.[13]

On the other side, Dvořák must have looked like the answer to Krehbiel's most ardent prayers. After all, the composer's aesthetic, conservative yet dynamic, corresponded perfectly to the critic's approach. Further, considering Dvořák's belief in national music and his inspiring attempt to create a work that reflected "American" energy, style, and variety, the composer's work was a concrete manifestation of all the goals for which Krehbiel had been reaching. That may be perhaps why Krehbiel ended his letter of December 16, 1893, thanking Dvořák for making notes on the symphony:

> I have had no greater happiness from 20 years of labor on behalf of good music than has come to me from the consciousness that I may have been to some degree instrumental in helping the public to appreciate your compositions, and especially this beautiful symphony.

Krehbiel on the "New World"

Krehbiel's December 15 article opens immediately with a discussion of national music and takes a neat slap at the way Creelman and the *Herald* misrepresented the affair in May. Here "yellow" journalism is taken to task by "responsible" journalism:

> The production of a new symphony by the eminent Bohemian composer would be a matter of profound interest under any circumstances, but to this occasion is given a unique and special value by the fact that in the new work Dr. Dvorak has exemplified his theories touching the possibility of founding a National school of composition on the folk-song of America. His belief on this point, put forth in an incomplete

and bungling manner through newspaper publications last Spring, created a great deal of comment at the time, the bulk of which was distinguished by flippancy and a misconception of the composer's meaning and purposes.

Krehbiel had a vested interest in the symphony's reception, since he, as much as anyone, understood the symphony as an object lesson for American composers:

> Only among his colleagues in Europe did his utterances find intelligent appreciation; for they knew what Dr. Dvorak had done for Bohemian music, and they also knew that if he said he had found material in America capable of being utilized in the construction of art-works distinctive in character, he would be able to demonstrate the fact.

And Krehbiel accused opponents of having "so long remained indifferent to the treasures of folk-song which America contains."

For Krehbiel, this discussion was not merely academic: he was at the time lecturing and writing regularly on the subject of national music. Indeed, in the *Tribune* on December 17, 1893, several pages after Krehbiel's second article on the "New World," there was a report of a lecture on folksong, given by the critic the previous day:

> Mr. Krehbiel explained the growth of the folk song in America, and showed the difference between it and the popular ballad. He said that the folk song composed itself; it was the product of the people, and came as an expression of their sorrows and joys. The identity of the author of the song was always lost. Its creation was a passing phenomenon; its music reflected the inner feeling of those among whom it found utterance.

Throughout his career, Krehbiel had an interest in African-American and Native American music, making arrangements, publishing tunes, and even sending several examples to Dvořák a week after the premiere. This interest may explain why Krehbiel virtually trumpeted his reason for penning such an ambitious article:

It is the purpose of this writing to enable those who shall hear the symphony this afternoon or to-morrow evening to appreciate wherein its American character consists. . . . There need be no hesitation in saying that the music fully justifies the title which Dr. Dvorak has given it. He has depended upon the melodic ideas and the spirit of the work to disclose its national character.

Krehbiel follows this passage with a detailed discussion of the symphony, focusing on two technical details that make it "American": the "Scotch snap" and the use of pentatonic scales. Both Krehbiel and Dvořák could have identified these devices through their reading of Mildred Hill's work. The first, a crisp, short accent on the first beat of the measure, was familiar to Dvořák before he arrived; it is also a feature of the Czech language.

Yet Krehbiel argues that these two devices should be understood as metaphysically American in this context:

The energy imparted to musical movement by the Scotch snap is, however, unmistakable, and Dr. Dvorak has well understood that its influence upon his work will be felt by its hearers as a natural expression of one of the characteristics of the American people.

This tricky point lay at the core of his squabbles with Huneker and Hale over the national qualities of the work.

The use of the pentatonic scale Krehbiel finds more ambiguous. He suggests that in employing it, "Dr. Dvorak is no more American than he is Scotch, Irish or Chinese, for the old music of these peoples and many others is marked by this peculiarity." He further notes the presence of this scale in the music of the Omaha Indians, referring the reader to a learned study.[14]

Krehbiel mentions that the scale is also used in many "slave songs of the south," identifies its African ancestry, and concludes the first part of the article by saying, "It is certainly aboriginal American, but that fact goes for little or nothing. Enough that it is popular here, and, therefore, justified in a symphony designed to give expression to American feeling."

The remainder of the article is devoted to a discussion and analysis of the symphony based on the notes Dvořák made for the critic, including several observations concerning the relationship between the Largo and *The Song of Hiawatha*, and some speculations about whether or not "Yankee Doodle" makes an appearance in the finale. He notes that the composer was, as usual, inscrutable, and would neither confirm nor deny the fact.

Two days after writing his long article about the "New World," Krehbiel penned still another review in the *Tribune*. Written as a direct result of hearing the premiere, it reflects his most heartfelt ideas about American music and Dvořák's symphony and comprises his definitive rebuttal to critics such as Huneker and Hale. First, he warms to his subject by alluding to critics of the symphony's American qualities:

> It is not to be imagined that the lovely triumph of the American symphony will close the mouths of the cavilers. It will be easy to say that it is a beautiful symphony, but that its character is not distinctively American. Some will call it a Celtic symphony: and they will not have to go far for arguments, for some of its elements are Celtic. Some will say that it is German in its structure, and they will have an easy contention, because the Germans having perfected the symphonic form, and Dr. Dvorak, with all his intense nationalism, being a conservative in this respect, has not deemed it necessary to smash any images in writing this work. He has, in fact, been more orthodox than has been his wont, possibly for the very purpose of making the object lesson which he set out to give native composers effective.

Only then does he articulate his main point, the essence of his argument:

> All that it is necessary to admit is the one thing for which he has compelled recognition—that there are musical elements in America that lend themselves to beautiful treatment in the higher forms of the art. . . . If the melodies which he has composed and moulded into a symphony contain elements which belong also to the music of other peoples, so does the American people contain elements of the races to which those elements are congenial. Let them be Scotch, let them be Irish, let them be German, let them be African, or Indian, in them there is that which makes appeal to the whole people, and therefore, like the people, they are American.

In his conclusion, he tries to explain, by inference, why the songs of Southern blacks are so critical to the formation of an American style:

> Being a hotch-potch of peoples, we cannot be said in a strict sense to have a distinctive style of melody. Being a vast population engrossed in conquering a continent through means that preclude that naive expression which is essential to the production of a folksong, we have been obliged to depend upon an element of the population that possessed the creative capacity. In the melodies of that element in our population there are features which the musician recognizes as characteristic, but the song in which those features are utilized is a product of American environment; that it is native is proved by the fact that it is congenial to American taste, that it touches the American heart.[15]

This passage contains two distinctive strains. The first, which is difficult to dispute, is his notion that just as Europeans have used "their" folk materials in musical works, so too should American composers and that there *are* American elements worthy of symphonic realization. We see clearly his attempt to throw off that sense of cultural inferiority that gripped many musicians and intellectuals.

His second argument is, despite the eloquence of his prose and the goodwill behind his intentions, harder to grasp and defend. He seems to be saying that because the American people are a polyglot crew, anything called "American" music may also have that character. He strays further into dangerous territory when he concludes that what makes the music most American is its appeal to the American soul. Even though both Huneker and Hale were quick to call him on this statement, he never backed down an inch on his main points. And perhaps he was correct to stand steadfast, for after all, the idea of national music has always been more metaphysical and even religious than technical: something becomes national because we believe it to be national.

Krehbiel continued to write about Dvořák's music while the composer was in the United States. Indeed, he penned three essays about Dvořák's American music in the *Tribune* at the beginning of 1894. On January 1 he contributed a piece titled "Dvorak's American Compositions in Boston" in which he castigated Paur, the conductor of the

Boston Symphony, whose performance of the symphony "misconceived the tempo of every movement so completely that the work was robbed of half its charm. It reminded one of the dinner at which everything was cold except the ice-cream." He also complained bitterly about Philip Hale's sarcastic dismissal of the work's "American" quality.[16] On the following Sunday, January 7, we find an essay called "Dvorak's American Compositions" that further amplifies comments made in other articles and offers a full discussion of the Quintet in E-flat Major for strings, Opus 97. Then, in a piece called "Dr. Dvorak's American Music," on Saturday, January 16, he discusses a performance by the Kneisel Quartet of Dvořák's "American" works, describing the composer's style as "full of ingenuity, replete with gracious fancy, clear as crystal and inspiriting in its unalloyed happiness." All in all, then, we have in the span of thirty-one days five articles by Krehbiel, consisting of over ten thousand words and almost thirty music examples, sure testimony to his deep interest in Dvořák and his works.

Henry Krehbiel's final article about Dvořák appeared in *The Looker On* in October 1896. In many ways it provides a point of closure to the episode. It begins by pointedly confessing that most Americans were unaware of Dvořák's visit:

> So far as the vast majority of the people of the United States are concerned, it would be entirely proper to say of them that from 1892 to 1895 they entertained an angel unawares. I refer to the sojourn in this country of Antonin Dvorak.[17]

Later he summarizes Dvořák's significance for the modern world, referring to him as "an ideal representative of the present" and saying that the composer

> helps us to keep up a love for music that is content to be music merely without striving to be philosophy and drama also; but at the same time he stimulates and encourages affection for the things which lie within the horizon of the broader vision of this latter day. Thus he robs two bugaboos of their empty terrors—ultra-radicalism and ultra-conservatism. Whether he gleans in the fields of the classics or cuts freshly in those of

the romanticists, the sheaf which he brings home is always a delight. He
is of all composers living, the frankest musician for music's sake.[18]

Journalism Now and Then

The premiere of Dvořák's symphony "From the New World" was a significant event in the history of American music, but in some ways it was
even more striking in the way it revealed the high level of American music
criticism. There were pages of newspaper space devoted to the subject.
While some accounts merely described the composer's appearance and
listed the society types who attended the premiere, more than ten major
articles gave the performance serious consideration.[19] Two newspapers
even printed music notation: Krehbiel's *Tribune* article appeared on
December 15, and the *New York Herald* on December 17 printed some of
Dvořák's sketches, taking up a third of page 5. The very cream of American music criticism wrote searchingly about the work and its ramifications, and there were brilliant contributions from Steinberg, Huneker,
Krehbiel, Hale, Henry Finck, Reginald De Koven, and Henderson.

What would Dvořák and Krehbiel see if they came back today? Certainly they might be perplexed by the role of music criticism in our society. They would see artists and their agents using critics as if their job were
to create puff pieces to stock résumés; they would see contests playing a
huge role in serious musical life; they would see a society that does not
support its young artists, and their dreams of making education available
to the poor would seem further away than ever. They might find, if they
had the time to explore, that the likelihood of encountering a music example in a major newspaper was, in spite of the monstrous technology available, just about nil, and that despite some conspicuous exceptions, the
overall quality of contemporary music criticism is about as low as the general level of musical literacy.

On the other hand, they might notice, as musicologist Charles Hamm
and conductor Maurice Peress have observed, that their dream of an
American art music based on native traditions of all kinds had come true;
that rather than taking their cue from Europe, many American composers
created musical styles based heavily on the music of African-Americans
and Native Americans, incorporating folk, popular, and art musics in an

astonishingly vibrant blend. Dvořák and Krehbiel, at least, would have been happy with that.

Postscript: A Handshake

Considering their warm and trusting relationship, it is fitting that the final epitaph from Krehbiel to Dvořák is undated and without context. In the Dvořák Archive in Prague there is one of Krehbiel's visiting cards with the critic's address, 152 W. 105th St. On the back of the card is written: "Dear Dr. Dvorak. You know how and when to give a handgrasp. I thank you for your kindness. H. E. Krehbiel."

PART IV

American Influences, American Landscapes

D vořák's "New World" Symphony and his American works in general have been criticized in various ways, but no one denies that they are "original" works. Yet it is astonishing how many kinds of models Dvořák used in creating them. There are musical models: moments from Beethoven, Schubert, Haydn, and Wagner abound. We have just explored the impact of Longfellow's *Hiawatha*, and seen how the article by "Johann Tonsor" stimulated the composer's imagination. There is a reasonable chance that the opening of the symphony was taken from Dvořák's aborted setting of "My Country 'Tis of Thee" (whose melody he later used as the theme for the variation movement in the Quintet in E-flat, Opus 97), and the Scherzo is probably modeled on Dvořák's idea of what Indian music might have been like, with a genuflection toward Beethoven and a possible borrowing from the first song in "Negro Music." Claims for Native American elements in the "American" Quartet and Quintet are hard to substantiate, but the composer said there were some. Add to that such things as birdsong, waterfalls, and the loneliness of the prairie and we have still only part of the gravitational pulls on Dvořák's imagination.

In the chapters of Part IV we will look at further instances of the impact that specifically American ideas, melodies, and images had on Dvorák's music.

9

Burleigh and Dvořák: From the Plantation to the Symphony

Dvořák arrived in New York at the end of September 1892. Let us try to imagine the atmosphere into which he came, and the sense he had that people expected great things from him. The Columbus Day celebrations were under way, the four-hundred-year anniversary being more celebratory and noncontroversial than that of a century later. The new arrivals were treated to three full days and nights of parades, speeches, and fireworks, all near Dvořák's residence. The composer was amazed by the scope of the event. "Think of it! Row after row of magnificent processions."[1] Within a week he heard Colonel Henry Lee Higginson, founder of the Boston Symphony eleven years earlier, give an oration, "Two New Worlds: The New World of Columbus and the New World of Music." The indomitable Jeannette Thurber was plying him with copies of American poems and taking him to see Buffalo Bill's Wild West Show. Czech immigrants were bursting at the seams with pride. Two months after his arrival, on November 27, 1892, he wrote to his friend Josef Hlávka: "America is awaiting great things from me, and mainly that I show them the way to the promised land and the realm of a new independent art: in short, to create [an American] national music."

So the seed had been quickly planted: Why not do for America what he had already done for the Czechs, that is, write standard European music with Americanisms instead of Czechisms? But where to get the Americanisms? Though Dvořák is rarely considered a realist, he had a realist work ethic, a credo we also perceive in Chekhov and Rodin: first immerse yourself in a particular "reality," then write! Dvořák, in the straightforward formulation of novelist Josef Škvorecký,

> had a rather simple theory about how great music should be written— a theory inherited from the German Romantic scholars. A composer must first immerse himself in the folk music of his nation. When he is full of that music, he should compose in the spirit of those tunes and melodies and harmonies.[2]

Probably less than a week after Dvořák sent his letter to Hlávka, James Huneker arrived at his door with a copy of "Negro Music." According to Dvořák's later statements, it was "Negro melodies" that were definitive in his creation of an American style. Yet how could he become "saturated" merely by looking at notated examples of six African-American melodies? And considering that he was happily sketching his symphony less than three months after his arrival in the United States, how could the saturation have happened so quickly? Indeed, confronted with this small window of time, many have wondered where Dvořák could have come up with "real" American models, and many others have doubted that there were such models, preferring to hear the work as "European."

I will argue that while the original stimulus for an American style based on African-American tunes came from "Negro Music," the melodies themselves were brought to life through his contact with Henry (Harry) Thacker Burleigh. While Dvořák most likely fastened on Burleigh *after* receiving the article from Huneker, it is appropriate to review the relationship between Dvořák and Burleigh and the documents that refer to it, and then ask some further questions about all the "Negro melodies" Dvořák might have seen or heard, what role they played in his symphony, and why he loved them so much.

Dvořák and Burleigh

Harry Burleigh was born in Erie, Pennsylvania, on December 2, 1866. His grandfather had been a slave and later worked as the town lamplighter. It is said that Burleigh learned many of the so-called plantation songs while accompanying his grandfather on his rounds. Burleigh's father was also a servant at the house of Elizabeth Russell, a wealthy woman with a great interest in music. Most likely, Burleigh heard many of the professional musicians who played at her house.

After singing in several choirs, Burleigh heard about the scholarships being offered at the National Conservatory in New York and scraped together enough money for an audition. He eventually was awarded a scholarship, and also worked both as secretary to Marian MacDowell (who later set up the MacDowell Colony for creative artists) and as a handyman while he studied a program of voice and other subjects at the conservatory. Eventually he also played string bass and timpani in the orchestra. He was already established at the conservatory when Dvořák arrived in 1892.

The problem that has always dogged anyone interested in pursuing the relationship between Burleigh and Dvořák is the lack of any document that allows us to establish exactly when the two met. It could have been within a few weeks of the composer's arrival, or, as I argue here, it might not have been until the beginning of 1893. Indeed, there are few sources that give us *any* detailed information about their interaction. The earliest is an article by Burleigh in the Philadelphia Orchestra Program Book, February 1911, about seventeen years after the fact. We don't really know why Burleigh broke what had been a long silence on the issue, but the first sentence suggests that people had begun to suppress the roots of the "New World" Symphony and write a new history for it:

There is a tendency in these days to ignore the negro elements in the "New World" Symphony, shown by the fact that many of those who were able in 1893 to find traces of negro musical color all through the Symphony, though the workmanship and treatment of the themes was and is Bohemian, now cannot find anything in the whole four movements that suggests any local or negro influence, though there is no doubt at all that Dr. Dvorak was deeply impressed by the old Negro Spirituals and also by the Foster songs.

It was my privilege to repeatedly sing some of the old Plantation songs for him at his home in E. 17th St. and one in particular, "Swing Low, Sweet Chariot" greatly pleased him, and part of this old Spiritual will be found in the second [closing] theme of the first movement of the

Symphony. It is in G major and is first given out by the flute. [Here he gives examples.] The similarity is so evident that it doesn't even need to be heard; the eye can see it. Dvorak just saturated himself with the spirit of these old tunes and then invented his own themes.

There is a subsidiary theme in the first movement in G minor with a flat seventh; and I feel sure the Doctor caught this peculiarity of most of the slave songs from some that I sang to him; for he used to stop me and ask if that was the way the slaves sang.

I have never publicly been credited with exerting any influence upon Dr. Dvorak, although it is tacitly believed that there isn't much doubt about it, for I was with him almost constantly, and he loved to hear me sing the old melodies. Walter Damrosch once alluded to my having brought these songs to Dvorak's attention, but there was so much discussion and difference of opinion as to the value of the intimation that in the songs of the negroes lay the basis for a national school of music and the controversy waxed so hot that all reference to the real source of his information was lost sight of.

In 1924 Burleigh again mentions his contact with the Czech composer: "Dvorak of course used part of "Swing Low, Sweet Chariot," note for note, in the second theme of the first movement of the New World Symphony. It was not an accident. He did it quite consciously. . . . He tried to combine Negro and Indian themes."[3] In a radio broadcast in the 1920s, Burleigh gave additional information about their association:

> The great master literally saturated himself with Negro song before he wrote the *New World*, and I myself, while never a student of Dvorak, not being far enough advanced at that time to be in his classes, was constantly associated with him during the two years that he taught in the National Conservatory in New York. I sang our Negro songs for him very often and, before he wrote his own themes, he filled himself with the spirit of the old Spirituals. I also helped to copy parts of the original score.[4]

More details emerged some twenty years later, in an article in the *New York World Telegram*, September 12, 1941:

Dvorak was living on E. 17th St., near the National Conservatory of Music that Mrs. Jeannette Thurber had invited him to direct. I was studying harmony, composition and voice there, Dvorak heard me, and asked me to come to his house to sing Negro folk music. . . . I'd accompany myself on the piano. Dvorak especially liked "Nobody Knows the Trouble I Seen," and "Go Down Moses." He asked hundreds of questions about Negro life. He would jump up and ask: "Did they really sing it that way?"

Mr. Burleigh, generally regarded as the father of Spiritual arrangements admitted the idea to salvage this Negro heritage came from Dvorak, who urged him to "give these melodies to the world."

This last testimony is straightforward except for one item. Burleigh mentions that Dvořák was "in his shirtsleeves with all his kids around him. There were lots of them." Could he have conflated some memories? Dvořák had only two children with him in 1892; the rest did not come till the late spring of the following year. So this memory of Burleigh's might well refer to the period after the composition of the "New World" Symphony. Whatever the case, Burleigh certainly spent a great deal of time with Dvořák and probably sang to him at the time he was composing the symphony.

Further corroboration regarding Burleigh's role comes from Victor Herbert, the well-known composer who taught cello at the National Conservatory:

Dr. Dvorak was most kind and unaffected, took great interest in his pupils, one of which, the very talented Harry Burleigh, had the privilege of giving the Dr. some of the thematic material for his Symphony—"From the New World." I have seen this denied, but it is true. Naturally I knew a good deal about this Symphony—as I saw the Dr. two or three times a week—and knew he was at work on it.[5]

There are further scattered bits of information about the two. Clearly, Dvořák had a special place in his heart for the brilliant young African-American singer and composer. Burleigh's friend and classmate Will Marion Cook, later a friend and sometime teacher of Duke Ellington, referred to Burleigh somewhat maliciously as "Dvořák's pet."

Finally, there is secondhand information from a person who, like Kovařík, had one foot in Czech soil and the other in American ground: the scholar-diplomat Miloš Šafránek, well known for his two books on composer Bohuslav Martinů. Šafránek had this to say about a meeting he had with Burleigh:

> Burleigh succeeded in getting a stipend at the conservatory, and immediately after Dvořák's arrival, he established an animated, cordial, and permanent relationship with his teacher. Dvořák's influence on the work of this significant American composer was decisive. Burleigh introduced Dvořák to Negro spirituals, which he himself, while preserving their traditional melodies, had adapted and published. His most popular adaptation is known as "Deep River." Several witnesses recalled that Burleigh, while still a conservatory student, and definitely before the Symphony From the New World was written, used to sing Negro spirituals for Dvořák.

Šafránek describes sitting in Dvořák's old apartment with Burleigh and Kovařík and adds a few details:

> I learned that Burleigh visited Dvořák quite often, perhaps daily, and sometimes the composer took him to see a new engine or to watch the departure of a steamship from New York.[6]

Saturation, Modeling, or . . .

If we believe that African-American songs were a primary source for Dvořák's symphony, we may wonder how the composer went about transforming them into his own "intellectual property." This process involves a touchy point concerning the issue of modeling and borrowing and takes us into an area of the "compositional process" not usually discussed. To some extent, writing a piece of music is like putting on a magic show. An illusion is being put forth—or, actually, many illusions: that the composer wrote the piece at a single go, that it has not been "stitched" together, that it reflects what the composer "feels." Further, especially in the late nineteenth century, the composer and audience together participate in the illusion that the work is "original," the product of an individual intelligence, and as with the form itself, there should be no sense that the ethos of the work is sewn together from diverse strands.

The classic view of Dvořák's encounter with "Negro melodies," advanced sometimes even testily by the composer, was that he simply heard all those melodies and then dreamed up his own. We may remember Dvořák's comments on an analysis of the "New World" by Hermann Kretschmar: "but forget that nonsense, the notion that I used Indian and American melodies, because it is a lie! I tried only to compose in the spirit of those national American melodies."[7] Such a forceful statement from the composer would seem to settle the matter: he composed only in the spirit of those melodies, that's it!

And yet there is a curious paradox. While granting that Dvořák synthesized the material he encountered, Burleigh and others insist that "Swing Low" was *quoted* almost verbatim, and we know that the tune appears in "Negro Music." If the composer is borrowing, would we really expect him to stop at only one tune? "So, I'll use 'Swing Low,' and the *rest* I'll make up!" Dvořák was an inveterate modeler, as were so many composers before him. When we imagine Dvořák sitting down to compose, we might picture him with a few scores lying about, works by Schumann, Beethoven, Schubert, or Smetana, with texts opened before him: Longfellow, Shakespeare, Erben. Is he telling the truth about his procedure with Burleigh's songs to the point that we may regard the appearance of "Swing Low" in almost all its glory as something that managed to slip out of Dvořák's mix partially undigested?

Let's go back to Burleigh's contribution and look at the situation in a more aggressive manner. What if we are bit skeptical of the various claims made and begin our investigation with the assumption that Dvořák has purloined "Swing Low" by lopping off the first measure of the song? His procedure is then exactly what one might do to disguise a borrowing just enough so that audiences are not scrambling through the work listening for famous tunes.

Yet aside from "Swing Low" and the other two melodies mentioned by Burleigh, how do we know what other songs Dvořák might have encountered? Aside from "Negro Music," a piece of evidence, albeit of a lesser order, is the collection of arrangements that Burleigh published many years after Dvořák's death, starting in 1917. These songs certainly comprised Burleigh's repertoire, and if Dvořák was as enthusiastic about his singing as the documents imply, he certainly heard most if not all of them. There are, of course, a few problems with using the collection. It was published more than twenty years after Burleigh's association with Dvořák, and the selections must have sounded very different when he first sang them for the composer. According to Burleigh, Edward MacDowell encouraged him to make his arrangements more complex and artistic, implying, of course, that Dvořák heard a much simpler version.[8]

Another problem lies in the very attempt to hear these tunes as the sources for Dvořák's symphony. Altogether there are almost fifty melodies in Burleigh's collection. Let us say we are trying to find out if Dvořák used one of Burleigh's songs for the main theme of the Finale of the symphony. A primitive thought experiment might have us begin our search by dividing the collection into two parts: one half that by any number of criteria is "less like" the tune in question and one half that is "more like" it. If we keep dividing our group of songs in this manner we will always arrive at a tune that sounds like *something* in the symphony, since many of Dvořák's themes, like Burleigh's, are pentatonically inflected. Because we know Dvořák was listening to Burleigh sing, indeed may have been saturated by Burleigh's singing, we might take such similarities too seriously.

Nevertheless, let's turn to the most famous tune in the symphony, the one that in effect *became* a spiritual: the main theme of the Largo. There is a persistent idea that Dvořák used an English horn in the Largo because it reminded him of Burleigh's voice. Certainly the only available recording of Burleigh singing does nothing but strengthen this assertion. His voice *does* sound like an English horn, reedy, sharp, and contained. So, if we imagine Burleigh singing a song to Dvořák that he remembers while composing the Largo, what is it? John Clapham has already noted the connection between the Largo and the song "Steal Away."[9] A closer exploration reveals an uncanny resemblance between the rhythms and harmonic profile of the two songs (CD 31).

Dvořák seems to "steal away" the basic harmonic shape of the tune. Although the melody is, of course, different, one can be superimposed on the other. Did Burleigh's performance of "Steal Away" lead to the Largo and could the main melodic gesture of the Largo have come from another song, "My Way's Cloudy," which is almost identical (CD 32)?

If there are two borrowings, why not three or more? One of the first tunes in Burleigh's collection is called "Don't Be Weary Traveler." This song has many of the same characteristics as the opening of the Finale (CD 33: *New World*; "Don't Be Weary"). The opening measures in particular are a microcosm of the theme Dvořák chose; the rhythm of the first two measures is identical, and they share melodic features. It is intriguing that Burleigh sets the tune in unison, also reminding us of the Finale of the "New World." Of course, we need to be a bit careful, for in his setting of "Swing Low," Burleigh's arrangement almost seems to be quoting Dvořák's use of it in the "New World" (CD 34: "Swing Low"; Dvořák's version; Burleigh's arrangement). If we continue further along this path, we might also discover that there are real similarities between the opening Allegro and "Hard Trials" (CD 35).

The above relationship is intriguing in another way. Although the final version of Dvořák's theme is in E minor, the original sketch was in F major. Could its original form have been the "missing link" between Dvořák's imagination and Burleigh's song? Finally, since we have Burleigh's record that Dvořák responded to "Go Down, Moses," might we not consider a possible link between the C-sharp-minor slow march in the middle of the Largo and that tune (CD 36: Dvořák; "Go Down, Moses")?

Returning to "real historical time," we can try to imagine just what happened during these days or weeks, perhaps even months, when Burleigh visited Dvořák in his home. Dvořák listens intently and may even make some notes. We might imagine that when Dvořák begins to compose he allows some condensed memory of Burleigh's singing, with pitch, rhythm, timbre, intonation, visual memory, the character of his own response, to enter his thoughts, and plucks harmonies, phrases, and shapes from it. Is it plagiarism, saturation, recomposition? Did Dvořák, as it were, become "obsessed" with this music, play it over and over in his head, and simply draw his "original" melodies from this process of thoughtfulness?

Or in the complete and utter privacy of his imagination, was he the "boned pirate" Huneker imagined who came to the United States to "rifle us of our native ore"? Did he cold-bloodedly lop off the first measure of "Swing Low," purloin the rhythmic shape of "Steal Away," and sneak "Hard Trials" into the minor mode? After all, aside from "Negro Music," Dvořák had no scores for any of these songs, so who would know? Perhaps one of the reasons he and his supporters felt so comfortable saying that he used no original songs was not only a result of his saturation, but because there were no written texts for potential source tunes.

Musicologist Richard Taruskin talks at great length about Stravinsky's "mendacity" when suppressing the extent to which he used folk music in *The Rite of Spring*. But composers can have many reasons for what they divulge. The most important may be their magician's reluctance to reveal too many of the secrets of their workshop, or, in more positive terms, their desire to control as much as possible the manner in which the work is received and perceived by an audience. Surprisingly often, composers succeed in this regard. So, did Dvořák, like Stravinsky twenty years later, dissemble in the service of maintaining the secrecy of the composer's inner workshop?

Yet even here we have counterarguments. We have seen that a song in Burleigh's collection, "My Way's Cloudy," begins with a conspicuous melodic similarity to the Largo. On the other hand, there is a moment in Dvořák's last mazurka that also forecasts the main tune of the Largo (CD 37).

Did Dvořák invent his Americanisms? Borrow little bits of them? Steal them? How do we work our way out of this dilemma? As I was considering these issues I had the pleasure of spending an entire evening playing Dutch popular music from the 1940s and 50s, lovely, somewhat jazzy waltzes with titles such as "Like a Wild Orchid" and a tango called "A Small Red Rose." I played for hours. The next day, sitting at the piano without any of the music, I found myself making up a song "in the spirit" of those Dutch songs and came up with what I thought was a decent tune. How much of it, I wondered, did I literally take from what I had played the night before (the plagiarist forgetting the quotes and gosh, just copying the stuff into a book by "mistake") and what was "original"? I obtained the Dutch songs again, and the results were a bit strange. I discovered that actually I had borrowed most heavily from two songs: the Dutch "Like a Wild Orchid" and an American song called "There's Only One Pal After All" (Mother, of course) that I had played several weeks before. Obviously,

I'm no Dvořák, but it is not hard to understand how Dvořák could have thought he'd merely saturated himself with these tunes, while all the while his mind was cold-bloodedly recording and rearranging them. Indeed, I will argue later that he did just that when he composed his famous Humoresques for Piano.

A Foundation for American Music

One thing, however, is beyond dispute. Dvořák found these "Negro melodies" deeply meaningful, whether it was Burleigh who introduced them to him or Huneker. In his famous manifesto in the *New York Herald*, Dvořák wrote, "It is my opinion that I find a sure foundation in the Negro melodies for a new National school of music." We are led to ask just why Dvořák seized on these tunes with such alacrity and what they meant to him.

The first point has already been covered: he needed some authentic American elements to make his "national " symphony, as requested—nay, demanded—by Thurber and others. What could be more American than tunes taken from the mouth of an African-American who had one foot in the cosmopolitan world of the conservatory and the other, as Dvořák no doubt imagined, in the mysterious plantation?

And yet the borrowed substance could not be too different from what he might normally use for thematic material in the symphony. It is all well and good to go on at great length about lowered sevenths as if they were an American invention, but we see the very same thing at the opening of Dvořák's Seventh Symphony (CD 38) and many other pre-American works—though, it is true, more often in the works composed in the United States.

Considering this problem recalls a series of commercials from the 1960s that showed a brand-new television set with a picture advertised as sharp and bright. These ads gradually became a joke, because people figured out that the picture on the advertised set could not be any better or worse than the television in one's own living room. If one's own set had "snow," then so did the set in the commercial.

Dvořák in America is like the viewer at home. His training and attitude are his own television, and America is the newly advertised set. He can see it only through the mechanism for perception he already has, and by the age of fifty he is pretty well "hard-wired." Of course, he may notice certain things about the new set—perhaps it is handsome, the picture may be larger, the shape of the new cabinet different, and it may even evoke strong feelings; but it can be perceived only through a screen that conditions its effect. Composers, then, can only formulate thoughts in the patterns that they have been using—with few exceptions, they can only *recognize* what they already know. The reason that certain rhythmic and melodic figures became Dvořák's musical Americanisms owes something to that ineffable combination of the exotic and the familiar.

There are several other reasons these tunes became so special to Dvořák. Music is not very good at rejecting impulses that are associated with it. So it is also likely that some of Dvořák's great excitement about being in the United States was translated to these melodies, which then took on a transcendent quality. They would not only symbolize America, they would now carry a personal stamp as well.

And yet there are some additional aspects to consider. Writing about the changing attitudes of whites to black music, Jon Cruz and others have used the expression "ethnosympathy."[10] This term refers to the relatively "new" idea in the nineteenth century that the sounds made by primitive peoples, formerly considered to be mere noise, actually contained vestiges of real human feeling. We get a taste of this belief in an article in the *New York Daily Tribune*, March 31, 1895, in which the great critic Eduard Hanslick, in commenting about the American sound, refers to the "ugliness" of Negro elements. The process of changing such a view is not merely auditory but social and political as well. Dvořák was surrounded by people like Henry Krehbiel and Jeannette Thurber, for whom the appreciation of "Negro" melodies was tied in with a broad progressive agenda. So we can assume that Dvořák's strong response to these songs was complex and multifaceted.

One last element must have struck the deeply religious Dvořák. The songs known today as "spirituals" were an overlapping of the sacred and secular worlds in which the composer traveled. With their allusions to Daniel in the lion's den, Joshua fighting the battle of Jericho, Moses going down to Egypt, and David playing on his harp, these were perhaps the original "biblical songs" for Dvořák. That they went far beyond biblical description into an exalted world of religious spirit—in such songs as "Swing Low," "Steal Away," and "Nobody Knows the Trouble I've Seen"— was surely the greatest attraction. Like Czech "folk music," they were anonymous, fresh, and honest, but unlike their Czech counterparts, they were also religious.

It is often implied that Dvořák made his reputation as a Czech composer by flavoring the High Hapsburg style with more than a dollop of an authentic Czechness gleaned from folk sources. But there was never anything like a Czech or Moravian Burleigh, never anyone who could share a vibrant repertoire of oral tradition with the composer. Thus, in the end, Dvořák probably had a more comprehensive and profound grasp of African-American music than he did of any folk music in the Czech Lands. There is a further irony here. It was Dvořák who first suggested that Burleigh give "these melodies to the world," and there can be no doubt that Dvořákian harmony played a role in Burleigh's wonderful settings.

10

A Spillville Pastoral

The process of writing the "New World" Symphony and the controversy about "Negro melodies" that erupted upon its completion had been demanding and even tumultuous for the composer. By the end of the academic year in May 1893, Dvořák needed a rest. The original plan had him returning to Bohemia for the summer, but chance intervened, and he found out from Kovařík about the existence of Spillville, an Iowa hamlet where he could see the exotic prairie and ease his longing for things Czech at the same time. The town had been established in the 1850s and had become a kind of "mother colony" for Czech immigrants who might eventually end up in other towns in Iowa, Kansas, or Nebraska.

Dvořák's time in Spillville is a legend wrapped in a legend: the world-famous composer, weary after months of teaching, conducting, and engaging in the arduous labors of the "New World," and suffering from homesickness for his native land, finds succor in the tiny Iowa hamlet. This Czech village, a literal home away from home, restores Dvořák's spirits and provides both him and the town with indelible memories.[1] In fact, the visit has taken on such a glow it is not surprising to find that two of the best descriptions of the town are found in a work of fiction, Josef Škvorecký's marvelous *Dvorak in Love*:

> They were standing on a treeless hilltop. Below them, across a wood that grew farther down the slope and stretched all the way to the meandering banks of the Turkey River, they could see the Spillville valley, fields of golden wheat, blue islands of wild asters, the red village

rooftops and beyond that, the far side of the valley rising again to meet the sky.

The moon was suspended in the sky and the spire of St. Wenceslaus's Church rose over Spillville like a black cut-out against the shimmering stardust. The pungent aroma of manure and the smell of wild roses reached them on a breath of air.[2]

Myth and fiction aside, there is no doubt about the impact that this town had on Dvořák. He was endlessly charmed by it, by its inhabitants—rustic Czech-American farmers—and by its fauna: cattle, the ever-present birds, and, if we are to believe the reports, skunks. When he first arrived he exclaimed: "I was walking in the woods by the stream and heard the singing of birds for the first time in eight months!"[3] It was here that he also heard the famous Kickapoo Medicine Show, and here where he wrote two of his most successful works, the Quartet in F and the Quintet in E-flat, both named "American."

In order to fully appreciate the release offered by Spillville, we may remember the happenings of just a few weeks before. Until the very moment he left New York, the composer had been caught up in the swirl of events surrounding his pronouncements about race and music as circulated by Creelman. The image of Dvořák sitting in a room with the lights out gritting his teeth may sum up the pressures that this controversy—so unusual for him—produced. Thus his flight into the country was not a mere vacation but an escape from a difficult and uncommonly stressful situation. Just how stressful we will see later.

Spillville had most of the qualities necessary for an Eden. First, it was very isolated, especially by Czech standards. Drop someone from a hot-air balloon almost anywhere in Bohemia on a cold winter's night, and within half an hour he will be warming himself by the fire of a cozy pub, a beer in each hand. Not so in the great open spaces of Iowa. Dvořák was amazed at the vastness. Too, since most of the inhabitants had left the old country a generation before, he would have found it quite rustic. The whole experience must have been a little like Wellsian time travel, an arrival at a place at once familiar and at the same time unbelievably quaint and strange.

Yet beyond the specifics of a return to Czech things, we have the great magnetic attraction of the countryside as a place of refuge. This is part of the legacy of romanticism: the dichotomy between the city as an arena of flux and change, tension and technology; and the countryside, where we commune with those things in the universe that are unchanging, find our real selves, and become rejuvenated. Whether in the pastoral poetry of Wordsworth, the discussions of nature in Goethe's *Young Werther*, or the paintings of Constable, the vision of rural sanctuary is a potent force.

The countryside also plays a significant midwifery role in the creative labors of such figures as Beethoven, Schubert, Brahms, and Tchaikovsky. Here the idea of walks in nature and summer searches for an idyllic space contribute to such compositions as Beethoven's "Pastoral" Symphony, Schubert's "Trout" Quintet, and Brahms's Horn Trio.

There is also a rich, specifically Czech, nature tradition as well. Not only does the second tone poem of Smetana's *Má vlast*, the famous "Vltava" or "Moldau," give us a snippet of country life, but the powerful beginning of the fourth, "From Bohemia's Woods and Fields," is, according to the composer, nothing more nor less than the "the impression as one steps into the country for the first time."[4] Here a dark and stormy opening gives way to a classic pastoral, with an endless drone.

For Dvořák this sense of the countryside was indeed profound, in two distinct ways. Not only was it a place where he could contemplate nature and rejoice in its power, it was also that the stresses he regularly endured in the city were absent. In other words, the countryside was a place where he could work undisturbed and be himself, and as I will argue, where he could calm his nerves.

Spillville was not, of course, Dvořák's first summer haunt. In 1884 he had purchased a parcel of land in Vysoká, near the estate of his brother-in-law, Count Kounic. This lovely summer retreat, near the town of Příbram, was a place he adored.[5] In the memoirs of his son Otakar we find the following description: "Vysoká was the place where he had the best feeling. In Vysoká he could stay relaxed even while working 12 hours per day on a composition." There he kept his flocks of pigeons and often was visited by friends. And there he completed many of his most important compositions.

Coming into the Country

"How beautifully the sun shines!" marvels the composer after the completion of the first movement of the "American" Quartet. It is difficult to know how to deal with the composer's two Spillville works. They were written one after the other—the quartet was sketched in the amazingly brief period of three days shortly after his arrival, and the quintet occupied the month of July. What they are seems so self-evident that we think it cannot be so simple, and yet from their first performances the works have struck audiences and critics much the same way. Dvořák is coming into the country. Clouds have lifted, darkness is gone. The sun shines. The musical lines are exotic, to be sure, "American," but so exuberant, so filled with spring and energy, that we hardly imagine this as a work consciously conceived, but rather one that circumstance brought into being.

Hartmut Schick insightfully argues that Dvořák virtually abandoned the European quartet tradition by banishing the very things that lie at its core: "seriousness" gives way to the cultivation of the bucolic; counterpoint and dialogue among the instruments is replaced by drones and ersatz drumbeats; "difficulty" and complexity are replaced by an almost amateur sense of ensemble; and musical logic yields to a *Hausmusik* aesthetic. It is reported that Dvořák, a violist, could just about play the *first violin* part of the quartet. Schick says that both Spillville works seem "to stand in direct opposition to the tradition of their genre, behaving decidedly anti-European that means, in this case, above all, anti-German."[6]

Although Schick rarely mentions Schubert in relation to these works, it is clear that he is a primary model. The two quintets, the "Trout" and the C Major, must have figured in Dvořák's mind as he wrote the Quintet in E-flat. Here we are reminded that in opposing Dvořák's Spillville chamber works to the mainstream of quartet literature, Schick neglects one other tradition of the quartet: its intimacy. Beethoven places his confessional "heilige Dankgesang" in the middle movement of a quartet, not a symphony. While the absence of the "learned" style in Dvořák's Spillville works may violate the quartet tradition, the aspect of deep personal feeling does not. That this feeling is primarily one of overwhelming joy should not distance it too far from the mainstream chamber tradition.

The quartet opens with a frame, a kind of murmuring of the violins, followed by the croak of a cello. The violist plays a rising line, a leaping figure that is not unlike the first theme of the "New World," except this theme, in F major, ends in an open rather than closed way and lurches into what sound like fanfares (CD 39).

We are always in search of moments when the material of music somehow penetrates into the real world. Do we have such a case here? Dvořák comes to Spillville. He is charmed, delighted. He is finally, after a difficult and fascinating year, relaxed and energized. He turns from the public sphere to the private, away from the reporters and the New York crowds, away from the grand gestures and complex organization of the symphony to the gentle, more subtle world of chamber music. Never has a quartet seemed more like a conversation among friends—but not a learned discourse, but a glorious communing. Still more: if we are considering this work as an utterance of Dvořák, perhaps less mediated by conscious craft than the symphony, it is not hard to feel that the bouncing, soaring viola line that opens the work is Dvořák himself, proclaiming, a Czech-American Whitman: I celebrate myself, I sing myself![7]

This opening gesture is also reminiscent of another famous Czech quartet: Bedřich Smetana's "From My Life." Both quartets begin with an assertive viola solo, cushioned by a bass pedal from the cello and two-note ostinati from the violins. Dvořák knew the Smetana quartet well—he was the violist at its first private performance. Perhaps this similarity is a gentle hint that the "American" Quartet, too, is from the composer's life.

The whole is set in the key of F major, like Beethoven's *Pastoral* Symphony, but more important, in the pastoral *tone*. As in the "New World" Largo (CD 1–2) we have the centuries-old sign of the pastoral: the repeated note, or drone, in the lowest part that provides a sense of standing still. The quality of this stasis is determined by the "sweet" consonance of the upper voices: we are standing still in a beautiful place. It is not that this realm lacks motion, it simply has no *forward* motion. Rather, the natural analogs to this sound, heard first in the madrigals of the late sixteenth century, are such images as sunlight glittering on a pond, the sighing of the breeze, shimmering leaves.

Pastoral vocabulary represents a timeless world, but not all timelessness is identical. One of Dvořák's greatest gifts is knowing how to create many different and distinct pastoral visions. The beginning of Dvořák's quintet, while it uses some of the same devices as the quartet, inhabits a different realm. The initial bars appear to be modeled on Schubert's Quintet in C Major, with its false adagio flavor and its alternation of major and minor episodes—even the rhythmic accompaniment resembles Schubert's model. Schick suggests that the solo viola at the beginning of the work (Dvořák again?) may be stylized African-American call-and-response singing, though we don't know whether the composer had heard such things. Open fifths in the cello enforce the bucolic flavor (CD 40). The eventual goal of this motion, however, is not a relaxed image of green pastures, but rather a Bacchanalian moment, a musical stylization of exquisite, almost unendurable bliss. The moment is prepared and announced with the broadest of musical colons (CD 41) and works itself into a passage that, while ostensibly keeping to the pastoral tone, threatens to explode the ensemble with pure abandon (CD 42). Thus the tone of the work is set with an unprecedented sense of celebration.

In these Spillville works, the different kinds of pastoral tone are reinforced by two basic strategies, the first harmonic and the second affective. Both works, particularly in their major-key movements, are buttressed by a series of tonal areas a third above and below the main key that define the harmonic profile of the compositions. In the Quartet in F Major, the second theme appears in the key of A major, while the last movement moves to A-flat major; A minor, D minor, and D-flat major are also favorite areas of inflection.[8] The quintet moves from E-flat to G minor in the first movement, possibly—as noted earlier—in response to Dvořák's source melodies. The B-major second movement tilts toward D major and B minor, while the last movement moves to a static G minor and then to G-flat major. These moves help Dvořák create short-term stasis by touching those keys least likely to suggest—as the dominant would—any real forward motion.

The second way to create large "pastoral zones" is through the presence of what we might call "anti-pastorals," those types of sound that conjure up opposing states. The character of the pastoral tone that dominates both movements is created not merely by "itself" but also by the way subsequent episodes subtly shade the primary material in retrospect. We have seen a special case of this phenomenon in the "New World" Largo, where the funereal atmosphere of the middle section darkens and slows down the composer's conception of the outer pastoral.

In the quartet, the sense of energy is heightened by moves to the key of A minor in the outer movements, the contrast of an F-minor trio in the Scherzo, and, most notably, by the D-minor lament that stands as the second movement (CD 43). The lament is a Schubertian-American one, with endless melody and lowered sevenths. It is tempting to consider this movement as one of Dvořák's stylized dirges. The two most suggestive funeral elements are the "drumbeats" of the viola partway through the movement and the dirgelike figures later (CD 44), suggesting something that goes beyond the merely sad and laps at the shore of tragedy. (The passages are at mm. 31–42 and 82.)

The comparable movement in the quintet, though less flashy as a "bearer" of emotional quality, is even richer in its attempt to turn away from the outer exuberance of the work into a more secret place. In this theme and variations the theme itself has a fascinating history. According to Kovařík, who quotes several measures of it with added text, it occurred to Dvořák after playing through "My Country 'Tis of Thee."

> I brought a few of these [patriotic songs] home with me; next day, the Master carefully studied those texts and made some comment that it was a pity for America to use an English tune for her anthem. He sat down at the piano, improvised a tune, noted it in his sketchbook and declared: "There! This is going to be the new American anthem for the future."[9]

If Dvořák actually did make such sketches at the time, they have not survived, at least not with the text to "America." Undoubtedly, though, the sketch in question is the one we have already observed when considering Huneker's contribution to the "New World" Symphony, the one marked "Motives, New York." Further evidence comes from a letter Dvořák wrote to his publisher offering him Opus 97:

> In this Quintet there is, in the second movement, an Andante with variations—its melody being part of an unpublished song composed to fit

an English text, which I intend to publish later as an independent composition.[10]

Though he never did publish the song, it is uncanny how clearly the words of "My Country 'Tis of Thee" fit the rhythms of the composition, and Jarmil Burghauser has even produced an arrangement of what Dvořák might have had in mind (CD 45). The theme, which was probably based on the first "Negro" melody Dvořák received from Huneker, features one of Dvořák's favorite devices: the alternation, as in the Symphony No. 8, from minor to major, from lament to celebration. The opening, with its low range, dotted rhythm, and unison descending bass line, suggests an inner world of conflict and pain, another dirge, while the shift to major suggests transcendent bliss. Their interaction creates the effect of emotional depth.

Much has been written about the Scherzo of the quartet, where the composer supposedly ingested nature literally. Kovařík described a scene in which the singing of a bird, probably a scarlet tanager, intruded into the scene and was absorbed by the composer into the work. Attempts to determine precisely what bird might have entered the composition have never been entirely successful, although tanager is the leading candidate.

In his stimulating article on the "American" Quartet, Alan Houtchens expresses some annoyance that commentators keep referring to the work as "simple" and "primitive."[11] Indeed, the work is anything but ingenuous, but it must be said that Dvořák is a master of illusion. That he intended to give the impression of effortlessness is seen clearly in the final movement, made up of a complex of thematic materials, including an embedded slow movement. Yet the impression we get when we initially confront the movement is one of seamless simplicity. Krehbiel noted, "The music is not profound or heavily weighted with emotion, but it is full of ingenuity, replete with gracious fancy, clear as crystal and inspiriting in its unalloyed happiness."[12]

Surely the gift of composition includes an acknowledgment that human memory is frail. Only certain details can be remembered: either we overload the circuits by making all material somehow "equal" in value or we create a hierarchy, whereby—to oversimplify only slightly—some material vanishes in our attempt to make other music memorable. If the first movement is to be really coherent, we must lose the A-major contrasting subject in the process of enshrining the outer shell as "the movement itself." No matter how much we point to the D-minor lament or the A-flat-minor variations, many listeners and critics will continue to agree with Krehbiel's assessment of these chamber works.

For centuries musicians have wrestled with the question, "How much of *this* do I need before I have to add some of *that* in order to achieve the effect I wish?" In other words, how can a composer be sure of creating a particular effect when the various parts of a work coalesce, first in "real time" and then in memory? If, let us imagine, Dvořák wants to create a sense of vitality and expansion in this quartet, and the function of the slow movement is to enhance this quality through contrast, how does he make sure that it is just long enough to do this without disrupting the effect? Or perhaps it is his *intention* to threaten the pastoral tone, to suggest that just underneath the expansiveness there is an awful yearning that will never go away, a yearning that coexists always with the idyllic spaces of the mind.

One listening is not enough to answer such a question—indeed, it cannot be enough. Too, it is also plausible that over the period of our relationship with the piece, the parameters change. So we can never be entirely comfortable with what a piece of music is or intends to do, for neither the "natural" response to a work or movement nor a carefully considered analysis can prove the issue one way or another. The "science" of creating musical effects is far more like metaphysical psychology than biochemistry; we could even argue that a composer simply designs a sonic substance, which then folds one particular way into the musical memory. We will see that the mysterious inner movements may continue to haunt us long after the outer shells have fallen away.

Among the Indians

One of the signal events of Dvořák's Spillville summer was the appearance of a group of Native Americans described by Kovařík as "Kickapoo," who "belonged to the Iroquois tribe." While Šourek, Clapham, and Sychra tried nobly to make some sense of this statement—the Kickapoo and the Iroquois are unrelated—Indianists have easily managed to sort it out. One of the great touring spectacle traditions of the late nineteenth century was the medicine show, and the Kickapoo show was one of the most popular of them all. This show used performance as a way to sell various "Kickapoo" products, actually manufactured in New Haven—a nineteenth-century version of the commercial-ridden television sitcom.[13] Although Dvořák might certainly have heard some interesting music, we must remember the commercial roots of the enterprise and speculate on the relationship between "national music" writ large and snake oil salesmen.

Dvořák was clearly taken with the performers he encountered. According to various accounts, he became friendly with the performers and had them sing for him—Burleigh-like. Because this event directly preceded the composition of the Quintet in E-flat, many have sought to isolate the repertoire of the troupe in the hope of connecting it with the quintet. This task has been almost impossible to accomplish, for as a commercial venture, the Kickapoo show did not bother with something as mundane as musical "purity." John Mack Faragher calls the music of the show "Pan-American," since it not only included the music of many different Indian tribes, it usually featured one or more African-American banjo players. Faragher concludes:

> The medicine show was American music-making in the mainstream of twentieth-century popular entertainment, a fact which makes it no less authentically American. Without knowing it, Dvořák was witness to the context out of which would come the miscegenated musical forms of the twentieth century: jazz, gospel, country and rock 'n' roll.[14]

And certainly the project of determining Native American influence on Dvořák is formidable. Unlike Dvořák's use of "Negro" melodies, documented by many observers and focused on the person of Harry Burleigh (and now, we may hope, the examples in "Negro Music"), the issue of Indian music is shrouded and confused. Dvořák did not, of course, help with his own remarks. After virtually ignoring the issue of Native American music in his controversial statements in May 1893, he suddenly made this comment in the *New York Herald* on the day of the "New World" Symphony's first performance:

> Now I found that the music of the negroes and of the Indians was practically identical. I therefore carefully studied a certain number of Indian melodies which a friend gave me and became thoroughly imbued with their characteristics—with their spirit in fact.
>
> It is this spirit which I have tried to reproduce in my new symphony. I have not actually used any of the melodies. I have simply written original themes, embodying the peculiarities of the Indian music, and, using these themes as subjects, have developed them with all the resources of modern rhythms, harmony, counterpoint and orchestral color.

Later in the same article he mentions the Spillville chamber compositions, saying: "They are both written upon the same lines as this symphony and both breathe this same Indian spirit."

As we have seen, Huneker made fun of Dvořák for seeming to mix up the music of African-Americans and Native Americans. Musicologist James Hepokoski has summed up Dvořák's attitude toward American music, saying that "apparently he judged it all to be collapsible, for his purposes, into rudimentary pentatonic or 'modal' formulas that could be taken as emblematic of non-European, racial others."[15] To some extent Dvořák's assessment may be correct, and if we examine the arrangements of Native American melodies in the work of collectors such as Alice Fletcher, they look similar to harmonizations of "Negro" spirituals. Dvořák probably knew these arrangements of Fletcher's: although her larger work was published only in 1893, excerpts had been available in journals such as *Century* from at least the 1880s.

Let us take a concrete example of a music thought to be among Dvořák's most "American," the Scherzo from the quintet. If we compare the opening of the movement with two samples of music that Dvořák is likely to have seen, one "Negro" and the other "Indian," can we speak with any authority about sources?

The first example, discussed earlier, is taken from Johann Tonsor's "Negro Music," which the composer probably received in December 1892

(CD 90). Now here is a bit of Alice Fletcher's transcription of the "Hae-Thu-Ska" dance song. Note the pulsing rhythm, and the specific accents she has placed in the upper part. Anyone playing the abrupt transition to G major would be forgiven for confusing "Indian" and "Negro" elements. But for the presence of repeated notes, the melody could easily be mistaken for a song by Stephen Foster (CD 46).

When Dvořák speaks about the similarities between various ethnic elements, he clearly has this kind of modal arrangement in mind. It is absurd to imagine that by the time he had been in the United States for a few months, he could not tell the difference between the two musics. Rather, in order to write a coherent work, any material he used had to be "collapsible" into his own existing language. In other words, he was not simply blurring distinctions between African-American and Native American music, he was, for the most part, taking those devices he could recognize as already belonging to him.

Perhaps for his own purposes he associated African-American music with "pathos" and Native American music with "rhythmic monotony." Thus the G-minor episode in the Finale of the quintet takes us into another world, which for Dvořák would have been simply "Indian" (CD 47). Obviously, Dvořák is neither the first nor last person to play with such materials. We are reminded here of Chopin trying to return to a more "salonized" world after dipping into one of his Polish peasant melodies, as in the following moment from the Mazurka in B-flat Major. Clearly, the dominant seventh is as uneasy following the drone as is Dvořák's dance tune after its static moments in G minor (CD 48).

At least three devices can be associated with Dvořák's musical view of "Indian." First, of course, are the real—or more usually imitation—"drumbeats," whether in the "New World" Symphony Scherzo, the Finale of the suite, or in the quintet. Second, we have the minor drone, something the composer never associated with "Negro" music. Finally, we have the possible borrowing of themes.

It is easy to dismiss Dvořák as naive, yet most of us do not know any more about Native American music than Dvořák did, and perhaps even less. Almost certainly, those repetitive rhythms and "monotonous" harmonies, primitive and powerful, were those elements the composer identified as "Indian," gateways to an idealized, exotic, and primitive past.

This characterization links Dvořák with a whole range of composers, including Rimsky-Korsakov, Saint-Saëns, and Ravel, who used a minor-key drone as a virtual symbol of the exotic.

How then do we characterize these two wonderful pieces of chamber music? Despite the sense of darkness in both slow movements, early listeners found them anything but tragic. Philip Hale, the critic who quarreled with the "American" bona fides of the work, nonetheless found the quartet "cheerful, delightful, tuneful and spontaneous . . . as frank and honest as a quartet by Haydn."[16] Henry Krehbiel also invokes Haydn in the *Tribune* on January 1, 1894, saying about the second movement and, by implication, the quartet as a whole, "It is absolutely void of all straining after effect, and in manner is as ingenuous and honest as a movement of Haydn's."

Perhaps the idea of Haydn as a model came from the composer himself. In an 1895 letter to J. B. Foerster, he said this about the quartet: "I wanted for once to write something very melodious and simple, and I always kept Papa Haydn before my eyes; for that reason it turned out so simple."[17]

Krehbiel thought that like the "New World" these two pieces might be intended as object lessons:

> The new compositions are compacter and simpler in form than the older one, and their expression is more direct. . . .One is even tempted, while listening to his Haydnlike frankness and simplicity, to believe that he has purposely reverted to the style of the father of the string quartet in order that the composers who may undertake to work on the lines which he has marked out may have the clearest model before them.[18]

Yet here, Krehbiel exaggerates. We have no sense of the composer writing any object lesson for American composers, of speaking in some accented foreign tongue. It is one of the astonishing but inevitable coincidences in the history of music that the pentatonically inflected dialect just invented by Dvořák before his arrival in Spillville is the perfect language capable of painting the relaxed, vibrant world that he had conjured in his imagination.

Dreaming of Spillville

Dvořák loved Spillville precisely because all the things that intimidated him elsewhere were absent. There were no reporters around, no high-society types to make him feel brutish, no critics to scrutinize him, no crowds to avoid. Just farmers drinking in pubs, simple folks to chat with, and a card game always in progress. But Dvořák's affection for the place goes even beyond these well-known factors. For all the talk of Dvořák's homesickness for his native soil, it comes as a surprise to find the following passages in Kovařík's letter written to Amy Balik of Spillville on April 17, 1933: " . . . upon his return to New York he missed Spillville, talked of nothing but Spillville, and said that 'Spillville is an ideal place, and I would like to spend the rest of my days there!' And the fact is, he intended to buy a place and live there."[19] Could Dvořák actually have contemplated settling in the United States? Kovařík says, somewhat elliptically, the matter "would be a long story," but adds that "had he his wishes, or rather dreams realized, he surely would have lived a happy life for a number of years more than he did, and would have enriched the musical world with many great works." Then we get a real surprise: "For as my friend Mr. Šourek told me, that Dvořák about a year before his death, while talking about Spillville, remarked 'that was an ideal spot, that's when I felt happy, and I should have stayed there.' "[20]

So Dvořák had found his only real earthly paradise, and the music he wrote there reflects it.

II

Inner and Outer Visions of America: Dvořák's Suite and *Biblical Songs*

On April 20, 1894, Dvořák described his current offerings to Simrock: "I have the Sonatina for violin and piano (easy to play), a Suite in A major for piano (of medium difficulty), then ten new Songs (two volumes) taken from the Bible, and I think that the Suite for Piano and the songs are the best things I have written in these genres."

Though they were composed consecutively, it would be difficult to find a more unlikely pair than the Suite for Piano and the *Biblical Songs*. The former is a "relaxed" work in the composer's somewhat extroverted American style, while the song cycle, often dark and chromatic, appears as a subtle exploration of the composer's inner world. The works give a remarkable view of some previously hidden landscapes.

Although most critics have validated Dvořák's high estimation of the *Biblical Songs*, his evaluation of the Suite for Piano, Opus 98 has not been confirmed. Indeed, no mature work of Dvořák's has come in for more frequent trashing than this one. Paul Stefan finds that it has neither the immediacy of the other American works nor their significance, while Gervase Hughes finds that "it is a work of little character apart from a few 'Negro' touches in the finale which might have been produced by any competent composer." Alec Robertson dismisses it as a "poor work," and John Clapham places it among the composer's "slighter compositions" in his first monograph and ignores it entirely in his second. The only faint praise comes from Šourek, who while viewing the work as minor nonetheless praises it as an example of Dvořák's "intimate" side.

Part of the problem, according to these critics, is that the piece exhibits no serious compositional touches; thus František Bartoš (using data from Otakar Šourek in the critical edition): "Apart from the finale of the last movement which repeats some of the musical material contained in the first movement, there are no signs of a closer thematic relationship which would link the movements into a complete whole." The theory rests on a peculiar premise—we do not necessarily expect close thematic relationships in Mozart in order to have a complete whole—and Bartoš is totally wrong about the facts in this case. Indeed, though its tone is relaxed and informal, this work is at least as carefully composed as any other piece by Dvořák. That Dvořák himself valued it highly would alone suggest that the work deserves a fresh look. Indeed, far from being a slight occasional piece, it is arguably the most characteristic and revealing work of his American period.

The broader concept of unity in music is almost impossible to grasp fully, since it exists on at least two levels. A more obvious kind of unification might refer to a series of repetitions, or near repetitions, involving such things as key structure, thematic shape, or harmonic gestures. This coherence is both easy to achieve and easy to spot. It is the second type of unity that is both more highly valued and more obscure, since it often involves the more intuitive sense that "this belongs with that" or illusions that "this theme grows out of that theme." We know that composers, for all their craft, are not gardeners. No theme really "grows" out of another. If we have such an impression, it is usually because the composer has carefully cultivated it. Proving the second kind of unity, the "more important" one, is impossible in the end, since so much of the process of both composition and listening is intuitive.

What is so strange about the disparaging reception of the Suite for Piano is that it displays all the outward signs of unity and compositional care. The most obvious of these is motivic. The opening movement has two main themes. The first grows out of a pentatonic four-note figure beginning on F-sharp while the second is based on a descending minor arpeggio (CD 49).

Variants and transformations of both these themes can be found throughout the work, and a sense of unity is also achieved by the pentatonic flourishes at the ends of several movements. In addition, almost all the secondary key-areas explored in the work derive from the first three notes of the first theme.

The other problem critics have had with the work—that it lacks a sense of drama and scope—is more difficult to dismiss. After all, the composition was written directly after the tumultuous reception of the "New World," where Dvořák was feted, in his own words, "like Mascagni in Vienna." Is not the suite simply an "occasional" work, as the Master pauses to catch his breath? Is it not at best a salon tidbit, long on sentiment and short on real seriousness? Before answering these questions, we might look at the fourth movement, which is arguably the most static and least dramatic part of the suite.

The movement, an andante, has been referred to as an "Indian lullaby." The character of the movement is determined by the alternation of chords a minor third apart—first A minor and C major, then C minor and E-flat major—that produce a sense of what we might call "pastoral displacement" (CD 50). Moving to chords a third apart is a bit like traveling in those "warp zones" so beloved of science fiction writers. It is as if one has arrived at a new place and created a new color without having moved at all.

The evidence of careful craftsmanship can be seen in the way the opening theme is varied slightly with each appearance and even more in the subtlety of dynamic indications. The main theme begins *piano* and in each of its three repetitions becomes progressively quieter, ending up with *ppp* una corda, or as soft as possible.

If we can agree that this movement is carefully, even painstakingly, crafted in order to achieve a certain effect, what then is the effect? Rather than moving forward tonally or otherwise, it creates a sense of standing still. One could object that the chromatic movement right near the beginning works against this sense, a view that is certainly open to debate. Yet it is more likely that this temporary invocation of an opposing affective world has the effect of reinforcing the primacy of the main theme each time it recurs. If composers are indeed illusionists, then in order to create a sense of stasis, metaphors of motion are usually invoked as necessary contrast. In the fourth movement of the suite, conventional tonal movement—with its tendency to move toward specific harmonic goals—is destabilized. Though Dvořák was no revolutionary, this piece in its own way challenges the tonal universe almost as forcefully as atonality did a decade later.

This process is not restricted to the fourth movement, but is present throughout the suite. Even the opening of the work, although clearly in A major, begins with an ambiguous F-sharp-minor chord that threatens the sense of forward drive wherever it occurs. (For all the talk about the work's lack of affective power, that opening "dissonance" is redolent with emotional possibilities.) The second theme involves no harmonic change, and there is a constant effort to stress harmonic color over forward motion. In sum, Dvořák has been trying to make a piece that, relatively speaking, stands still.

This new and expanded approach to tonality suggests why Dvořák composed the work as a suite. The suite is a genre that implies a cyclic whole, but one that is free from the fairly rigid tonal and formal expectations of symphonies, sonatas, and quartets, all of which carry with them considerable historical implications. That Dvořák wrote the work for solo piano further suggests that he wished to separate this utterance from the public grandeur of symphonic work into, as Šourek says, a world of intimacy.

What then, is a suite? If it does not base its rationale on a certain type of musical logic that stresses the inevitable unfolding of certain ideas or abstract principles, what does it do? More than anything else, a suite is a collection of interrelated pictures. The composer of such a work is not bound to forge inevitable and dramatic connections between the different sections: by choosing a suite or a serenade, it is understood that different principles hold.

Indeed, the Suite in A Major might be considered a series of pictures from Dvořák's inner world. Some of those pictures may indeed have been affected by his contact with America. As we have seen, Dvořák adores playing the "Indian drum" and creating ostinato passages that invoke tom-toms. These may be powerful and warlike, as in the second theme of the first movement, or sinuous, as the exotic minor drone in the third movement (CD 51).

Another level of inquiry involves the landscape itself. It may be a self-fulfilling prophecy to claim that the "loneliness of the great prairies" made a deep impression on the composer and then search for examples to confirm it, but we must wonder how else to explain the pared-down, Shaker-like language that Dvořák uses in the suite and elsewhere in his American works. For a sense of just how different the language is from the composer's earlier works, we can simply turn to the second volume of Dvořák's piano works as published by Supraphon and contrast the suite with the work that precedes it in the collection, the *Poetic Tone Pictures*. One passes from a world of virtuosity, chromaticism, ghoulishness, bacchanale, funeral marches, and weird recollections of the past to a clean, open space only slightly tinged by the pathos of the work's opening gesture. Here there is no bombast or striving after effect.

Dvořák located and observed the pastoral spaces in the United States, but they were very different from those he had encountered before. At the core of the pastoral is an urban image of country life. Yet country life in the European sense was almost always populated. An inn, a village green, peasants dancing. The American West offered no such homey comforts. Thus, on the basis of his encounters, Dvořák created a specifically American pastoral. The motifs become more drawn-out and relaxed, resulting in greater use of the patterns we term "pentatonic," and the range becomes wider. We may also hear the exquisite minor-mode stasis in the third and fourth movements as related to the composer's impression of the sadness and stillness of the prairie, as implied in one of his most revealing letters home to Emil Kozánek, which includes the words "few people and a great deal of empty space."[1]

Dvořák loved composing pictures, scenes from *Hiawatha*, Erben, Hussite legends, and heroic evocations. He was filled with American images—indeed, they had been thrust upon him constantly since his arrival. Considering the way episodes of the piece are strung together and the sometimes obviousness of transitional stitching, we can easily consider this suite to be a series of unknown American pictures. These might be landscapes, Indians, perhaps a passage or two from *Hiawatha*, a fleeting version of a song heard on a New York street, all hovering on the cusp between abstraction and concrete reality. The "frame" of the suite, which opens and closes the work, is both celebratory and expansive—its most penetrating and characteristic gesture is the plagal motion in the first few seconds of the piece, which adds a prayerful glow to the proceedings.

That the composer bragged about the suite to Simrock and later lovingly orchestrated it suggests that he had no doubts about its value, that he had said what he had to say. It is no exaggeration to hold that this work most vividly reflects the American contribution to Dvořák's style: this completely unpretentious vision, devoid of romantic flourish and cliché, rejecting bluster and offering a simple yet subtle and variegated series of resonant landscapes, both inner and outer. In his letter to Kozánek he alluded to the "many curious things" he could say about America. Certainly he said at least some of them in his suite.

Oh That I Had Wings Like a Dove

At first glance, nothing could be further from the "Shaker" harmonies of the Suite in A Major than the sound world of the *Biblical Songs*. Though the opening of the first song describes a downward fall similar to that of the suite's beginning, the work speaks a different language. The chromatic harmonies used throughout the song cycle are musical metaphors for innerness, awe, and torment. Death hovers around the cycle, and not by coincidence does the first composed song, number seven in the set, begin as a wrenching funeral march. Of course we can still find hints of the American sound here and there, in the opening of the second song, in the bouncy tune that closes the set, and even in Dvořák's beautiful setting of the lines "Yea though I walk through the valley of the shadow of Death . . ." There are even some delightful quotations, probably coincidental: the final three notes in the vocal line of Song 8 on the words "For I put my trust in Thee" are identical, in both key and rhythm, to the first three notes of the English horn solo of the Largo.

We do not know exactly why Dvořák decided to write his *Biblical Songs*. Most critics think that it had something to do with the death of some of Dvořák's friends and colleagues, like Hans von Bülow, and more immediately, the illness of his father, who died shortly after the songs were completed. Critics tend to create a parallel to the idea of "Czechness"— the notion that Dvořák has special insight into anything considered "Czech"—by suggesting something we might call "religiousness," implying that because Dvořák was a religious Catholic, these songs are necessarily honest, profound, and intensely personal. That they are personal is beyond question, and because the composer chose not only the psalms himself but fastened on specific verses we can argue that Dvořák chose precisely the texts he wanted to use.

At the end of the sixteenth century, a group of Czech translators and scholars finished their translation of the Bible. The vitality and poetic beauty of the Bible of Kralice is one of the great treasures of Czech literature, easily the equal of the roughly contemporary King James Version of the Bible. The immediacy and power of this language, as much as anything else, caught Dvořák's imagination, especially at a time when he was so involved in American things. Though Dvořák's personal circumstances have been closely linked with the *Biblical Songs*, we might also argue that the whole cycle has been objectified and concretized as a stone carving of a simple, strong man struggling to understand his life and fate. This may be so, but since virtually all the critics have considered this cycle a work where the compositional and personal come together, it is appropriate to ask some personal, and of course compositional, questions about a passage in Song 3.

That the song occupies an inner place in the cycle leads us to consider interiors and middles, whether the middle section in a movement or song or an entire inner movement within a larger composition. Middles in music present a paradox. In the hierarchy of musical repetitions they are clearly less important, so it is sometimes easy to conclude that the central *point* of, let us say a scherzo and trio is the scherzo, and that the trio is of lesser moment. We realize, of course, that there are no absolute laws that govern the regulation of meaning. We could argue as easily that the trio is what the piece is "really about," just as someone could suggest that Shakespeare's *Hamlet* might be understood in terms of the minor courtiers Rosencrantz and Guildenstern.

Though this argument may be counterintuitive, there are many places where the material in the musical middle is something hidden, artfully tossed to the center precisely because it may be too real and too profound for the composer to feature, but too important to banish. So let us look at the middle of one of the inner songs of the cycle and see if we can find evidence of an American landscape lurking there.

Song 3 was among the last group sketched and completed. Psalm 55 might at first seem to be a strange choice for a setting, since the anguish expressed in the opening lines is not generic, but rather is associated with betrayal. There is no sense, however, that this meaning was significant for Dvořák, though it might have been.

The song opens ominously, with dark chromatic harmony, before yielding to the repetitive insistence of a simple, heartfelt prayer. The musical language following the opening chords, with its simplicity and pathos sounds like something that should be sung by the Prince at the end of *Rusalka* (CD 52). Things start to go to pieces in the middle section as two separate sequences of third-related harmonies appear, creating a sense of disjunction on the words "Attend to me and hear me: I mourn in my complaint, and make a noise," and it all comes to a compressed and powerful climax on the words, "Pained and sore is my heart, and the terrors of death have fallen upon me. Fearfulness and trembling are come upon me, and horror hath overwhelmed me" (CD 53).

After this tumult, the voice is silent for three beats, the harmony moves toward resolution on the words, "And thus I spake," and we reach the still point of the song. "Oh, that I had wings like a dove! for then would I fly away, and be at rest." The passage that accompanies these words is introduced with a timeless trill. The texture shifts up an octave, and a charming pentatonic rill unfolds over a static bass. This is a hidden world of childlike delight, of escape to perfect calm. It lasts a mere seven measures, seven measures of perfect harmoniousness, and closes with a descending pentatonic frame (CD 54).

At first it appears that the song will end by referring obliquely to the tone of the opening, but there is a dark parallel to the dove's idyllic escape, and the song ends with its most terrifying and unexpected notes on the words "I would hasten my escape from the windy storm and tempest," with downward lashing vocal lines and an octave-and-a-half chromatic descent in the keyboard part before concluding in a hushed and dark whisper (CD 55). What interior landscape is this? If it is indicative of the composer's state of mind, whence comes the fear and trembling? Dvořák's fears will be taken up in a later chapter, but let us for a moment return to Eden. At this point we can understand that when seeking a perfect, restful place, Dvořák dips into a variant of his American style. That this paradise is delicately poised between the fear of death on one side and a terror of storms on the other is, I believe, a truly autobiographical statement, made all the more revealing for being hidden in the middle of the cycle.

12

Some American Snapshots

The works written with America in mind display an amazing compositional variety. The "New World" Symphony and the Cello Concerto are massive works, marking the period at each end, with the imagined Hiawatha opera hovering in between. There are public display pieces—*The American Flag* and the Te Deum; multimovement works, such as the Sonatina for Violin and Piano, the "American" Quartet in E, the Quintet in E-flat, and cyclical works like the *Biblical Songs* and the Suite in A, which give the impression (not always strictly true) of a more relaxed tone and more casual construction and linking.

Interspersed with these are pieces that stand alone, independent of the movements or works that surround them. These American snapshots are revealing, for—from a paraphrase of "Swanee River," to a hidden lullaby, to an exalted moment at Minnehaha Falls—they offer glimpses of inner spaces that the composer rarely showed.

Deconstructing Foster

The Humoresques for Piano are, by almost anyone's standards, a bit hard to figure out. They were written in the summer of 1894 in Vysoká, as the composer pored over his American sketchbooks. Looking among these piano pieces, we find a speeded-up funeral march (No. 1), a Gershwin-like bluesy number based on a sketch titled "Hiawatha's Youth" (containing a fragment from a work that the composer wrote in 1875: No. 4); a slice of Americana that is almost a literal shadow of the A-minor finale from the

Suite in A, with an A major section containing a quote from "Oh! Susanna" (No. 5); some inexplicable Indian bird passages (No. 2); a little church chorale, supposedly heard on a New York street corner, surrounded by weird "spiritual" music (No. 6); and a bizarre final movement that sounds like something out of Mussorgsky and concludes in a way too strange even for that Russian composer. Most of these pieces have an ABA or rondo form and are in duple meter, but otherwise there is little connecting these works to each other—they are more like a patchwork quilt.

Tucked in an inconspicuous position in the lineup—as the penultimate selection—is the most famous piece of the lot, the Humoresque in G-flat. By the turn of the century, it had become a staple of the light-classical repertoire, heard most frequently in arrangements for violin and piano by either August Wilhelmj or Fritz Kreisler and later arranged for countless other instruments, often in the "easier" key of G major. Aside from the "New World" Largo, it is the composer's most popular American work and the best-known of all his works. Although the Humoresque in G-flat seems fairly straightforward, we may not know it as well as we think.

Like most war horses, or in this case a "war colt," there is something familiar about it from the start. How do we come by the sense we have heard it before? It has long been noted that the melody of Foster's "Old Folks at Home" can be sung over the first part of the humoresque. Rather than seeing a direct influence, conductor Maurice Peress sensibly writes, "I'm not saying that Dvořák . . . has the Foster thing in his mind, necessarily . . . but artists like Dvořák will hear music and then it imprints itself onto the conscious and subconscious mind."[1] If Peress is right, there is no need to look at the relationship any further, but if there is one American piece we are sure Dvořák knew—more surely than "Go Down, Moses," "Swing Low," or "Steal Away"—it is "Old Folks at Home."

We have already imagined what it must have been like at the benefit concert for the Herald Clothing Fund in Madison Square Garden in January 1894. The newspapers had done their job and the hall was packed. Dvořák was conducting the orchestra of the National Conservatory, the African-American choir was excited and resplendent. Burleigh and the great Sissieretta Jones offered solos. And the Master himself was "leading for the fund," as one of the newspapers put it, with his own arrangement of Foster's tune for full orchestra.

If we now look at Dvořák's arrangement and compare it and Foster's tune to the humoresque, we see that the two pieces have the same harmonic structure, but we also see a very similar accompanying pattern (CD 56: Dvořák's arrangement; Humoresque; "Swanee River" and Humoresque superimposed). We could easily stop there, but there are more similarities. One of them is obvious: Dvořák has used the same pentatonic inflection as Foster. Only slightly less obvious is that virtually every note of "Old Folks" can be found in each corresponding measure of Dvořák's. While the octave leap (on "Swanee") in Foster is more striking, Dvořák gets us up there as well. In fact, with the exception of the first measure, the first notes of each measure are the same for both Dvořák and Foster. And the octave leap *begins* the second part of the humoresque, which too has elements in common with the second part of Foster's song (CD 57). Finally, the characteristic "snap" rhythm (on "Ribber") from "Old Folks" can be found in the second measure of the F-sharp-minor middle section (CD 58).

We might say that Dvořák inhaled, or ingested, the work and transformed it after his own vision. Yet what *is* his own vision? We are thrown back again, almost helplessly, on issues we have pondered before. How do we decide which parts of a composition are most "important"? Which passages are what the piece is really "about" and which are foils? In most ABA compositions, whether a minuet or a *da capo* aria, there is a basic assumption that the outer, or A, section is paramount, and that the middle exists for the purpose of contrast. Yet there are numerous times when the "inner" part carries more weight, and stands as a vulnerable core, protected by a more brittle outer shell. It is very tempting to take such a view of the humoresque.

One aspect of Foster's song is in no way represented in the first part of Dvořák's piece: its pathos. If Dvořák borrowed the surface harmonic patterns of "Old Folks" for his outer section, surely the F-sharp-minor part is his reading of the inner depths of that song, with its tone of longing, nostalgia, and the "sad weariness" of the text. And if this is the case, the growing intensity of this section may well represent the natural tendency for this middle section to want to "break out" and take over the piece. But it cannot. This desperate sadness remains isolated while the somewhat insipid dance (of life?) reclaims the stage.

Of course, all of the above may be fiction, but if Dvořák was planning to reset "America" according to his own light, why not "Old Folks"? Too, when there are secrets, Dvořák, like anyone else, likes to hide them, and what better place to hide them than in the middle?

Only one question remains. Where did Dvořák get the famous rhythm, halfway to ragtime, that carries the piece forward? One possibility is Maurice Strathotte's "Plantation Dances," but another source, which has just come to light, is more likely. The Dvořák Archive in Prague contains a volume titled *Minstrel Songs Old and New*, published in Boston by the Oliver Ditson Company in 1882. It is a wonderful compendium of popular American songs, especially minstrel songs. On the front page in Kovařík's hand is written: "I am sending you this volume of 'Minstrel Songs' that belonged to the Master and that he left here." The first piece in the collection is Foster's "Old Folks at Home," and Kovařík says that Dvořák used this version as the basis for his arrangement.

But there is more. Many songs have the famous dotted rhythm, including "Good Sweet Ham," on page 60, and the "Louisiana Lowlands," on page 72. Most interesting, however, is "Nicodemus Johnson," on page 116. Not only does it begin with the dotted rhythm, which goes all the way through, but the "Master" has marked it with his telltale blue pencil (CD 59). This likely is the main source for the famous rhythm.

We come away from this account of the G-flat Humoresque with the clear impression that Dvořák simply thumbed through a book of minstrel songs for inspiration, choosing a little bit here and a little bit there, some Foster, then some Nicodemus Johnson. Dvořák's charmed and restless searching through the possibilities for American music could easily serve as a metaphor for the Master's entire visit.

A Lullaby

There is a further level of American ephemera beneath the slightly disconnected world of the Humoresques. After Dvořák finished a first set, he promised Simrock another collection of similar smaller piano works, but he composed only two. Perhaps preparations for his return to America in October 1894 obliterated any other plans, or maybe he just lost interest. Whatever the case, the pieces were found among Dvořák's manuscripts only in 1911, when they were edited by the composer's son-in-law, composer and violinist Josef Suk.

The two pieces are charming, easily the equal of their predecessors, yet they are even more enigmatic. While the first piece, in G major, is shaped like a humoresque, the second, in G minor, is more ornate. Both have middle sections in the parallel key, and both have similar almost unprovoked outbursts in the middle sections. There is little "natural" growth from one idea to the next; we find, instead, sudden shifts that often evince some hidden extramusical meaning. In order to explore what one of these secrets might be, let us take a brief look at the first piece, titled "Lullaby" by the composer.

At first sight the piece appears unproblematic. In its transparency it resembles several other American works, but it lacks the conspicuous use of pentatonic writing, except at the end of the opening phrase (CD 60). Two distinctive features of the piece are the open fourth at the beginning of the main theme and a persistent G pedal that accompanies the first section, even in the more chromatic passages (CD 61). Surely if this is a lullaby, as the composer tells us, it is a pastoral one that has something to do with America, but we don't need to search nearly that far for a model. The lullaby and pastoral elements are tied neatly together in the Czech tradition, most notably by the song "Hajej můj andílku," an eighteenth-century melody that appears prominently in Smetana's opera *Hubička* with a similar drone accompaniment (CD 62).

The pastoral section of the Dvořák lullaby is followed by an abrupt shift to G minor and something that sounds "Indian," with its monotonous pounding, combined, oddly, with a triplet motive that Dvořák often associates with death (CD 63). This theme is treated almost developmentally until there another shift, and now the opening idea is developed and passionately intensified until it reaches a climax on the high b. Over the next measures it falls almost two octaves until the main theme reappears.

Readers unfamiliar with Czech traditions might wrongly assume that it is normal for Czech lullabies to feature passionate outbursts in the middle sections. So what is going on in this piece? Do we again have evidence of the gravitational pull of the program?

To answer this question, let us go back to the beginning of the work and consider what kind of source Dvořák might have used. The familiar influence of pastorals and Indians suggests we look at *Hiawatha* again. Is there a lullaby in Longfellow's poem?

Chapter 3 of *Hiawatha*, "Hiawatha's Childhood," offers a charming passage in which we learn that Hiawatha's grandmother, old Nokomis,

> *Nursed the little Hiawatha,*
> *Rocked him in his linden cradle,*
> *Bedded soft in moss and rushes,*
> *Safely bound with reindeer sinews . . .*
> *Lulled him into slumber, singing,*
> *"Ewa-yea! my little owlet!*
> *Who is this, that lights the wigwam?*
> *With his great eyes lights the wigwam?*
> *Ewa-yea! my little owlet!"*

Indeed, we can hear the words of the lullaby embedded in the tune and imagine, as Dvořák might have done, the primitive pastoral spaces in which the action took place (CD 64).

A *Hiawatha* reading might explain the next passage as well. For directly following the lullaby are references to the things Hiawatha learned from his grandmother:

> *Many things Nokomis taught him*
> *Of the stars that shine in heaven;*
> *Showed him Ishkoodah, the comet,*
> *Ishkoodah with fiery tresses . . .*

Immediately following is a description of the "Death Dance of the Spirits," which could explain both the "interrupted" lullaby and the presence of the "triplets of death" in this more dramatic section. The climactic part of the middle section could refer to

> *Warriors with their plumes and war-clubs,*
> *Flaring far away to northward*
> *In the frosty nights of Winter;*
> *Showed the broad white road in heaven,*

Pathway of the ghosts, the shadows,
Running straight across the heavens,
Crowded with the ghosts, the shadows (CD 65).

In a charming speech at the Dvořák Centennial Conference in 1993, the novelist Josef Škvorecký described different kinds of creative artists. There were those, like James Joyce and Henry James, who put all their love and genius into a few truly great works. Dvořák was, he felt, of another type, which he also identified with the Czech writer Karel Čapek: one who put his genius into everything he touched without regard for whether it would be a great work or not.

These two pieces of ephemera from the American years bear out Škvorecký's thesis. They are filled with the requisites for greatness in miniature, perfectly capturing something that is both tangible and forever shrouded in mystery.

Standing at Minnehaha Falls

Aside from a short trip to Chicago at the beginning of August to celebrate Czech Day at the World's Fair, Dvořák spent the summer of 1893 relaxing, going on long walks, talking to the local farmers, and playing his beloved card game, an almost-forgotten one called Darda. But at the beginning of September he was on the move again, having accepted invitations to visit Nebraska and Minnesota.

It is no exaggeration to say that one of Dvořák's loveliest experiences in the United States was his trip to St. Paul. "An exquisite town!" he gushed in a letter to his friend Antonín Rus. Part of the reason for the trip was to do some advanced scouting for his *Hiawatha* opera, which he hoped to write on returning to New York. Thus his greatest joy came from visiting a special place nearby: "We went to the valley and saw little Minnehaha Falls, a place that Longfellow celebrated in his famous poem. It is not possible to express how bewitching it was."

There was even a hint of musical inspiration in the experience. Dvořák's secretary and companion Kovařík reports that the composer took down a theme on his cuffs while standing amid the spray; he also states that the melody later became the theme of the slow, "Larghetto" movement of the Sonatina for Violin and Piano, completed in November 1893.

Finally, an article in the *Dacorah Republican* of October 19, 1893, contains a passage that further illuminates Dvořák's experience in St. Paul:

> Dr Dvorak exhibited several new compositions for chamber music. One was a quintet and bore the name of "Spillville." Another was a quartet for strings. Other pieces of work were still unfinished. . . .

The writer then quotes Dvořák at length:

> I have read the poem of Longfellow and now that I have seen the falls, it has suggested to me a composition in which I hope to express all that I have felt. I will make it a rhapsody probably, or a fantasy, and into it I shall try to put the mighty rumble of waters, and the gentle lapping of the little waves, and all the iridescent hues that lie over the waters, and it shall bear the name of Minnehaha.[2]

Let us travel back to the very moment, more than a century ago, when Dvořák stood gazing at the waterfall, and use it as a prism to explore some of the issues and ideas raised by the composer's American years. By expanding from his inner imagination to the outside world and back again, we can unabashedly mirror the simple form of the sonatina's middle movement and solve a small musicological problem as we go.

So there is Dvořák, standing and watching the falls, transfixed. Suddenly a theme occurs to him, but he has no paper. He dashes off a few notes on his cuffs. . . .

The first conundrum, and one that I doubt can be solved to anyone's satisfaction, involves the issue of music and depiction. Most of the music scholars with whom I have discussed the matter feel extremely ambivalent about the idea that music can "paint" or "portray" objects, ideas, or visions from the so-called real world. Thus the tendency would be to couch Dvořák's "sleeve notes" in the context of the composer giving utterance to his immediate sense of being—in other words, expressing himself, or "expressing his emotion," or translating his experience into a musical code that an audience might be able to decipher. Of course, the idea of "expressing" or "encoding" is about as mystifying as the notion of "depicting."

As we ponder this phenomenon we might move back from Dvořák to Mendelssohn, to a parallel moment at the beginning of the nineteenth century. On August 7, 1829, the composer stood on the shores of the Atlantic looking out at the Hebrides Islands. He captured the view in a well-known sketch. More famously, however, at almost the same instant, he jotted down a musical theme, which occurred to him as he took in the scene. The theme, of course, is the opening of what later became the *Hebrides Overture*, almost unchanged. Mendelssohn seems to have thought that both sound and image were depictions of the scene, a musical sketch and a pencil sketch, and despite any reservations about what music can and cannot do, which of us would want to go back in time and explain to him, "Music can't do that, Felix"?

Surely, though, Mendelssohn's pencil sketch has identifiable objects and the music doesn't. Would we know anything about the musical idea if Mendelssohn had not placed it, programmatically, on the gloomy coast of Scotland? Perhaps not, but I believe that one could say the same thing about the pencil sketch. Without any information about its location, we might well take the "water" for a meadow, and the castle could place the scene in Germany, Italy, or even New Jersey. Actually, if we wanted to be bloody-minded, we could argue that because of Mendelssohn's limitations as a graphic artist the sketch carries none of the artist's point of view, the musical snapshot is infinitely richer—in fact, simply a better sketch of that place.

Let's return now to the beginning of the Larghetto from Dvořák's sonatina and see if we can figure out just what the composer might have had in mind. In a charming display of self-effacement, Dvořák dedicated this, his one hundredth opus, to his children, and in a letter to his publisher he described it as "for children but suitable also for adults." In keeping with this statement, the movement opens with a figure whose simplicity and repeated notes evoke the rhythms of childhood (CD 66).

Yet there is more: the style is also in keeping with the composer's American style, particularly his reading of Indian music as something magical, repetitious, and monotonous. The first two measures have this quality, and the larger theme extends it through almost literal repetition, completely in keeping—actually almost a textbook case—of musical exoticism. Whether the monotony is masked (as in the dull pedal in Borodin's "Polovtsian Dances") or the repetition takes on the element of caricature (as in Gilbert and Sullivan's *Mikado*), such repetitions are a key strategy in depicting strangeness.

This sense of tableau is enhanced, in turn, by a second repetition of the entire theme, in which Dvořák brilliantly extends this sense of monotony to the harmonic language. A series of third-related chords—F–D–B♭–D–F—moving in a tonally "meaningless" sequence trace the cyclical time of the exotic world as a colorful spiral creating an ecstatic glow. This is the kind of thing that Mussorgsky did so brilliantly and that Dvořák himself plays with in creating certain "Old Slavonic" moments in his works (CD 67).

Though Dvořák never divulged any program for the Larghetto, the movement became known, through the interventions of Fritz Kreisler and others, as the "Indian Lament," or "Indian Wail." Yet hearing the movement as "Indian" involves a certain misunderstanding of what Dvořák did to create his "American" style. Although the repetitions at the beginning of the Larghetto may be a shorthand for tom-toms, at least part of the modal sheen has another source, and while Dvořák may well have been thinking "Indian" in his slow movement, inevitably it came out somewhat African-American as well, since the opening idea bears a real resemblance to various elements from "Negro Melodies."

If the timelessness of the movement's opening is achieved through contrived monotony and through melodic and harmonic spirals, the movement's middle uses even more traditional means to signal space rather than forward motion. Indeed, we might easily argue that this passage is the most idyllic and timeless moment in all of Dvořák's music (CD 68).

We have seen several cases, most particularly the "New World," where Dvořák hides things in the middle movements. Could there be some program, or image, hidden in the middle of the sonatina's movement? In order to explore this question further, we must consider the nature of music, in both its formal and its affective status. *Speaking* in instrumental music is both speaking and not speaking. You can confess a great deal in a musical work without really letting anyone know what you are doing.

And composers, like everyone else, have lots of secrets, and lots to confess. How better to get it all off your chest than to put it in your works.

Such intimate ideas, however, cannot be placed too conspicuously, lest they lose their sheen. But how do you simultaneously hide and reveal? Certain basic tendencies of perception affect how we listen to music. There are no *laws* about such things, and we have already referred to a minuet or a scherzo as a series of sandwiches where the form of individual sections is a microcosm of the whole. In general, the trio does not challenge the affect or identity of the A section. Rather, the B section has a tendency to actually vanish in the memory, an act of almost Wagnerian self-immolation, in the service of the surrounding sections, which are strengthened through contrast. On a larger scale, the same principle operates in the relationship between middle movements and a whole work. In multimovement compositions we tend to privilege what we hear first and last. Middles have a strange habit of disappearing, which is why, from my viewpoint, they are an excellent places to hide things, being inner, interior, and tending to evaporate; a good place to squirrel things away because no one will look for them there.

So what exactly do we find in Dvořák's middle movement? Since we know that the composer was more or less obsessed with *The Song of Hiawatha* and made a special trip to see the falls for inspiration, we can try to connect the movement with the poem.

Reference to the waterfalls occurs after the agonizing fight between Hiawatha and his father, Mudjekeewis, in Chapter 4 of the poem. Hiawatha departs for home but stops first in the land of the Dacotahs, "Where the Falls of Minnehaha / Flash and gleam among the oak trees / Laugh and leap into the valley." Hiawatha has come to buy some arrows from the ancient Arrow-maker, but he has a secret reason for stopping. The Arrow-maker lives with his dark-eyed daughter:

Wayward as the Minnehaha,
With her moods of shade and sunshine,
Eyes that smiled and frowned alternate
Feet as rapid as the river,
Tresses flowing like the water,
And as musical a laughter:

And he named her from the river,
From the water-fall he named her,
Minnehaha, Laughing Water.

Let us return to Dvořák standing at Minnehaha Falls. He hears something and writes it down. But how can images of rapid feet and flowing tresses possibly be squared with the opening of the sonatina's Larghetto, which usually suggests the idea of lament to listeners and arrangers? Before answering this question we might note that there is something elusive going on in Dvořák's music concerning the relationship between G major and G minor. While the oscillation is obvious in such moments as the *Slavonic Dances*, it takes over in the Eighth Symphony, which is truly in the key of G major-minor. This tendency becomes amplified in several of the American works. The second and third themes of the "New World" use this key pattern, and it is at the core of the programmatic disturbance in the slow movement of the Cello Concerto. We have just encountered two small piano pieces that Dvořák wrote in the United States that go easily back and forth, once again, as if G major-minor were a single key.

If we go back to the passage from Longfellow armed with this knowledge, we find that the appeal of Minnehaha is not her shining disposition, nor is it solely her merry laughter, but rather her complexity: She is "wayward" with moods "of shade and sunshine"; she both smiles and frowns.

Is there any evidence beyond the circumstantial and geographical (and, of course, wishful thinking) to connect this movement with the image of Minnehaha? Let us remember that Dvořák's most ambitious American project, the *Hiawatha* opera, was never completed. As far as he was concerned, parts of the now famous "New World" were but sketches for this great Indian epic. When we hear the composer say that the trip to St. Paul involved Hiawatha, we should take him seriously. Should we now conclude that this G-major-minor oscillation is a double portrait of Minnehaha in all her moods?

Perhaps, and we should keep it in mind as we try to unravel our minor musicological mystery: Kovařík tells his charming story about Dvořák's cuffs and claims that the composer wrote down the "theme" of the movement. But as we know, the movement has two themes. Are we sure that Kovařík was talking about the first? I think not, and I offer two pieces of evidence to support my view as well as the notion that the movement was inspired by Minnehaha. First, about a month before completing of the sonatina, the composer sketched a suite in D minor. The second movement, an adagio, is a version of the sonatina's first theme, but in F major.

Is it likely that Dvořák would have taken down this tune on his cuff to use, and manage to get it in the "wrong" mode first? Besides, as we have noticed, this stylized and elegiac passage is hardly in keeping with the composer's supposed ecstasy while beholding the falls. Tucked away, though, among the sketches for the unfinished *Hiawatha* opera is a theme labeled "Minnehaha" (CD 69).

There is a similarity, both in key and shape, to the middle section of our sonatina movement that makes it utterly obvious that it was the second theme that Dvořák wrote down on his cuffs; it is his portrait of the waterfall and the woman for whom it was named. This is his "water music," and the gentle lyrical song that goes with it. This is the great illusion of the pastoral mode: sparkle without movement.

It is fitting, then, that Dvořák went against the grain by conspicuously marking his inconspicuous sonatina as Opus 100 and then hiding his exquisite portrait in the middle of its middle. This lovely secret in the midst of his one hundredth work is at once noticed and effectively hidden from view.

We have proceeded from considerations of landscape, to secrets, to questions of specific programs. But these programs are still external— Dvořák paints the American landscape, he paints Minnehaha. One cannot help noticing, though, that the Larghetto shows hints of the funereal with its dotted, sometimes plodding and marchlike countenance, and the *sforzandi* near the end seem almost out of place in their tragic weight (CD 70).

The movement almost inverts the mood of the "New World" Largo, whose middle section was surely inspired by the forest funeral of Minnehaha. But who was Minnehaha, where's the tragedy, and, to paraphrase Hamlet, who was she to Dvořák that he should weep for her?

Minnehaha is, of course, the central *romantic* interest in Longfellow's poem, but tragedy clings to her name and image. As we have seen, in the chapter called "The Famine," she dies of starvation and fever while

Hiawatha is hunting in the woods, and her forest funeral is one of the most memorable moments in the poem.

I have argued that Dvořák spent a great deal of time in the United States coming to grips with *The Song of Hiawatha*, especially the characters of Hiawatha and Minnehaha, and that his vision of America was intimately bound up with them. This vision involved broad external landscapes, tender wooing, and the waterfall, but it ultimately had a personal and intimate core. Thus we can also say that the G-major center is a self-portrait of Dvořák bewitched by the shimmer of laughing water in a meeting of the real and the imaginary adventures of his American exploration.

That is why the slow movement of the sonatina is so special. Inner movements are a nice parallel to *Innigkeit*, innerness, in general. They are often the white dwarf stars of music, packed too closely with multiple meanings, which leads us to end with a paradox. It is easy to say that Dvořák's music needs no commentary, especially of the kind I have offered, that it exists on a "purely musical" plane. I don't disagree, but focusing on this static G-major center, this sparkling musical image of the Minnehaha Falls, reminds us of something that is counterintuitive. On the one hand, slow movements are hidden, protected from the rest of the world by outer movements, but because they are repositories of so much that cannot be said, they gain a special power. We can argue that the true character of a work such as the sonatina lies is the way the Larghetto invisibly shines its sun and shadow on the rest of the work. Thus Dvořák, standing at this still point of his exquisite vision, paints the surrounding world as well from this silent ecstasy.

PART V

The Hidden Dvořák

To some extent, studying Dvořák is like observing a planetary body acting under the gravitational pull of an invisible force. Despite their vaunted lyrical beauty, many of Dvořák's most famous compositions reveal a world of conflict and tension that seems to be absent from the composer's life. In the previous three sections, we have seen how Dvořák interacted with texts (such as *The Song of Hiawatha*), with journalists, and with aspects of American landscape and culture. In the chapters that follow we will look behind the curtain at some of the incidents and predispositions that shaped the character and approach of his later years.

13

The Master Is Not Well

In the middle of September 1893, Dvořák and his family made their way back East after a splendid and restful summer in Spillville, Iowa. Traveling past Niagara Falls, where Dvořák was said to have exclaimed, "This will make a symphony in B minor," they eventually arrived in New York at the end of the month. Dvořák was to resume his activities at the National Conservatory soon, and within less than three months the symphony "From the New World" would have its magnificent premiere in New York City.

Yet all was not as it should have been, as the composer was behaving strangely. According to Kovařík, "A whole week after the return from Spillville, Master was very unsettled, in short, he was homesick for Spillville, for the country, he missed his 'triad of old men' with whom he was in daily contact throughout the Summer." Šourek, and others who followed, have explained this simply: Dvořák was longing for Bohemia, and after the bucolic world of Spillville, the bustle of New York was a shock to his system. That this was the case is undeniably true, yet each year thousands of people make the transition between country home and the bustle of the city without such difficulty. Dvořák's malaise was a sign of something deeper and more profound.

A more graphic description of Dvořák around this time was provided not by his protective amanuensis but by his adoring son Otakar:

Under the influence of stress my father increasingly smoked and started to have problems with his nerves and depressions. After Spillville's quiet the rush of the big city changed him and brought me a new task—to accompany Father to the conservatory. Sometimes he was afraid of the tram's electric wire. Other times he was afraid of the wagons and other vehicles on the streets. Never before had he expressed so many fears to me.[1]

Otakar's testimony is particularly convincing: he obviously has no idea that it might be stigmatizing to present his father in such a way, and it rings true at least in part because it is precisely the sort of thing that would make a lifelong impression on a young boy.

Nerves

That Otakar uses the expression "nerves" is entirely appropriate, since that word was enjoying currency at just the time Dvořák was visiting the United States. In writing about a range of disorders he observed, the neurologist George M. Beard concludes:

In this country nervous exhaustion is more common than any other form of nervous disease. With the various neuroses to which it is allied and to which it leads, it constitutes a family of functional disorders that are of comparatively recent development, and that abound especially in the northern and eastern part of the United States.[2]

Although one might think so, this passage does not describe today's world; rather, it refers to what was considered in the late nineteenth century to be a virtual epidemic of non-psychotic mental disorders. In 1869 Beard coined the term "neurasthenia" (literally "nerve weakness") to describe a broad range of mental disturbances. Never completely alike in different people, such mental states as disorientation, acute distress, and extreme unhappiness merged with physical symptoms ranging from insomnia, nausea, and diarrhea to numbness, headaches, and muscle weakness. It was Beard's conceit, in his classic pamphlet *American Nervousness: Its Philosophy and Treatment*, as it is ours, that these supposedly stress-related disorders are of recent origin.[3] But, of course, they have probably been around since the beginning of human time.

Beard tried both to classify the symptoms for appropriate treatment and to destigmatize such conditions. After all, to be declared insane was to be discredited, turned into a nonperson, and, inevitably, institutionalized. Once neurasthenia was associated with both the upper classes and with the "nervous exhaustion" that one might get from being a bank president, a physician, or a stockbroker, the ailments acquired a certain status. Along with this theory came both a classist and a sexist corollary: many neurologists divided cases up into three main categories. Upper-class men were thought to be suffering from "cerebral neurasthenia," while the plebes were diagnosed with "spinal neurasthenia." The causes of the former were the stresses and strains of modern life; for the latter, sexual excesses and physical exertion.[4] Women who displayed the same symptoms were invariably diagnosed with "hysteria."

Serious studies and popular works on the subject multiplied, with titles like *The Nervous Life*, *Nervous States: Their Nature and Causes*, *The Treatment of Neurasthenia by Means of Brain Control*, *Nerve Exhaustion*, *The Nervous Breakdown*, and even *Confessions of a Neurasthenic*. Both doctors and patients offered their opinions on the subject, but most agreed that they were facing a new epidemic, a result of the stress of modern life.

"Dvořák Never Walked Alone"

Is there any way to determine whether any of this applies to Dvořák? Throughout his later years, we find several offhand accounts by students and friends attesting that Dvořák was often unable to walk about or travel without a companion. Barushka Klírová, who lived with and worked for the Dvořáks in New York after they returned from Bohemia in the summer of 1894, wrote about the composer in her memoirs:

After he returned from the conservatory, sometimes he composed, and when he had somebody to go with, he went for a walk. It seldom happened that he walked alone. He did not like loneliness, and therefore, Mrs. Dvořák or Prof. Kovařík went with him. Once Dr. Dvořák wanted to go to "Perinas" to get his cigars. That was quite far from us, and Mrs. Dvořák was not available, so I offered him my company. On the way home I wanted to stop to see some friends. . . . When we got the cigars, on our way home, Dr. Dvořák advised me that it was time to leave him. However, because I knew how much he disliked being alone, I decided to accompany him back. His pleasure was apparent when he gave me a big smile as a reward. All the same, he instructed me that I was to explain this to his wife. She would probably be upset that he did not allow me to leave him. And indeed, when Mrs. Dvořák opened the door, and was welcoming us, she smiled, and said to me: "Of course, Barushka, I had a pretty good idea that you would be coming too." They knew and understood each other very well, and it helped them with such problems.[5]

This "problem" is put more succinctly in the memoirs of one of the students who studied with Dvořák in Prague:

The Master sent me (certainly because I was the youngest) to look in front of the Rudolfinum and see if "his Mary" was waiting there. She was a servant who waited for him—Dvořák never walked alone.[6]

On the surface, none of the witnesses—Otakar, Kovařík, or Klírová—thought too much about Dvořák's behavior. But we should. Although it seems obvious, walking around outside by oneself is a key sign of adulthood. Yet there are many grown-ups who, for various reasons, are not always up to the task. How and why is it that a stocky, healthy, grown man like Dvořák was not capable of walking the streets by himself, and what does it have to do with Beard's neurasthenia? The answer points us to a syndrome that today is designated as agoraphobia. John Clapham used the word in connection with Dvořák more than thirty years ago:

From time to time Dvořák suffered from anxieties of one kind or another, and these were often connected in some way with the unknown. When going on a long journey he liked to have a companion, and he needed to be assured well in advance about travelling instructions. He took a long time to reach a decision when invited to America and in later life showed signs of agoraphobia. He was also apt to be concerned about his family's and his own health.[7]

I also used the word in my introduction to *Dvořák and His World*, although I did not understand its full implications. Agoraphobia is commonly thought of as a fear of open spaces, but that is only the iceberg's tip. If, as seems certain, Dvořák did suffer from agoraphobia at times, what is it really, and what impact, if any, could it have had on the composer's everyday and creative life?

Several criteria allow for the diagnosis of agoraphobia. The condition involves "anxiety about being in places or situations from which escape might be difficult (or embarrassing)," and "agoraphobic fears typically involve characteristic clusters of situations that include being outside the home alone; being in a crowd or standing in a line; being on a bridge; and traveling in a bus, train or automobile."[8]

But agoraphobia is not simply an isolated phenomenon. The agoraphobe fears "open spaces" not necessarily because there is anything intrinsically scary about the space itself but usually because "help may not be available in the event of having an unexpected or situationally predisposed Panic Attack or panic-like symptoms."[9] Furthermore, many studies suggest that panic disorder and agoraphobia are intimately connected: "In clinical settings, almost all individuals (95%) who present with agoraphobia also have a current diagnosis (or history) of Panic Disorder."[10] In other words, what most agoraphobes worry about is feeling severe discomfort or even having a panic attack in a public place.[11]

Although for some people the condition is chronic, for many individuals such states come and go, and we can assume that when Dvořák was comfortable, as we assume he was at home or walking the grounds of Vysoká or Spillville, he was completely asymptomatic.[12] Yet it is possible, though not certain, that there was some residual difficulty. Someone who has repeated panic attacks over time is considered to have a panic disorder, and *DSM-IV*, the bible of American psychiatry, goes on to describe the condition: "In addition to worry about Panic Attacks and their implications, many individuals with Panic Disorder also report constant or intermittent feelings of anxiety that are not focused on any specific situation or event. Others become excessively apprehensive about the outcome of routine activities and experiences, particularly those related to health or *separation from loved ones*" (italics mine).[13]

Performance Anxiety and Thunderstorms

If Dvořák suffered from such a condition, we would expect to notice other aspects of his behavior that were affected by anxiety, and this is indeed the case. First, Dvořák suffered from severe, even debilitating, performance anxiety. Kovařík describes the symptoms:

> Before each concert, Dvořák felt sick. The day before the last rehearsal was the most difficult, not only for the composer, but for everybody in the household. He could not work or read, and became incurably restless. To relieve the tension we would go for a walk together but when we had made two or there trips around the park just outside our house in Stuyvesant Square, he would be in a hurry to return home.

Dvořák's nervous behavior was hardly limited to those times when a performance was looming, but was far more general. In fact, according to Kovařík:

> The Master, who was a tireless worker, at once fell into a bad mood if he was without employment. He was more or less irritable, bad tempered, distraught, there was, so to speak, no making anything of him sometimes. The most trifling question put him in a fury.[14]

And then we find the classic agoraphobia tagline: "I had to be with him all day long."

There are other aspects of Dvořák's behavior that suggest someone suffering from anxiety. For example, the composer was terrified of hail and hated storms of all kinds.[15] In the words of his American student Hopkins, "If there were an electric storm which Dvořák feared, there could be no thought of a lesson till it passed. These storms were the bane of his existence."[16] This condition may stem from a heightened startle reflex; in other words, loud noises become simply intolerable and terrifying to the sufferer. In separate reminiscences, Hopkins described Dvořák's behavior in the face of approaching storms as "frantic," and said that the composer would bang on the piano to drown out the sound of the thunder. He also mentioned that the composer had a deep-seated fear of fire and thieves.[17]

When and Why Did the Anxiety Begin?

If we can accept that Dvořák was in the grip of this condition for at least some of the time he was in the United States, we might ask when it began: whether it might have been brought about by his trip to the United States, or whether it worsened here. The evidence is that he had it earlier. In his reminiscences, Kovařík notes that Spillville was such a wonderful place for Dvořák because he could go out by himself: "He usually went alone—here he had none of the nerve storms which he sometimes suffered from in Prague."[18] This statement implies not only a preexisting condition but one associated, at least in Kovařík's mind, with the need for companionship. A letter from Dvořák to his friend Antonín Rus in 1889 suggests that it appeared around that time:

> I have been at Vysoká since the 6th May and have not been to see you yet! It is terrible! But what's to be done when I am not as I used to be. To travel—what a delight it was for me formerly—and now? I am glad when I can sit at home.[19]

It is difficult to understand Dvořák's condition fully from the distance of a century, but there is little doubt that he suffered from agoraphobia. Most discussions of the disorder suggest that it is caused by some combination of heredity, chronic stress, and traumatic events. In Dvořák's case, we can surely point to chronic stress. Even though Dvořák was no peasant, he was hardly sophisticated, yet he found himself in an elite world, both within the Czech Lands and in Vienna, England, and the United States. A variety of passages attest to his sense of insecurity—indeed, we read of Dvořák's own sense of shame when he received his honorary doctorate. Though he certainly was able to find ways of minimizing that shame, it must have caused him great embarrassment at the time. In a later chapter we will see that Dvořák was caught between "a Ring and a hard place." Though given the role as a classicizing figure (as opposed to Smetana at home and Wagner abroad), Dvořák was becoming more and more of a Wagnerian and wrote nothing but operas and tone poems in the final eight years of his life, despite his reputation as a composer of symphonies and chamber music.

But even these conditions do not necessarily create the stress that causes anxiety. Dvořák was working constantly, trying to improve his family fortunes, and trying to make a career as a composer. Finally, several of his children died in infancy. All these factors combined could easily have produced, in conjunction with genetic predisposition, his problems with anxiety.

Homesickness and Other Maladies

The information assembled here strongly suggests that Dvořák suffered from a garden-variety anxiety disorder, as do five to ten percent of the population at one time or another. But can we, or should we, expect more from exposing this? In other words, if we establish Dvořák's condition beyond a reasonable doubt, would it tell us anything that we really want to know?[20]

At the very least, an awareness of Dvořák's agoraphobia provides simple answers to several biographical questions and explains certain behaviors and activities that have not been well understood. For example, it has always been a puzzle why Dvořák decided not to attend the first public performance of the "New World." According to Kovařík:

> Master did not attend the very first performance of his symphony on December 15th—it was a general rehearsal, something which has since been discontinued. The Master came with family to hear the symphony at the Saturday evening concert.[21]

Though this performance was billed as an open rehearsal, it was treated in many ways as a premiere. Several critics reviewed the symphony at that time, and many prominent people were in attendance. It is unthinkable that Dvořák would miss the performance. Burghauser says, ". . . there is also the story of a young girl, perhaps a pupil in the conservatory, whom Dvořák sent in almost by force."[22] This is all very strange stuff, and much easier to understand if we imagine that Dvořák was having a great deal of trouble with his nerves at the time.

We have also seen that one of the most astute observers of Dvořák was James Creelman, who more than almost any of his contemporaries showed an ability to ferret out hidden facts. In this context his description of Dvořák's behavior during the controversy over "Real Value of Negro Melodies" is especially telling: "Well, when Dvorak realized what he had done, he locked himself in a room and turned the lights out. For an hour he remained alone. No one knows what he did, but I strongly suspect that he folded his arms, set his teeth and stared at the darkness. It is a way he has when the world is too much for him."[23] At first the suggestion that Creelman actually was privy to any special information about Dvořák's condition may seem to buy into the reporter's own conceit, but when we remember that Creelman was literally in the pay of Jeannette Thurber, who certainly knew about the composer's condition, the words take on a special meaning.[24]

Creelman was not the only one to notice that Dvořák sometimes displayed unusual behavior. František Šubert recalls:

He used to come and see me at my office at the National Theater either when he had finished some work—something new or the revision of an old work—or when rehearsals of his works were on. I do not remember him ever sitting down. He usually walked to and fro or stood at my desk or at the window, gazing into space, now in one direction, now in another, spoke or listened. And it would happen that in the middle of a sentence he would suddenly break off and become lost in thought. In his mind some musical idea had taken wing and was soaring and singing like a skylark and sometimes he straight away began to whistle it. Only after a while, and as if there had been no interruption, he would return to reality and to what he was saying. Or during a conversation about a certain subject, he would suddenly start speaking about something quite different, his mind fully occupied with it. And sometimes, in the middle of a conversation, he would turn on his heel with a greeting, or even without, and be gone. And he would maybe return in a few days "to finish what we were talking about."[25]

Dvořák was considered a genius, and therefore people tended to regard such behavior as curious or even colorful rather than disturbing. That is certainly the case with an incident (to be discussed in the final chapter) mentioned in Kovařík's description of a trip to the opera with Dvořák. There is little doubt that the composer suffered a panic attack at that occasion, or at least felt acute public discomfort.

Other aspects of the biographical record are in need of reevaluation in light of Dvořák's condition. The relationship between Kovařík and Dvořák has always seemed like a natural one: the older man's somewhat gruff affection suggests a father-son relationship. Yet *DSM-IV* notes of agoraphobia that the various conditions that cause it "are avoided (e.g. travel is restricted) or else are endured with marked distress or with anxiety about having a Panic Attack or panic-like symptoms, *or require the presence of a companion*" (italics mine).[26] We have already seen how important it was for Dvořák, whether in Prague or New York, to avoid being outside by himself. In this context it becomes clear that Kovařík was not merely Dvořák's helper, but was essential to his ability to function.

An even broader topic involves Dvořák's famous homesickness. Here is a description in the words of his son, Otakar:

> Then homesickness struck again; he missed the other members of our family, and of course Vysoká. In letters mailed to his friends he mentioned that Vysoká was the place where he had the best feeling. In Vysoká he could stay relaxed even while working 12 hours per day on a composition. The best medicine against his homesickness was his composition. His job helped him overcome such longings and the depressing thoughts that accompanied them.[27]

This homesickness has always been central to any discussion of the American years, and the pathos of the famous Largo is usually attributed to it. It has been part of a campaign to mark Dvořák as a Czech family man, who, when deprived of his brood and his country, simply languishes. This characterization may be true, but a key part of anxiety is a frightening kind of obsession known as "catastrophic thinking." When one is in the grip of such thinking, each pimple becomes an omen of terminal cancer and loved ones become the subjects of unrealistic and agonizing worries. Further, someone who suffers from anxiety likely suffers from depression as well. In other words, "homesickness" might be considered a code word for what today we call "depression."

Finally, a whole range of Dvořák legends, from his love of cards with the Spillville farmers, to his interest in trains and pigeons, to his abhorrence of public speaking, may also be related to his anxiety. That he chose physical retreats from stressful urban environments and found restful idylls like Vysoká and Spillville is more than just a country man seeking his own; these locations served as a necessary escape for his psychological health by allowing him to avoid precisely the kinds of stresses that set him off. The pigeons and trains calmed him and took his mind off other worries, but, particularly in the case of trains and their numbers, they may also have been an obsession, and according to many students of psychology, obsession is at the root of many of these disorders.

His Last Two Beers

Another area of the composer's life is also problematic. In his memoirs, Otakar throws in an offhand comment about his father's drinking:

> He would describe fantastic stories about ocean liners, New York streets, the zoo, and so on. But in the end, before finishing his last two glasses of beer, Father always confessed to the fact that not all of the stories were true.[28]

I leave it to others to speculate how much beer Dvořák was drinking if his son could so routinely refer to "his *last two* glasses of beer," but I do not think we are talking about three or four beers here.

Certainly there is and was a great deal of drinking in the Czech Lands, and there is no proof that Dvořák was anything more than a "normal Czech drinking man"; but Dvořák was not just a normal Czech man: he was a world-famous composer and, as such, a public figure. A national hero stumbling around is different from a workingman doing the same thing. Although Kovařík insisted that Dvořák did not imbibe too much, there are several references, some anecdotal, to his drinking. Some of the Spillville stories involve excessive tippling and paint pictures of the composer passed out along the Turkey River.[29] In his reminiscences, Ladislav Dolanský recalls the following incident, which combines the idea of drinking with the desire not be alone:

Once on a Sunday morning we met at Velebín Urbánek's shop. Dvořák invited me to go to a wine-shop. I was not accustomed at that time to drink anything in the morning, and was not very willing to agree. But Dvořák insisted: "Please do me the favor, I should not go alone."[30]

They sit in the wineshop together, Dvořák has his drink, and despite Dolanský's attempt to start a conversation, the composer does not reply. They sit together silently. Dvořák finishes his wine and they get up to leave. "In the street he shook me warmly by the hand and said: 'You don't know how grateful I am that you went with me; you have done me a great service.' " It is hard to escape the conclusion that Dvořák needed a companion to escort him to the wineshop, where, having had a drink, he felt much better and able to walk by himself.

We are already familiar with James Huneker's reminiscence about his devastating pub crawl with Dvořák in New York.[31] Dvořák scholars have tended to dismiss such accounts as scurrilous, but need we brand Huneker a liar to save Dvořák's reputation? As we have seen, Huneker turns out to be a remarkably reliable, though acerbic, witness. Huneker *was* a big drinker, and if he was intimidated by Dvořák's drinking, that says something. Paul Polansky argues that the diaries kept by the composer's wife in New York reveal that an enormous amount of money was spent on beer per week, almost five dollars, about a quarter of what it cost to rent his flat.[32] Finally, we are told that according to family members, Dvořák had "consumed beer over the measure" at the time of his final illness.[33] We often have the idea that people drink because either "they want to get drunk" or they are "addicted" to alcohol. But many people, then as now, drink to relieve tension and anxiety. Considering Dvořák's agoraphobia, we could look on his drinking as self-medication for anxiety.

There is a general sense that while the short-term effects of alcohol may produce a sense of relaxation, in the long term it definitely exacerbates the condition.[34] Tchaikovsky, who may have had a similar disorder, is a case in point. He fell into the syndrome of drinking excessive amounts of alcohol in the evening followed by excessive amounts of caffeine in the morning. This habit could not possibly have benefited any nervous condition he had, and over time it would likely worsen it.

Several of these themes—fear of travel, general anxiety, and alcohol—come together in Kovařík's reminiscence about the train ride to Spillville through the "dry" state of Pennsylvania.[35] In the course of Kovařík's record there is an oblique reference to a thunderstorm "which came earlier than expected " but "was not too bad and . . . ended well." Then Dvořák throws a fit because he cannot get a beer, screaming, "So, this is America, the land of freedom! A free country! And one cannot get his glass of beer!" Kovařík finally finds him a drink, but Dvořák does not want it because he has thrown *another* fit: "The situation in our car was terrible! . . . He was running back and forth like an angry lion, and as soon as he saw me coming he shouted 'You, go away! I don't want to see you Indian!' (He called me Indian because of my American origin.)" It turns out that the train had been moved to another track, and when Dvořák thought that Kovařík had disappeared, he became apoplectic.

Did Dvořák Ever Consult a Doctor for His Condition?

If Dvořák did suffer from anxiety, did he try to seek out help for his condition? Doctors' records from a century ago are difficult to come by, and I have not been able to locate any notes on the matter whatsoever. There is, however, one unusual piece of information. In Dvořák's *Letters and Reminiscences* we find the following reminiscence by Otakar:

> Something that is perhaps quite unknown to the general public is that Father was very keen on gymnastics which at first consisted in taking a chair and doing arm exercises with it. Later he got himself dumbbells and exercised with them early in the morning.[36]

The spectacle of Dvořák's weightlifting may have been a naturally occurring phenomenon, yet it is precisely the kind of activity that doctors at the time prescribed to relieve tension and quiet anxiety.

Anxiety and the Creative Mind

It is no secret that more than a century after their birth, psychiatry and psychology are imperfect sciences. The fact that Prozac and other antidepressants are being used by millions does not really mean we understand any more about the way the mind works and what begins, continues, or ends the kinds of conditions we have been discussing. If our information about so called mental disorders is sketchy, how much more so is our understanding of how such states might interact with a broad range of creative impulses. Yet this lack of knowledge should not deter us from posing certain questions, at least about what the possibilities for such a thing might be, and whether there is a marginal relationship, no relationship at all, or a fundamental relationship between illness and activity.

While the search for microscopic details that reflect "Dvořák's disturbance" would ultimately result in a *reductio ad absurdum*, where every diminished chord or dissonant passage could be considered evidence of the disability, there are other ways in which such observations can become part of our larger picture of the composer. If we accept that Dvořák suffered from anxiety, it is likely that the morbidity, depression, and pain that the composer experienced became part of the emotional palette out of which he composed. Whether or not he was actually feeling such things as he worked—and it is as likely as not that composition actually offered a *respite* from such feelings—he knew them and could use them. On the other side, we have evidence, in the glorious ecstasy of the Spillville works, of just what happens to someone when the gray cloud suddenly lifts and we get a (pathological?) surge of joy.

Whatever the case, there is no doubt that Dvořák's mental state was considerably more complex and variable than we have heretofore thought. Although his condition was not at all uncommon, this in no way implies that it was easily tolerable for him. There are recorded cases of agoraphobia without symptoms of panic, but the great likelihood is that Dvořák was terrified at least some of the time and must have suffered greatly. I believe that his fear and suffering played a significant role in his coming to grips with his creative personality.

In the following chapters I will allude to some of the conditions that caused the Master to become anxious, or, in the parlance of his time, "to weaken his nerves," and I will suggest that secrets, death, and Wagner were both significant responses to and causes of his stress. But I must point out that there are those, particularly in the Czech Republic, who object to this kind of inquiry, who view a discussion of Dvořák and anxiety as intrusive, disrespectful, willfully iconoclastic, or simply beside the point. But it is none of these. If Dvořák really was a man of the people, someone who could sit down with farmers more easily than with princes, and if he was truly someone who could express things to all of us, it was not only because he was Czech, or Catholic, or unpretentious, or the product of a small-town upbringing, it was also because of his fears, which alone gave him something in common with all of us in a way both simple and profound.

14

A Cello Concerto, a Death— and Secrets

In the spring of 1894, Dvořák heard a concerto for cello by one of his colleagues at the National Conservatory, Victor Herbert, the future composer of *Babes in Toyland* and other successful operettas. According to witnesses, he was impressed by the work, coming backstage after the performance and exclaiming, "Splendid, absolutely splendid!" He could have added what Brahms was reported to have uttered after playing through Dvořák's Cello Concerto: "Had I known that such a violoncello concerto as that could be written, I would have tried to compose one myself."

Dvořák spent more than four months in Bohemia that summer, where he completed the Humoresques for Piano, returning to New York only at the end of October to start his new term at the National Conservatory. Within a few weeks he was at work on a composition that would be the other great "bookend" of his American stay and one of his most ambitious and significant efforts. A magnificent work of epic proportions, filled with broad, seemingly public gestures, the concerto has also been associated with the composer's romantic life.

Let us begin with a testy letter that Dvořák wrote to his publisher Simrock. Here he categorically forbids anyone, including the work's dedicatee, the cellist Hanus Wihan, from adding any material whatsoever to the end of the concerto:

> I must insist on my work being printed as I have written it. . . . I shall only then give you the work if you promise not to allow anyone to make changes without my knowledge or consent—including my friend

Wihan—and this includes the cadenza which Wihan has added to the last movement. . . . There is no cadenza in the last movement, either in the score or in the piano arrangement. I told Wihan straight away when he showed it to me that it was impossible to stick something like this on. The finale closes gradually dimenuendo—like a sigh—with reminiscences of the first and second movements—the solo dies away to pp, then swells again. The last bars are taken up by the orchestra and the whole concludes in a stormy mood. That was my idea and I cannot depart from it.[1]

Even though it is perfectly understandable for a composer to want a work played the way he intended, Dvořák's biographer Otakar Šourek felt a need to explain Dvořák's behavior:

Dvořák must have found this interference [Wihan's cadenza] unpleasant, especially since it involved that part of the final movement which he rewrote after his return from America (the beginning of May, 1895), and in which he piously alluded to the death of his sister-in-law, Josefina Kounicová-Cermáková (d. May 27 of that year), whom he highly esteemed not only as a dear friend, but also as the charming young actress who, long years ago, when he was still a viola player in the orchestra of the Provisional Theater, had awakened in him a secret passion [the expression of this unrequited love was his first cycle of songs, *The Cypresses*, in 1865.] With the thought of her in mind, he had already introduced into the second movement of the concerto a theme which is a paraphrase of his well-known song "Leave Me Alone," from four songs Op. 82, of which Josefina was particularly fond, and then, under the impression caused by her death, there appears a fragment of this melody at the close of the work.

For this reason he insisted on his own definitive conclusions and for this reason he was determined to counter any interference with his conception.[2]

These passages are the main source for almost all the speculation that has taken place regarding this concerto. Šourek's account contains certain provable facts: Dvořák's letter to his publisher is extant, everyone agrees that Dvořák quotes one of his songs in the second movement, and we know that he made changes in the coda of the last movement after the completion of the work, sticking in another reminiscence of the same song. But Šourek's discussion also contains assertions for which we have virtually no corroboration: he is the only one to tell us of Dvořák's "unrequited love" that supposedly gave rise to *The Cypresses*, and also the only source for the idea that Opus 82 No. 1, "Leave Me Alone," was one of Josefina's favorite songs, placed into the concerto "with her in mind." Where did Šourek hear such things? Was it "well known" by all the Master's intimates, or was it a chance piece of information Šourek was lucky to get? Could he even have heard it from the composer's widow, or perhaps one of the children?[3]

We may never be able to answer these questions, and thus the relationship between Dvořák and his sister-in-law will likely remain a matter of conjecture, and to a certain extent a matter of secrets. What is unusual is that these secrets have become an integral part of the Cello Concerto, and a cursory sampling of program and liner notes suggests that today almost every audience encounters the work through the blurry scrim of Josefina. To probe the matter, we can briefly trace the musical issues related to the song, explore possible connections with Josefina, and then expand to a broader consideration of the concerto's character, including a look at Dvořák's language of dying, funerals, and lament.

Šourek's first point about the music, that the concerto quotes Opus 82 No. 1, is certainly correct. Actually, Dvořák quotes two different parts of the song, written by him to a German text. The first quotation, which occurs in the second movement, is not the beginning of the song, but rather a variant that occurs at the text "Lasst mich allein! Verscheucht den Frieden nicht in meiner Brust mit euren lauten Worten" (Leave me alone! O banish not the peace within my breast with words so loud; CD 71). The similarity between the two passages is obvious (CD 72). Later, in the coda, Dvořák quotes the beginning of the song, "Lasst mich allein in meine träume geh'n" (Leave me alone with my dreams; CD 73).

When we consider these facts in the context of Dvořák's relationship to Josefina, at least four scenarios are possible.

1. There is no connection between the concerto and Josefina. Someone gossiped; Šourek got it wrong; it has all been a big mistake.

2. Even though Dvořák had never been in love with Josefina, they were dear friends, Opus 82 No. 1 was one of her favorite songs, and he included it in the concerto in her memory.

3. Dvořák had been in love with Josefina when he was a young man, and remembered this love as a tribute to her.[4]

4. The romance-novel plot: Dvořák had been in love with Josefina as a young man and carried the torch for her always. (There are, of course, variant scenarios of this last hypothesis: she knew, she didn't know, she loved him too, it was a secret until his death, a select group was in the know, etc.)

None of these scenarios can be proved unequivocally. For each argument, there is a counterargument, and little documentary detail to back any of it up. Let's explore these possibilities one by one. Could the whole thing be a giant mistake? Could the concerto have absolutely nothing to do with Josefina? For this to be true, Šourek, the official biographer, would have had to be completely wrong; we would also have to turn up a suitable reason to explain why Dvořák rewrote the end of his concerto on the heels of Josefina's death and placed a love song in such a conspicuous position. Also, if there was not a shred of truth in Šourek's story, one imagines there might have been some outcry on the part of the family when the third volume of his biography was published in 1930.

Yet a non-Josefina approach to the concerto is possible. Finding her in the second and final movements could simply be a matter of wishful thinking and inverse logic: because Dvořák's insertion of the coda and his behavior regarding the cadenza loomed conspicuous to Šourek, he may have had a natural tendency to allow gossip to play an outsized role in the matter. Today we do not have trouble understanding why Dvořák simply wanted the conclusion of the concerto *his* way, as he claimed to Simrock. There is nothing odd about writing one's own coda. After all, he was a world-famous composer—why shouldn't he have the work the way he liked? So it is possible that the Dvořák–Josefina myth occupies the same stature as the Court of Honor in Tchiakovsky's supposed suicide. It's a myth and nothing more.

The second theory, that Dvořák did quote the song as a tribute to a dear sister-in-law and an old friend, is also possible, if a bit far-fetched. Of course, Dvořák might have included the song in the second movement simply because his sister-in-law liked it, and then added another reminiscence after her death. Yet it would be odd to quote a love song for the death of a relative. Too, if the quoted song was to be an innocent tribute to his sister-in-law, why not say something about it? Now, it is possible that all the relevant family members—including his wife—*did* know, and that's how Šourek found out: the use of the tune may have been the equivalent of a funeral for family only. In that case, though, we might have expected others besides Šourek to have heard something about it, and no one else has ever come forward—Šourek is apparently the only one who found out.[5] Also, the original placement of the melody in the middle of the middle movement adds a tone of mystery—it is both hidden and exposed. There is a bit too much secrecy in force for the kind of innocence implied by the second hypothesis. Quoting such a moving love song in such a vast epic work is an unlikely gesture toward a departed family member.

The third theory is in some ways the most attractive, since a reminiscence involving the composer's youthful infatuation satisfies the romantic angle of the affair without compromising the normative view of Dvořák as a Victorian paterfamilias. At the same time it would validate Šourek's information, leaving his position as a responsible biographer unchallenged. Yet arguments for this view are not airtight either. If, as Šourek tells us, the songs from *The Cypresses* had such a special place in Dvořák's heart, it is peculiar that he would have reworked several of these as late as 1889 as the Love Songs, Opus 83, unless the songs still meant something to him. Further, both the theme and the text of "Leave Me Alone" are closely related to No. 14 of *The Cypresses*, "Zde v lese u potoka" ("By the Brook"), which Dvořák rearranged as No. 6 of the Love Songs.

Indeed, it is difficult to escape the conclusion that there is a core relationship between these two songs. Not only are the melodic lines similar, so are the settings. (The main difference between the two, the octave leap in "Leave Me Alone," may come from the tenth measure of "By the Brook.") Both songs begin in a pastoral world with descending parallel thirds, and in both the main theme is presented twice, but altered (in Opus 82 it moves from F-sharp major to F-sharp minor, in Opus 83 it moves a third higher). Both songs leave their world of serenity and bliss to explore an opposing state of torment, marked by chromatic movement, and both seek release in a climax, on the word "love" in Opus 82, and the disintegrating "rock" in Opus 83.

If Dvořák is still recalling his youthful love for Josefina in *both* Opus 82 and Opus 83, and later placing traces of it throughout his concerto in ways both conspicuous and secretive, we can hardly call the relationship over and done with. If someone is thinking continually about an "innocent" early romance it cannot be that innocent. But these arguments too, have problems. Even if *The Cypresses* was originally intended for Josefina, its republication as Opus 83 might simply be an attempt by Dvořák to provide Simrock with the smaller pieces he requested so often. And we must understand that not a single document has turned up implying anything but filial affection between Josefina and Dvořák.

It is the fourth scenario, which sees a good deal of torch-carrying over the decades, however, that many have found so compelling. It explains more easily why Dvořák couldn't simply tell Wihan why his additions were especially unwelcome and why this particular song, with its aching text, was used. It also explains why any information about the situation was hard to come by. It might even explain why Vysoká, where his sister-in-law lived during the summer, was so special to him. But before jumping to this conclusion, let's explore further some of the musical gestures of the concerto.

John Clapham has offered one explanation for the insertion of the song in the second movement.[6] He quotes a letter in which Josefina, writing in a distraught tone, chides Dvořák for not writing, and intimates that her health is deteriorating:

Dear Anton!
Forgive me for not writing to you for such a long time. But I have been continuously confined to bed and unable to do so, and for the same reason I have nothing important to report which would be of interest to you. . . . I have not heard from you for a long time. This is not as it should be! However, I shall have to resign myself to the fact that I have nothing to look forward to anymore. . . .[7]

This letter was received in November 1894, just before the first sketches of the concerto. Let us look at the second movement in that context and see what Dvořák might have had in mind.

The movement has several types of material. There is a chorale-like main theme, which has a kinship to such things as the slow movement of Beethoven's "Emperor" Concerto (CD 74). There is, of course, the song fragment, but there are two other ideas before it occurs. The first is something that sounds like a reminiscence, a sigh of memory (CD 75), and it is easy to hear this as a reference to the second measure of "Leave Me Alone," with its plagal sigh (CD 73).

The second idea is the most striking and provocative (CD 76). Indeed, we might say that this interruption is a key to the nature of the entire concerto. Its range, mode, and dotted rhythm take us into a realm distant from the opening of the movement and mark a kind of affective space that had become one of Dvořák's favorite expressive tools. It will be useful, at this point, to explore the relationship between this sound world and the state that, no matter what else we do, we will all one day achieve.

Music and Death

Music does many things well. It can serve as accompaniment to grief and horror, celebration and ecstasy, religious adoration and sexual jealousy. It can suggest waterfalls, thunderstorms, and carnivals. Because composers have no trouble using music to stand in for any kind of kinetic process, there are countless musical analogs to *dying*—chromatic descents, the sound of an orchestra "dying out," the agonizing downward spiral of Desdemona in *Otello*, or Mimi in *La Bohème* gradually going to "sleep." Yet Death itself, as the absolute cessation of movement, defies sonic characterization. But since the issue of death is central to Romantic thought, composers had to find some solutions to the problem of musical death. What they eventually negotiated with their audiences is both simple and elegant.

To see how it started, we must return to the days of the French Revolution, when public secular ritual was a keystone of the new regime. Among the many celebrations of civic virtue were ceremonies devoted to honoring the martyrs of the revolt. The music that accompanied many of these, with its combination of somber memorial and grand public display, was codified and stylized by some of the best composers associated with the Revolution. Something of that spirit is heard in such works as the *Marche Lugubre* of François Josef Gossec.[8]

The slow tempo, minor key, dotted rhythms, and conspicuous drum stylizations, which, taken together, suggest physical staggering and represent an archaic Baroque gravitas, create a world of resonant sound that simply had not existed previously.

Credit for taking this language into the mainstream must surely go to Beethoven, whose "Marcia funebre" from the "Eroica" Symphony, while perhaps intended to evoke the public ceremonies so beloved of Napoleon, also became associated with the death of a more generic hero and, eventually, with death itself (CD 77, arranged for piano).

Beethoven's work filled a gap in the musical imagination and provided, by popular consensus, a symbol for our unutterable fate. Although it is, ironically, a march—one of the musical stylizations most notably associated with *movement*—that so potently became associated with the motionlessness of death, it is appropriate. The musical funeral is but a military march slowed down and "minorized," replacing the heroes of battlefield action with the contemplative martyrs of the graveyard. Yet death is not only undepictable, it defies comprehension. It therefore must have something to stand in for it: a visual sign, like a skull or skeleton, or in this case, the aural symbol of a slow, dotted rhythm played on a timpani.[9]

If Beethoven was a pioneer in bringing musical funerals into the mainstream, both Schubert and Berlioz avidly followed his lead.[10] But it was left to Chopin to create the most potent musical presentation of the funeral march. Not only is the famous march the most notable part of Chopin's piano sonata, but it was the part of the sonata that was written first, and the other movements were "written around it." It is not by coincidence that funeral marches are found almost exclusively in inner movements. While the slowness of the march mandated its position in a multimovement design, it also led to the mystique and mystery of the genre.

At first blush it is odd to think of Dvořák as a master of the funeral march. After all, his pedigree as a merry, lyrical, straightforward Czech is still widely accepted. Yet from the beginning of his career to the end, he used funerals and funeral imagery in works large and small.

Dvořák: Death, Dying, and Lament

The only instance in Dvořák's works where a funeral march is clearly marked by both programmatic association and tempo indication is his 1896 tone poem *Holoubek*, which is marked "Andante, Marcia funebre," and is meant to depict a widow following her husband's funeral cortege (CD 78). *Holoubek* opens with the classic dotted rhythm in third and fourth horns. A recent rash of books bear titles such as *Seven Habits of Highly Effective People*; someone should publish a musical version called *The Habits of Highly Effective Composers*. One of these is certainly the "habit" or principle of compositional economy. Since audiences are unlikely to want to sit around forever to get the message, composers usually try to choose musical images that can accomplish many things at the same time. The arresting opening drone fifths in Beethoven's "Pastoral," for example, suggest, simultaneously, a "new" world, the creatures that populate the world (the bagpipe and shepherd beyond), and the timelessness of the realm itself, all in less than a second. Dvořák takes only slightly longer in *Holoubek*. The repeated notes in the muted horns have a noble lineage, suggesting, as in the first temple scene in *Zauberflöte* or Schubert's song "Der Tod und das Mädchen," a speaker or voice from another world. We know that muted brass was associated with ceremonies marking fallen soldiers, and thus marks an additional funereal association. Further, the use of the horn also suggests the outdoors and the forest location of this particular funeral.

This gesture is followed a measure later by the characteristic timpani tattoo, which adds its hints of rumbling thunder, gloom, and public memorial. This touch is certainly part of Beethoven's legacy: drumrolls are a prominent feature of the "Eroica" funeral march, where they appear at the very opening and help to provide the movement with its sense of urgency and forward motion. Indeed, this rhythmic gesture has become one of the most pungent musical spices in the composer's pantry, so potent that even one measure of it carries enormous representative weight.

It is also, curiously, one of the few absolute equations in musical depiction: a drum playing the role of a drum. We will see, though, that Dvořák sometimes assigns this figure to the strings.

Already we have seen how funeral imagery made its way into the "New World" Symphony, from the work's opening, through Minnehaha's forest funeral in the middle of the Largo, to the Finale funeral. And we have seen that even in his most lighthearted compositions, such as the "American" chamber works, there are hints of the funeral in the slow movements. But these are not merely isolated incidents, for we find funeral marches in all genres. For example, Dvořák's incidental music for the melodrama *J. K. Tyl* (1882) features a funeral march based on the song "Kde domov můj." At the words "add text," the song by František Škroup that would later become the Czech national anthem appears in funeral guise. Here the drumrolls are particularly conspicuous, occurring in both the timpani and the cellos. The use of drumroll or tremolo figures in the lower strings are a staple of Dvořák's funeral style.

There is a funeral march in the Symphony No. 3—in a parallel spot to where Beethoven placed his march in the "Eroica"—and another one in *The Specter's Bride*. Funerals are both covert and actual. While we can all clearly hear that the *Rusalka* leitmotiv is cast as a funeral march after the death of the Prince, it is not so obvious that the motive, which appears more than a hundred times, and more than anything else sets the tone of the work, has *always* been a funeral march.

Funeral marches appear where we expect them to—in the "Lacrimoso" section of *The Hero's Song*, the Requiem, and the *Stabat Mater*—but also where we least expect them, as in the slow "Dumka" movement of the Piano Quintet, Opus 81. According to David Beveridge, the piece was modeled on Schumann's Quintet in E-flat, and the second movement of that work is clearly in the funeral march mode (CD 79).[11] The slow movement of the Dvořák work is quoted in one of the composer's Love Songs, Opus 83, a piece updated from the cycle *The Cypresses*, written in 1865 supposedly for Josefina Čermáková. The passage, a descending triplet rhythm, occurs during a pause between the lines "In the sweet power of your eyes" and "I would gladly die." The figure, which also occurs in a sketch for the first humoresque labeled "Marche funèbre" is clearly associated with the idea of death (CD 80).

Indeed, while the dumka has become known as a folksy artifact with alternating fast and slow sections, the entire dumka subgenre is nothing more or less than a series of funeral gestures—the word itself derives from a Ukrainian elegy.[12]

Two of the most conspicuous unidentified funeral marches in Dvořák occur in two G-major works, the Symphony No. 8 and the String Quartet Opus 106. In coming to grips with their meaning we may do well to listen carefully to the words of a British reporter who spoke with Dvořák when the G-Major Symphony was premiered:

> The Adagio is exceedingly original in character and treatment. There is a story connected with it, which, however, the composer keeps to himself, and his audience would gladly know, since it is impossible not to feel that the music tries hard to speak intelligibly of events outside itself. Wanting the story, one must be content with picturesque utterances, a great deal of absolute beauty, and the fresh aroma which the whole work gives forth.[13]

Why did Dvořák write so many musical funerals, even when they are not called for by any program? Especially in the composer's last years, these laments multiply and move toward center stage. We have seen that Dvořák suffered from anxiety for at least the last fifteen years of his life. Since many of his funerals occur in those last years (Requiem, *Rusalka*, *Hero's Song*, String Quartet in G Major, Symphony No. 8, "New World," *Holoubek*, *Armida*, etc.), it may well be that the thoughts of death and illness that accompanied his condition became a more significant part of the composer's creative personality. To put it another way, Dvořák's need to meditate on questions of mortality became ever deeper, until the abstract and spiritual merged with the biographical.

Dvořák's musical meditations on death are not, however, all cast as funeral marches or funeral march stylizations; he regularly employs two other kinds of gestures. While the inertness of death requires some kind of symbolic language, dying lends itself to more traditional musical behavior. In fact, the Cello Concerto, the "New World" Symphony, and *Rusalka* all share the trope of what I call a "sighing/crying/dying" musical set followed by a funeral march, as we saw in Chapter 2. We will see the role played in the concerto's second movement by the chromatic descent with decrescendo.

Finally, Dvořák's arsenal of styles contains something we might call the language of lament. In addition to passages associated with funeral marches, conspicuous examples can be found in the *Biblical Songs*, in Dvořák's various "dumky," in the C-sharp-minor passage preceding the funeral march in the Largo (which Shelley identified as the "lament of the Indian Maiden"), in the opening of the Sonatina for Violin and Piano's slow movement (which Kreisler titled "Indian Lament"), and in the slow movement of the "American" Quartet, whose main theme Dvořák referred to as a *Klagemelodie* (mourning melody).[14]

A Death in the Family

We interrupted our discussion of the Dvořák Cello Concerto at a point of musical interruption, as the pastoral tone of the movement's opening was cut off by a G-minor outburst. This passage has the dramatic function of both introducing the song fragment and, in its second incarnation in the key of B minor, dismissing it, as if forever banishing the world of idyll and romance implied by the innermost part of the movement. The whole movement is touched by a sense of anger and lament. Indeed, one of the most prominent passages in the movement is a quintessential crying/sighing/dying passage played in the cello with a striking diminuendo from F to what must, from all the decrescendo signs, be a pianississimo (CD 81). Previously this "dying" passage had led to a funeral interruption in B minor, and now it appears to lead to a restatement of the main theme. But with what a difference! With its lugubrious French horns the pastoral chorale has been transformed into a funeral dirge, complete with the dotted rhythms in the bass (CD 82). Only after an extensive cello commentary on this passage can the work return to a pastoral G major, with drones, singing birds, angelic bliss, and a rhapsodic cello line, with intimation of a darker world sneaking back shortly before the end.

So the movement appears to tell a story of musical death and transfiguration. The quote of "Leave Me Alone," may certainly be intended as a memorial to Josefina. But there is a problem: she wasn't dead yet! We have read her distraught letter on the subject of her health, but she was not quite on her deathbed. What is going on? We will take up this matter a bit later, after seeing how the composer did respond to her death, in May 1895.

Surely nowhere in his works does Dvořák comes closer to speaking himself than in the coda to the final movement. We may remember that Dvořák added this section to an already completed concerto. While the passage in the brass (at measure 421) may originally have been intended as a moment of closure, in the later version of the concerto it acts an introduction. In some ways it is analogous to the framing at the start of Smetana's "Vyšehrad" or the "New World" Largo, providing a kind of "once upon a time," an introduction to a world of "Legenda," where time passes in its own special way. The cello is here introduced as narrator, commentator, and guide (CD 83).

First the cello accompanies us to the Elysian Fields. Then we hear a B pedal that is sustained for twenty-three measures, ensuring a pastoral tone. Over it the strings oscillate between B major and its subdominant, E major, lending the whole a plagal, almost religious flavor. Gradually the cello begins to add a languorous triplet, taken from the harsher version of the Finale's main theme. The sense of timelessness is amplified by the entrance of the woodwinds, pianissimo with various syncopations, as muted trumpets create an impression of distance.

The cello begins to modify the idyll, moving to a pedal F-sharp and introducing a series of recollections. The first remembered item is the very opening of the work, presented as a quasi-interruption by the clarinets— yet the recollection does not completely undercut the pastoral tone (CD 84). Then the soloist, as a kind of Ghost of Christmas Past, takes us to the key reminiscence. Once again we hear "Leave Me Alone," but this time it is the very beginning of the song, the part that speaks of ecstasy. The melody is taken by a solo violin, and in this context it is easy to imagine that it is the immortal beloved (Josefina?) herself singing, timelessly, over a dominant pedal. It is a lovely gesture, yet seen in the context of the song, it is even more deeply moving. "Leave Me Alone" is a complex song. We have noted that the more idyllic aspects of the opening give way to a turbulent middle section that resolves into a lament, as if the hopes of the singer have been crushed (CD 85).

Dvořák's setting in the concerto bypasses the torment, and the gesture at the end of the phrase seems to say, "Now it's over, the song is over, the pain is over; this is the way it all ends, simply and correctly, settling back to the F-sharp major it has always wished to find" (CD 86). This meditation is followed by another recollection of the concerto's opening theme (CD 87). This time it is truly an interruption of memory and idyll. Any doubts about its function as a requiem vanish when the elegiac triplets appear in the timpani (CD 88), telling us what we should know already. Like the Rusalka motive, the main theme of the Concerto for Violoncello has always been a kind of funeral march. Although it is marked "Allegro" we can easily hear the work's opening at half speed, that is, as an adagio, like the Funeral March from the "Eroica" Symphony or Dvořák's own Symphony No. 3. It is not until we have passed the first moments of the movement that we sense its velocity and power. The use, once again, of lower strings and bassoon, together with the stark rhythms, suggests that Dvořák's decision to quote his song as a memorial is not an accident that occurred as he reminisced about Josefina but is part of a much larger plan.

The coda proper concludes with several extraordinary passages. After the second quote of the opening theme comes an exquisite moment where two mutually exclusive elements are somehow combined and reconciled. While the cello continues its tortuous funereal descent over the throbbing timpani, the strings restore the pastoral mode. The opening theme gradually dies out and vanishes with a pizzicato, setting the stage for the astonishing *andante maestoso* that must be heard as an anticipation, several years before the fact, of the last kiss of Rusalka and the Prince (CD 89). Only then do we arrive at another series of chords that end the timeless stretch of this coda and restore us to the real world and also mark the concerto's end.

Though the personalization of the added coda is unusual, it merely reinforces in microcosm the whole theme of the work. The composer-as-cellist-as-hero leads us through a series of events in which he participates and on which he reflects.

I have used three types of evidence in my discussion of the Cello Concerto: scuttlebutt, or who told what to Šourek; documents, in the form of letters and sketches; and the music itself. There is one more kind of evidence that, while it ought to be justly treated with *great* skepticism, nonetheless belongs the mix. It is a photograph taken of the Dvořák family in Vysoká in the summer of 1894, that is, just before the composer's return to America, the last summer he would see his sister-in-law. [15] Such a photograph is difficult to read, and any readings are no doubt prey to our dispositions, but it does appear that many of its subjects have been caught off guard. It may be a trick of light or angle, or simply an extraneous moment that caught her attention, but Josefina seems to be gazing with consummate fondness at Antonín while the composer looks rather confidently at the camera—the great man and his family. Above him, just to the right, his wife scowls. The photo tempts us to ask, in conjunction with other evidence, what if everyone got it wrong? What if Josefina never "rejected" Dvořák at all, but always adored him from afar? Was she indeed his Minnehaha? And he her Hiawatha? While it is heartwarming to think of any relationship they might have had as something beautiful and sustaining, perhaps it was a source of constant pain as well. Who else but someone in pain would choose "Leave Me Alone" as a memorial to a loved one?

Yet, Josefina was not the only person close to Dvořák who died during his American years. On November 6, 1893, Tchaikovsky succumbed to cholera, and on February 12 of the following year, Hans von Bülow died. Finally, on March 28 the composer's father, František Dvořák, died. The frequent references to homesickness in discussions of the Cello Concerto makes it seem humble and very "Czech," but this massive work has such a monumental quality that it could more than anything be considered the composer's second Requiem. The majestic tragic march that opens the work may be a memorial to all those who have departed and, more important, the composer's meditation on the themes of life, love, and death. That he cast himself as the narrator-cello hero of the piece at first flies in the face of the image of a "modest" Dvořák; but several years later we find him composing the autobiographical *Hero's Song*, with its musical commentary on romance and mortality, and still later *Rusalka*, with its themes of love, restless wandering, death, and tormented erotic love.

Finally we may ask the most difficult question: If parts of the concerto, beginning at least with the second movement, were inspired by Josefina, why did he write her funeral months before she died? The easy answer is that he thought she would die and was inspired to memorialize her—

whether he was ever in love with her or not. And of course, it is possible that he was so distraught by Josefina's letter and so moved by it that it was *as if* she had died.

Yet there is a more logical explanation. We have tested the hypothesis that the piece was somehow "about" Josefina, that the composer wished to honor his sister-in-law, his great friend or his great love. But what if, in the end, Dvořák is a composer first and last? What if Josefina's illness, however greatly he responds to it, creates in him a rhapsody, a fantasy that ignites his imagination? Bluntly, what if he recalls his memory of her in order to find material for his concerto? What if the second movement is an imaginary interlude inspired by Josefina, just as the center of the Largo was inspired by Minnehaha? Would this scenario diminish the composer or his work?

And this is where we must leave it. For even if Dvořák was recalling an innocent early love in his concerto, is not a composer a kind of actor, and would he not have had to reenter the emotional world of his early romance in order to write passages of such originality and richness?

Secrets

Some issues relating to the Cello Concerto may become clearer in the future, as other documents and interpretive strategies emerge, but for the moment, there is no unequivocal solution to the puzzles that have been raised. That we have not been able to penetrate Dvořák's intimate world matters not at all, for it is not Dvořák's secrets themselves that are so compelling, but the very idea of Dvořák as a man of secrets. Of course, everyone has secrets. Hamlet had them, and so did Macbeth; Faust lived by them, and so did Emily Dickinson. Clinton could not keep them under continued pressure. Beethoven had his Immortal Beloved, Tchaikovsky his gay life, Janáček his Kamila Stösslová, and Martinů his Vítězslava Kaprálová. Writers and composers, such as Kafka and Berg, have placed codes in their work that refer to distant lovers. The history of humanity is also the history of secrets: romantic and sexual, venal and mercenary, criminal and depraved, interesting and trivial. So was Dvořák a family man first? Or a lover? Or a consummate composer, ready to sublimate any aspect of his life into a musical moment? We cannot know, but in my view, the Cello Concerto is a great repository of secrets and as such is in no way an exception among Dvořák's works. Rather, it is evidence that Dvořák lived in a world where unresolved and hidden things flit like moths on a summer evening. While some of these create torment and anxiety, they also, not incidentally, can make life somehow bearable. Dvořák's music is filled with such things, and thus part of coming to a deeper understanding of his music is a belief in the importance of these secrets, of listening to his music as if it is filled with them, even if they cannot—and perhaps should not—ever be known.

In the end, though we cannot prove that Dvořák's fundamental conflicts had to do with romance. We know he was struggling with other matters as he wrote the Cello Concerto. One of the most important was whether to follow in the footsteps of Brahms and continue to write symphonies and chamber music or to emulate Wagner in forging a direct connection between musical language and a range of literary and dramatic programs. In the next chapter, I argue that in the end, Dvořák chose to follow Wagner. Yet the particular magnificence of the Cello Concerto results from the idea that, probably for the last time, he still wanted to be both of them.

15

Between a Ring and a Hard Place: Dvořák's Homeric Wagner

Dvořák returned home to Bohemia in April of 1895. Though he discussed the possibility of resuming his position in New York as late as 1897—in one letter telling Jeannette Thurber that she could use his name for advertising purposes—he never went back to the United States. Within the year he completed a new quartet in G major and finished another in A-flat begun in the United States. With these pieces he bid farewell to the tradition of classicizing "absolute" music. In the nine years of life remaining to him, he wrote nothing but music associated with a story or plot, including five tone poems, three new operas, and several revisions. Although extramusical ideas had, to a great extent, influenced the works of his American years, this break is striking.

One aspect of America that must have played a great role in Dvořák's new artistic vision was its distance from Europe. Surely Dvořák felt enormous pressure from friends at home and in Vienna to conform to a certain vision of what a composer must be. Ironically, we get a glimpse of this view when we read Hanslick's response to Dvořák's tone poems, his sense that the composer "was taking a downhill path that leads directly to Richard Strauss." Kalbeck went further, asking, "How does Saul come to be among the prophets and Antonín Dvořák among the program musicians?"[1] But what, after all, was Dvořák's vision, and where did it come from?

One of his clearest statements of aims comes from an oft-quoted interview he gave to the Viennese newspaper *Die Reichswehr* in March 1904:

In the last five years I have written nothing but operas. I wanted to devote all my powers, as long as God gives me the health, to the creation of opera. Not, however, out of any vain desire for glory, but because I consider opera the most suitable form for the nation. This music is listened to by the broad masses, whereas when I compose a symphony I might have to wait years for it to be performed. I got a request again from Simrock for chamber works, which I keep refusing. My publishers know by now that I shall no longer write anything just for them. They bombard me with questions about why I do not compose this or that; these genres no longer have any attraction for me. They look upon me as a composer of symphonies, and yet I proved to them many years ago that my main bias is toward dramatic creation.[2]

This statement announces, without any hesitation, the orientation of the composer. Though he died later that year, he believed he would have many more years of life and write many more operas. Once again, the many programs in his music, hidden and otherwise, suggest that this "break" is hardly what it seems, but it certainly entailed coming out of the musical closet. How did Dvořák come to see himself in this light?

Some Influences

If we look at the main influences on Dvořák's life and music as from the gondola of a balloon at a great height, several figures loom large. To be sure, Beethoven is visible (or should I say audible) in many places. The symphony "From the New World," for example, is riddled with reminiscences from the "Pastoral" Symphony and the Ninth Symphony as well. Certainly Smetana was a significant figure in Dvořák's development: Dvořák's *Hussite Overture* echoes the older composer's *Má vlast*, and many moments in the operas recall Smetana's example. Mozart and Haydn appear, particularly in the symphonies and chamber music. As we have seen, several critics, and even the composer himself, framed their discussion of the Quintet in E-flat Major and the "American" Quartet by referring to the works of Haydn. Dvořák also had a deep fondness for the music and person of Tchaikovsky, and the two became great friends during the Russian's visit to Prague. Several scholars have argued that parts of Dvořák's symphonies or operas were based on passages from Tchaikovsky.

Schumann and Schubert were also particular favorites of Dvořák's. The Quintet in A Major for Piano was modeled on Schumann, and Schubert's voice can often be heard in the symphonies and chamber compositions (we may remember Huneker's simultaneously admiring and disparaging words: "He was an imitator of Schubert and didn't use quotes.") The gorgeous "endless melody" of the second movement of the "American" Quartet recalls moments in Schubert's Trio in B-flat, and the opening of the Quintet in E-flat may be modeled on the Schubert Quintet in C. Also, we may note that Schubert is the only composer about whom the enormously reticent Dvořák actually wrote a whole article (coauthored with Henry Finck).[3]

But a casual look through the Dvořák literature would confirm that according to most commentators, Brahms was the composer who was most important in shaping Dvořák's orientation. The story is endlessly told of how Brahms was the first composer of any note to recognize Dvořák's genius and how he encouraged the young musician. We have letters from Dvořák to the older composer in the most obsequious language, thanking him for a recommendation to his publisher Simrock.[4] Dvořák also bathes himself in humility, apologizing for some carelessness that evidently made Brahms a bit grumpy.

There was extended contact between the two figures, and a real Brahmsian influence in the symphonies and some of the harmonic gestures in the piano pieces. Finally, the two were friends, and despite Brahms's occasional griping, they held great admiration for each other. Brahms amazed Dvořák by undertaking the tiresome task of checking the proofs of the "New World," and he told a friend as he was about to hear the Cello Concerto, "You will hear a piece today. A piece by a man!" Dvořák believed that Brahms was a great master, and Brahms thought Dvořák to be his greatest living contemporary.

Yet after carefully going through the literature—primary, secondary, real and apocryphal, scores and words—I have concluded that the most profound influence on Dvořák was none of these figures but rather someone who has either gotten too much credit for influence or not enough, depending on whom you believe: It is, of course, Richard Wagner.

I use the word "influence" rather glibly, as if I knew what it really meant, but its meaning is far from clear. What is influence? The writer Leonard Michaels once said that real influence is terribly difficult to gauge because it acts upon the recipient for a long period of time and from a great distance. The greater the distance and the more time, the more difficult it is to pinpoint the source. Here we can make an unscientific but real differentiation between impact and influence, the former being something more immediate and the latter more subtle and profound. While other composers made their impression, Dvořák struggled with the image of Wagner for the greater portion of his creative life.

"The Great Little Man's Face"

In order to understand the context in which Dvořák first encountered Wagner, we must look briefly at musical life in Prague at the time. Particularly at the conservatory—where not all that many decades before, Václav Tomášek, a fine proto-Romantic composer, had enforced a Mozartian cult, at the expense of Beethoven—Prague remained conservative, suspicious of "progressive" music. It was only by participating in an outside ensemble around 1857 that Dvořák encountered Wagner's music for the first time, playing *Rienzi* (and later probably also *Tannhäuser* and *Lohengrin*).

Dvořák's most important early contact with Wagner himself came on February 8, 1863, when the German composer appeared in person to conduct a concert of his own works, some completely unknown in Prague. It is almost certain that Dvořák himself played in this concert. The program consisted of *A Faust Overture*, "Entry of the Mastersingers," and "Pogner's Address"; the Prelude to *Die Meistersinger*; the Prelude to *Tristan*; "Siegmund's Love Song"; and the overture to *Tannhäuser*—a composition that became one of Dvořák's favorite pieces. Dvořák wrote of his reaction: "I had just heard *Die Meistersinger*, and not long before Richard Wagner himself had been in Prague. I was perfectly crazy about him, and recollect following him as he walked along the streets to get a chance now and again of seeing the great little man's face."[5]

Despite this love for Wagner, Dvořák was somewhat afraid of him, as this reminiscence makes clear:

Although I am not from the bottom of my heart a Wagnerite, I still love and esteem him, and I am glad that I saw him with my own eyes. It happened when I received my Stipendium, on account of which I had to go to Vienna. They were just studying *Tannhäuser* and *Lohengrin* and Wagner conducted the rehearsals. Of course I heard about them and although the public was not allowed to attend, I got in with another man. The rehearsal was in full swing. I spied Wagner immediately. He was in the parterre, a stick in his hand, and was walking the floor, watching and listening. But he looked cross, and was all the time discontented. Every little while he would poke the conductor in the back with that stick. As I said before, I am glad to have seen him, but I would have been still more pleased could I have talked with him. However, at that time I had not the courage to introduce myself to him because Wagner was then already at the zenith of his glory and of me the world knew very little as yet.[6]

As I have suggested, Dvořák's biographers over the last several decades have been determined to place him in a hermetic "Czech" context, so his love and reverence for Wagner has received mostly negative attention. For example, John Clapham keeps Dvořák away from the Teutonic taint of Wagnerian magnetism, making Dvořák appear more original and certainly more "Czech" than he otherwise would. So to cure himself of Wagneritis, Dvořák is said to draw on the example of the elder Statesman of Czech music:

. . . he was well on the way towards a partial renunciation of Wagnerian influence and an acceptance of a good measure of classical ideals, helped by the example of Smetana.

We are also told that even when Dvořák drew on the works of others, he was in no way defined by them:

Dvořák's harmonic vocabulary undoubtedly owed a little to the chromatic harmony of Wagner and Liszt, yet we find that when he wrote chromatically it was normal for his music *to remain highly personal.*

Yet we read that "the choral-like introduction to the Adagio of Symphony No. 1 borrows from the Tarnhelm motive." A few pages later, it seems that the whole thing is about to blow over:

The noble sweep of the principal theme, turns of melodic phrase, harmonic characteristics, the inclusion of a cor anglais in the first two movements, a harp in the second and a tuba in the Finale, and in some instances the method of writing for the instruments, all betray a continuing, but diminishing, admiration for Wagner.

After which the battle is won—or is it?

The Fourth Symphony comes at the beginning of "a decisive reaction against the influence of Wagner and Liszt—Wagner's influence is still strongly felt in the Andante.

Two pages later, the great sage of Bayreuth has been vanquished—"the retreat from Wagner was complete, and henceforth the work of the Viennese composers was to serve as his principal model"—only to return three pages later with the influence of the "Magic Sleep Motive."[7]

Like the "rise of the Middle Classes," which lasted for centuries (and perhaps continues to this day), the "renunciation" of Wagner lasts for Dvořák's entire career. It is no secret that Wagner's—and Liszt's—influence on early Dvořák was staggering and immediate. We can easily hear the Wagnerian voice in some of Dvořák's operas and in the early chamber music.

We could, of course, go through Dvořák's works seeking Wagnerisms and find them in abundance. But instead we will look at some stories involving Wagner and Dvořák. A close reading of these reveals some of the essential qualities that marked Dvořák's Wagnerian turn.

Escape from the Met

The first story comes from the pen of Kovařík, who describes a slightly unusual trip to the opera:

In the afternoon the Master used to visit the (former) Fleishmann café at the corner of Broadway and 10th Street where he met Anton Seidl, then the conductor of the New York Philharmonic and, at the same time, conductor of German and mainly Wagner opera at the Metropolitan Opera. Seidl was an outstanding conductor, especially of Wagner—he had lived in close contact with that musical giant for some considerable time—and so the Master very often asked Seidl about Wagner—how he worked and so on. They had very interesting conversations and also discussions which not seldom became decidedly "heated"—but in the end everything always ended well—both it seems thought over their conversation and then when they met the next day, one or other admitted that he had been "partly" mistaken—and it was all right.

One day the Master asserted that the best of Wagner's operas was "Tannhäuser"—with this Seidl did not agree and it gave rise to a long debate which did not finish that day. As soon as they met the next day, however, Seidl began—"Well, I was thinking over our yesterday's discussion the whole evening, I considered it from every angle and I admit that you are right—from the point of view of opera Tannhäuser is the best.—But do you know Siegfried?" When the Master said that he had seen it only once, Seidl promised to send tickets for the next performance at the Metropolitan when he would be conducting.

The tickets came for seats in a box in the so-called "Diamond Horseshoe," a row of boxes whose holders arrive at the performance at the last moment or usually even after it has begun, bedecked and overloaded with diamonds—all in evening dress. Of all this, however, we at this time knew nothing. The Master put on an ordinary dark suit, I chose from my modest wardrobe the darkest I had—but it was still pretty light. Whenever the Master was to go anywhere, he was always in a hurry to be there in time, and on this occasion he made more than usual haste. The attendant looked at us in considerable surprise—perhaps because of our dress, perhaps because he was not accustomed to show people to their boxes half-an-hour before the beginning of the performance. The auditorium was still practically empty and the Master, having pulled out his watch and looked at it said: "We've been in rather too great a hurry." Then we watched the stalls gradually filling up and that helped us to pass the time. Suddenly voices were to be heard in the neighboring box—the Master looked round and immediately moved one seat back—I followed suit. The neighbors had come in evening dress and those who came after them the same. And so we finally reached the wall—each in a corner and waited for the lights to go down.

At last the opera began. Round about ceaseless chatter. The Master "looked" at the talkers but it had no effect. So he paid no more heed to them and, although their talk was disturbing, listened attentively. After the first act we went home. Our attendant again looked at us curiously—perhaps thinking to himself: "Strange customers these—when others are only beginning to come, they go home."

At their usual meeting, Seidl asked the Master the next day what he thought of "Siegfried." The Master confessed straight away that he had gone home after the first act. The rendering, what he had heard of it, was excellent, but that he had enough of that perpetual and constantly repeated rhythm.[8]

There are several strange things about this passage, the strangest of which is that no record exists of any performance of *Siegfried* at the Metropolitan Opera conducted by Seidl during the years Dvořák was there. While there is some slight possibility that a special performance was held that was not publicized, that seems unlikely. Perhaps Kovařík has conflated two episodes, something he has done in other cases. The only record of a performance of the opera is the following announcement from the *New York Herald* in March 1894. The headline is "Siegfried Revived."

That the return of Wagner's "Siegfried" to the stage of the Metropolitan Opera House would be signalized by a joyous demonstration might easily have been predicted. The mere announcement that it would be given at the second representation of Mr. Damrosch's German season must have set thousands of hearts to fluttering under the stress of delightful recollections and more delightful anticipation. It is the drama in which Mr. Alvary first reached his artistic maturity and throughout the two seasons in which he was the representative of the youthful hero no more picturesque figure or one more calculated to warm the hearts of sentimental maids and matrons was to be seen on our stage.

One thing is clear: he left before the end of the performance, possibly because Damrosch conducted the work and Damrosch's Wagner was not especially well regarded. On the other hand, Kovařík reports that Dvořák had no problem with the performance. But there are other peculiar things going on, and the story has a bizarre flavor as poor underdressed Dvořák gets pushed farther and farther back in the box.

Another version of the same story was told by Kovařík to Alice Masaryková, who published it in *Hudba ve Spillville* (Music in Spillville):

> Dvořák never bothered about his clothes. One evening we went to the opera. He was wearing a light grey suit. We had seats in a box, in the diamond circle as they used to call it. We were early and when the ladies with their diamond tiaras and grand evening gowns appeared, Dvořák looked round, feeling very uncomfortable. The opera was Siegfried. I think Dvořák's favorite Wagner opera was Tannhäuser. All we listened to that evening was the first act. Then he got up from his seat and we started to leave. I asked him how he liked Siegfried. "We sat there a whole hour and that was enough," he answered, and back home we went.[9]

Whether or not Dvořák really left the opera because he felt uncomfortable about his clothing, this appears to be a clear case of anxiety. For whatever reason, Dvořák became severely uncomfortable and left. Yet his anxiety may have had a more specific source.

Although Masaryková's version is ambiguous ("enough is enough"), Kovařík's own memoir suggests that Dvořák had enough of the Nibelung motive. Certainly the beginning of the first act, where the motive is repeated almost one hundred times before Siegfried's entry, could try anyone's patience. But the first act has marvelous scenes in it, culminating in the forging of the sword. Even if Dvořák had been bothered by the repetition, it is not something that would have affected his response to latter portions of the act.

Perhaps he left because of something he would never have admitted, even to himself—and it could have been the source of his anxiety. In order to maintain his sense of power as a composer, he needed to give a wide berth to influences that might overwhelm him. Quite possibly his departure was occasioned by his finding the work, and Wagner, too overpowering at this point in his career. And, because of other factors mentioned in contemporary reports, he was already feeling exposed, as if he was being stared at. And now Wagner's music on top of that! It must have been intolerably disturbing.

A Bust of Wagner

The next story comes from a book of reminiscences by one of Dvořák's pupils at the Prague Conservatory, Josef Michl. Writing about Nietzsche and Wagner he says:

> From the conversation which followed, I saw that the Master was very interested in Nietzsche: He put one question after another which exhausted practically all I knew about the philosopher and a good third of his questions remained unanswered. Finally the conversation concentrated on the essay "Nietzsche versus Wagner" and here Dvořák said: "I think nobody in the world has written anything like it *against* Wagner. Nietzsche must have had a great mind and in many respects he is right. But in some things he does him injustice and great injustice. You know you can talk a great deal about Wagner and you can criticize a great deal, too—but he is undefeatable. What Wagner did nobody did before him and nobody can take it from him. Music will go its way, will pass Wagner by, but Wagner will remain, just like the statue of that poet from whom they still learn at school today—Homer. And such a Homer is Wagner!"[10]

This seemingly straightforward passage, a simple paean of praise, also contains some strange elements. First, there is the comparison with Homer. Why does Homer come to mind when Dvořák looks for an image of comparison? Even more curious is the way Dvořák frames the comparison: it is not initially with Homer himself, but the statue ("Wagner will remain just like that statue"). In what sense is this a clue to Dvořák's view of Wagner?

The first point yields more easily to exegesis. Homer was not merely an immortal poet, but the greatest of bards, and this leads to two further items. First, Dvořák considers Wagner's achievement ("What Wagner did nobody did before him") to be analogous to that of a bard, putting the nation's legends into an artistic form so that they may endure for all time ("Nobody can take it from him"; "Wagner will remain"). More important, though, it gives us further insight into Dvořák's own ambitions and, to a certain extent, his achievement.

As Dvořák's 1904 interview makes clear, the composer considered opera to be "the most suitable form for the nation." Dvořák's self-image as a Slavonic bard should not be underestimated. He was always fascinated by epic tales and legends, and the word "Legenda" appears in Dvořák's works over a span of decades.

Immediately after returning to Bohemia, Dvořák embarked on a project of setting the ballads of K. J. Erben as tone poems, continuing a fascination with Erben's work that includes *The Specter's Bride*. Most telling, perhaps, is the composer's final enigmatic tone poem, *Píseň bohatéýrská* (usually translated as *The Hero's Song*). Dvořák chose the title carefully; *bohatýr* is a Slavonic word for a mythical bardic hero. Quite likely, the work is an autobiographical portrait, complete with death and resurrection, having a firm connection with *Tannhäuser*.[11]

The operas Dvořák composed after his return similarly lay claim to a position as a national poet: *Rusalka* deals with the mysterious world of myth and fairy tale, while *The Devil and Kate* appropriates the model of the village opera. Despite his apparent modesty, it is Dvořák who would be Homer.

And yet, why does he refer to a statue, why not simply say, "Wagner will remain . . . just like that poet." His reference to Wagner as a statue suggests that Dvořák, perhaps unwittingly, was ceding to him the central place in the pantheon. By configuring him as a bust, a traditional object of worship, he suggests that Wagner is more than a flesh-and-blood composer, he is a concrete immortal. "History may pass him by," but he is always there—in Dvořák's view, history is the viscous fluid, Wagner the solid. This passage may even suggest that Wagner was the most revered of all the composers on whose works and ideas Dvořák drew.

There is something vaguely Talmudic about late-nineteenth-century music. So much of what we call influence is in reality a dialogue between masters reaching back for centuries. We understand that Beethoven comments on the works of Bach and Mozart, and that Brahms carries on discussions with Palestrina, Buxtehude, Haydn, and Beethoven. Dvořák's dialogues, commentaries, and annotations involve among others Beethoven, Smetana, Mozart, Schubert, and Brahms. Perhaps, in all his modesty, he views them as equals. But Wagner seems to be something else: he is the icon to whom one prays, the most sensational force of all.

Composers and Religion

Dvořák made a most interesting observation about Wagner in an article on Franz Schubert that appeared under his byline in *Century Magazine*. The magazine was running an innovative series featuring composers writing about composers, with articles on Liszt by Camille Saint-Saëns; Schumann by Edvard Grieg; and Grieg by William Mason. Despite his affection for Schubert's music, Dvořák informed the magazine that he could not write an article by himself, and refused to contribute until the critic Henry T. Finck agreed to work with him. The collaboration consisted of an interview in which Finck tried to elicit interesting testimony from the composer, which he then surrounded with his own ideas.

While it is difficult to separate who said what, some of the opinions are so unusual and characteristic that we can be confident they represent Dvořák's thinking. For example, the following must have come as the answer to a question by Finck about which composers were most honest and effective in writing religious music. The first two names might be expected, but the third is a surprise:

> To my mind, the three composers who have been most successful in revealing the inmost spirit of religious music are Palestrina, in whom Roman Catholic music reaches its climax; Bach, who embodies the Protestant spirit; and Wagner, who has struck the true ecclesiastic chord in the Pilgrims' Chorus of "Tannhäuser," and especially in the first and third acts of "Parsifal." Compared with these three masters, other composers appear to have made too many concessions to worldly and purely musical factors.[12]

It is easy to believe that Dvořák's fondness for Wagner has to do with his dramatic gifts, his sense of scope and display, and his fearless cultivation of a national idiom, but harder to imagine that it was Wagner's ability to convey "the inmost spirit of religious music." But in reconsidering the relationship between Dvořák and Wagner we may wish to count these words as among the most important.

Now Dvořák did have an irascible sense of humor about the subject, although it may reveal something about his own habits. The following passage reports a short discussion between the composer and one of his students:

> Generally Dvořák spoke of Wagner in terms of the highest admiration and respect. At one of the Wagner chats a student allowed himself a remark which displeased Dvořák very much.
>
> "If you please, Doctor Dvořák, I heard that Wagner liked a drink now and then, and that when he was composing he always had a glass of wine near him."
>
> To which the highly displeased master retorted snappily:
>
> "That is none of your business—whether he drank wine or not—but I bet you—black on white—that you could never compose anything like his music, no matter how much you drank."[13]

Standing on the Mountaintop

Dvořák has frequently been compared to Brahms, and I have suggested that he really wanted to be Wagner all along. Perhaps, though, the best composer parallel to Dvořák was Tchaikovsky. Not only was he an almost exact contemporary, but the two shared the sense of being caught between different worlds, one national and the other cosmopolitan. So let us close this study with two stories, one about Tchaikovsky and the other about Dvořák and Wagner.

It is well known that the "Pathétique" Symphony received a lukewarm reception at its first performance. The composer himself said, "Something strange is going on with the symphony! It is not that it wasn't liked, but it has caused some bewilderment."[14] Quite simply, people were puzzled by the composition. Yet when the work was performed just a few weeks later it was an enormous success, and everyone seemed to understand it. Indeed, all the things that were puzzling to the first audience somehow made sense to the second. What had happened in the meantime? Only this: the composer had died suddenly of cholera. The second audience "discovered" that there was a correspondence between the inner life of Tchaikovsky and the "codes" of expression he was using. The *Russian Musical Gazette* summarized the feeling about the new symphony: "It is indeed a sort of swan song, a presentiment of imminent death, and from this comes its tragic impression."

I believe that this story has much to say about Dvořák. Here we have two exact contemporaries going through many of the same emotional experiences as they travel throughout Europe, trying both to use and to transcend the merely national while remaining truthful to a personal vision. Tchaikovsky, considered the quintessential "emotional" composer, is thought (like Beethoven) to have only one subject: himself. There is little sense in Dvořák criticism that the composer might somehow be *living* the material of his compositions, beyond some abstract imaginative connection. Why is this so? The question can be answered by the second story, in a memoir by Karel Sázavský about Dvořák's journey to Southern Moravia and his ruminations about the landscape:

> In the meantime we, along with Dvořák, had reached the Pálavské hory. "What is that?—I never noticed it before. What a curious thing!" I told him all I knew about the hills, about where you go to climb them, I mentioned the legend—but the Master no longer seemed to be listening. Knowing his way, I was sure that he was turning something over in his mind and that in a little while he would come out with something original—the result of his cogitations. I was just beginning to think I had been mistaken, but in a little [while] the Master began: "I always envied Wagner that he could write. Where would I be today if I could write! And I can't speak either. —But listen," and he raised his voice under the stress of some strong emotion, "if I could speak I should call our nation here and I should climb up that hill and from there I should tell them something, and tell it to them straight, but I can't speak." And then he relapsed once more into silence and for a long time gazed out from the carriage at the "Pálavské hory."[15]

This is the most telling of all the Dvořák legends. Here the composer confronts the strange hills in Southern Moravia, near today's border with

Austria. Cloaked in mystery and myth, the three cliffs supposedly represent three women. The contemplation of this natural phenomenon spurs him to thoughts of Wagner. Although Dvořák has been seen as a modest creative personality who avoids conflict in favor of lyrical gestures, the desire to speak from a mountaintop is hardly a sign of modesty, leading us to wonder whether he is referring here to more than his well-known fear of public speaking.

I have already argued that Dvořák wished to emulate Wagner in a musical sense, and there are many passages in his works that allow for such a conclusion. But the shadow cast by Wagner was not merely musical. Indeed, some of the dramatic tension in Dvořák's work may stem from his sense of "muteness" in a historical time when he is being pressed to speak. Perhaps Dvořák really has figured out what national music is and what music means in both a national and an international context. But he can't speak. He envies Wagner because he would like to be for the Czech nation, and perhaps even for the modern world, what Wagner was for the Germans: a Homer, a visionary, a prophet who speaks to the population, like Moses atop Sinai, tablets in hand. And like Moses he is mute, but also like Moses he has a deeper power.

When we look at his music and see the scope and conflict of the last symphonies, with their programmatic yearnings, we find the story about Dvořák's urgent need to speak out both touching and powerful. Dvořák is, then, very much like his character Rusalka—a classicist who transformed himself into something else and in the process became a mute and a keeper of secrets.

The story also reveals Dvořák's sense of how important it is for creative figures to write their own histories, lest others write it for them. Wagner leaves no doubt about his thinking at different times in his career, sometimes to our despair: Dvořák leaves us to guess. The mantle of the abstract formalist, the Czech patriot, and the conservative Romantic have all been placed on Dvořák's shoulders.

Dvořák occupied a niche that was simultaneously created for him and that he created within the ecosystem of nineteenth-century music: "Hear, hear! We have an opening in the composer's pantheon for an ethnic lyricist. Please submit your compositions to the nearest German publisher with a recommendation from a bona fide German composer." Dvořák was invited to the Great Composers party on the condition that he arrive in national dress. His ambivalence about doing so was extreme, but he acquiesced, at least in part because he was something of a nationalist, in part because the success was too much to turn down, and in part because like most of us, he was insecure.

In the process, though, he had to submerge part of himself. Too, he was within the Viennese orbit and had assembled for himself a formidable arsenal of supporters. Most important of these was Brahms himself, the virtual dean of German composers. But he also had the support of Joachim, one of the great virtuosos of the time, and Hans Richter, a preeminent conductor. Hanslick, the influential critic, was behind him, as was Simrock, among the most respectable publishers of the century. No better team could have been put together for promoting the composer. But in taking their support, and shaping his aesthetic, he had also suppressed his natural dramatic tendencies. His American journey gave him a taste of standing astride the world like a colossus. He was king of the mountain, the biggest *hombre* in the country, and he could, by God, do what he wanted to do.

And what did Dvořák find in America? Wagner, and lots of it! As Joseph Horowitz has shown in *Wagner Nights*, New York was "Wagnerland."[16] The composer was everywhere; his disciple, Seidl, was Dvořák's main champion, and a drinking buddy to boot. The irony is that even though Dvořák had known Wagner's music for most of his life, it was only in New York that he was immersed in it. Thus Dvořák returned to Prague far more Wagnerized than he was when he left. According to Horowitz, "You could even say that however 'saturated' with Negro melodies he may have been in the United States, the Wagner saturation in New York was even more profound. It was perhaps even more enduring because it was more deeply resonant both with Dvořák's musical language and his agenda as a cultural nationalist."[17]

Upon returning home, Dvořák dropped chamber and symphonic music forever in favor of first the Erben tone poems and then a series of operas and opera revisions. Perhaps his goal all along had been to *speak* in music—*and* be understood.

My earlier "thought experiment" of associating passages from *Hiawatha* with the Finale of the symphony despite any firm evidence may be viewed as a metaphor for what I have tried to accomplish in these pages. By what right do I come along and suggest that the main theme of the "New World" Symphony might be a *leitmotiv*, or that the Finale is a famine or a battle, or that Dvořák suffered from serious anxiety, or that he speaks boldly as hero of the Cello Concerto? Does it not somehow *taint* the music to imagine such unproved and even unprovable associations? Dvořák would have known better; he said it himself about another composer: "Wagner will survive." Dvořák will also survive, especially considering that he has already survived an incarnation during which it was often thought that his music meant, basically, *nothing*. I trust I may be forgiven for suggesting now that it means too much.

Postscript

Research into the life of Dvořák has been both exhilarating and humbling. As Richard Feynman once said, scientific articles are a pack of lies and distortions. They appear to present our calculated and inevitable path to a correct conclusion when the actual process is usually tortuous, filled with countless wrong turns where we ignored obvious data, elevated material that was clearly beside the point, and in general made fools of ourselves.

More than three years before this book was completed I took seriously James Huneker's claim that it was he who introduced to Dvořák the idea of composing a symphony on African-American themes, and the result may be seen in Chapter 6. Yet Huneker's description of his encounter with Dvořák ends with another hint: "At all events he accepted some specimen themes and also a book on the characteristic songs of the American birds."

With some shame I confess that for two years I pursued the African-American tunes and left the birds alone, thinking that Huneker was simply being a wag. However, as time passed, my faith in Huneker's veracity increased, and since he was clearly telling the truth about his "specimen themes," the birds gradually began to nag at me. But it took until September 2000 for me to do something about it. I finally stood in the Dvořák Museum in Prague and asked if they had any books of birdsong. After looking at me dubiously and muttering something about its not being an ornithology museum, the curator went off to look at the catalogue. And there it was: *Wood Notes Wild*, a book of birdsongs by Simeon Pease Cheney, published in 1892, complete with notation![1] Considering the evidence, there was no doubt that Dvořák had brought the book back with him to Bohemia when he returned home.

I raced through the volume looking for the Master's characteristic blue pencil, hoping for a little bit of marginalia. Nothing. Then I went through theme by theme looking for anything familiar or suspicious. The first two birds were the bluebird and the robin, and the latter's song leaped out at me. Certainly this snippet must have been the inspiration for the famous bird passage from the "New World" Largo in C-sharp major. Didn't Dvořák tell Krehbiel that this moment represented the "awakening of animal life on the prairie"? As further evidence of the sometimes inexplicable carelessness that accompanies various discoveries, it was not until more a month *later* that I reread the passage that I had, years before, identified as the source of the birdsong in Chapter 2:

Pleasant was the journey homeward!
All the birds sang loud and sweetly
Songs of happiness and heart's-ease;
Sang the bluebird, the Owaissa,
"Happy are you, Hiawatha,
Having such a wife to love you!"
Sang the robin, the Opeechee,
"Happy are you, Laughing Water,
Having such a noble husband!"

It was the robin after all! And probably the bluebird as well, and Lord knows which other American birds were imbibed and transformed in the same way that Dvořák had ingested African-American and Native American song, Hiawatha, Minnehaha Falls, and the great prairie.

We live, we love, we create by breathing. For a time, Dvořák sailed across the ocean, set himself down in New York City, Iowa, Boston, Chicago, and St. Paul. He inhaled all the America he could find, including these birdsongs, mixed it with his own craft and soul, his love and his fear, and exhaled some extraordinary music—extraordinary not only because of its beauty and power, but because for every birdsong we can identify, for every secret we can pierce, there are hundreds more that remain hidden, and will doubtless remain so forever, or at least until a new generation of passionate investigators looks this way again.

Appendix

NEGRO MUSIC.

To one who has passed his childhood in the South, no music in the world is so tenderly pathetic, so wildly, uncouthly melancholy, so fraught with an overpowering *heimweh*, as that of the negroes. When he hears one of these quaint old airs, he needs but to close his eyes and the potent spell of the music revivifies the past. Old memories, that he had deemed forgotten, rise as if obedient to the voice of enchantment. He is again a child in the cradle, and his faithful old "mammy," as she rocks him, bends over him in the firelight and croons:

CD 90

Again he sees the dark river, lit up by the flare of burning pitch, and the dusky figures of the roustabouts, their white eyeballs gleaming, singing with stentorian voices while they load the boat with cotton, solo alternating with chorus:

CD 91

O, far' you well old mistis.	Wa-a-aw.
I ai'n' come home tel Chrismus.	Wa-a-aw.
I'm gwine fer ter bring some money.	Ya-a-as.

Or it may be that he is sitting upon the broad piazza in the moonlight, and there is borne to him by the evening breeze a distant chorus, rising and falling in unearthly,

NOTE: The following words may be sung to this air:

> "O, de mugwump roosts on de hollow log,
> And de snagwap sits in de tree;
> And when I hear dat migfunk sing,
> My heart is sad in me."

229

NEGRO MUSIC.

plaintive cadences, like the moaning of the wind or the cry of a lost spirit.

CD 92

Genuine negro music is invariably in a peculiar minor, which differs from the civilized scale in two particulars; the sixth note of the gamut is omitted and the seventh is half a tone lower. Try over the specimen given above, making the F sharp, as it would be in modern music, and notice how completely the peculiar, plaintive charm vanishes. There are some other differences which cannot be represented in musical notation. For instance, the A in the fourth bar of the passage above is neither A nor yet A flat, but between the two. This scale is said to be that of the primitive races —of the Esquimaux, the Egyptians, the South Sea islanders. Traces of it may be found in Meyerbeer, Chopin and Grieg, composers who have made free use of *volkslieder.* I have no doubt that this music, like Voodooism, is a remnant of former idolatry. Doubtless many of these hymns have been sung for centuries before the shrines of fetishes in the dark jungles of Africa.

As to rhythm, a certain syncopation, represented by an eight and dotted quarter is common.

When the blacks came into contact with the major scale of the whites, they adopted it, preserving still the syncopated rhythm and the omission of one note of the scale (the seventh in the major.) For example:

"Swing low, sweet chariot."

CD 93

There is the same omission of the seventh in Scotch music.

Much of the so-called negro music is as little like what it is intended to represent as the words are like negro dialect.

It is quite a common thing for the negro women to im-

NEGRO MUSIC.

provise words and music while they are at work, a sort of Wagnerian "melos," or endless melody, as it were. I have often heard them drone softly thus all through the livelong, bright summer day.

The music is an important factor in their religious (?) revivals. I shall never forget my experience at one of these meetings. The negroes had been wrought up almost to a pitch of frenzy by the fervid declamation of a "colored brother." They were all standing; the women kept up a continuous, subdued droning—their emotional state required some outlet: a huge stalwart darkey began a hymn in which all speedily joined; about fifty of them crowded about a young girl whom they wished to "bring through," singing at the top of their voices and swaying their bodies rhythmically to and fro. The object of their solicitude sat for a time in a sort of stupor. Everywhere she looked there were gaping throats and fierce eyes glaring at her like those of wild beasts. She was the center of attraction. Gradually she joined in the song and ended by falling into a convulsion of such violence that five of the men could with difficulty hold her. This "new birth" was received with many pious ejaculations of "Praise the Lord!"

"Previous condition of servitude" in certain reformatory institutions of the state, or porcine or other petty peculation does not in the least debar a brother from active participation in these exercises.

Various attempts have been made at collecting these our only *volkslieder* but they have not been very successful, for the reason that the tunes are usually arranged in four parts by the collector. Now, in the first place, these airs are always sung in unison, and in the second place the flatting of the seventh, as every musician will immediately perceive, renders it well-nigh impossible to harmonize them. As it is, the melody is usually sacrificed to the harmony. The melodies, pure and simple, with no attempt at improving them, should be collected and preserved; for, like Caucasian church music, they are rapidly disappearing before the triumphant march of "Gospel Hymns!"

When our American musical Messiah sees fit to be born

In the left margin: "I love you, Daddy," written by Dvořák's son.

NEGRO MUSIC.

he will then find ready to his hand a mass of lyrical and dramatic themes with which to construct a distinctively American music.

I have said nothing of Gottschalk, since his music, so far as my limited acquaintance with it extends, seems to be rather that of the Cubans than that of the negroes.

In conclusion, I give two tunes, one of them almost purely African, the other evidently composed in the transition period between the old and new schools.

"I would not live always."

CD 94

"I will arise and go to Jesus."

CD 95

JOHANN TONSOR.

LOUISVILLE, KY.

Notes

See Bibliography for complete listings of cited works.

Chapter 1: *A Composer Goes to America*

1   I am grateful to David Beveridge for his perspective on this issue.

2   Dvořák, *Letters and Reminiscences*, 142.

3   Kovařík was an American-born Czech who studied violin, first in Milwaukee and later in Prague. He helped Dvořák's family and eventually became, in effect, a secretary to the composer. Much of the evidence regarding Dvořák's sojourn in America comes from a series of letters between Kovařík and Dvořák's biographer Otakar Šourek (1883–1956). These letters were part of Šourek's estate and were in the possession of Jarmil Burghauser, to whom I am grateful for granting me access to this material and for helping me throughout this project. Some parts of the correspondence have been published, but unless otherwise indicated, the portions I quote have not. The notes consist of thirty communications (letters, etc.) containing about 192 written pages dating from March 6, 1927, to November 17, 1945.

Chapter 2: Hiawatha *and the Largo*

1   All the statements in this interview can be corroborated, and the language itself hardly seems the work of a ghostwriter, unlike several other interviews that appeared in American newspapers. Dvořák's English was fairly decent, as good as that of any of his continental contemporaries. He read widely and corresponded in English, not without mistakes, but with a certain authority.

2   *Dalibor* 1 (1879): 191–92, written by Dvořák's friend Václav Novotný, with music examples.

3   In notes for the Philharmonic Society on November 12 and 13, 1897, Krehbiel wrote, "It is Dr. Dvorak's musical publication of the mood . . ."; on December 1 and 2, 1905, he wrote, "By his own confession the slow movement is Dr. Dvorak's musical publication. . . ." By March 14 and 17, 1911, this had become "According to Dvorak's statement to this writer the Largo is a musical publication of the mood. . . ."

4   This and other citations from Krehbiel's letters are taken from documents deposited in the Museum of Czech Music (Muzeum ceské hudby) in Prague, Czech Republic, which is now named the Czech Museum of Music. There are eight letters and one visiting card in this file (numbered 788–96). The letters range from brief notes of inquiry or thanks to a note asking Dvořák not to call for his scores because of some fear about scarlet fever infection. I am grateful to Dr. Markéta Hallová, director of the Dvořák Museum, for making this material available to me. I am also indebted to the conductor and scholar Maurice Peress for information about Krehbiel's analysis and for alerting me to the existence of the Krehbiel letters. The letters are published in Dvořák, *Korespondence* 7:142–43, 150–51. The editors assume that the second letter was written on December 30, but the content, with its reference to the "New World" Symphony performance, makes it clear that it was written on December 16.

5   Francesco Berger (1834–1933[!]) was a pianist and composer who served for twenty-seven years as secretary of the Royal Philharmonic Society. Dvořák wrote to him many times on business matters and they became friends. This letter is published in Dvořák, *Korespondence*, 3:268.

6   By contrast, when Dvořák *is* dissatisfied with a critic, he notices and objects, as in this letter of February 1900 to Oskar Nedbal: "I'll send you Kretschmar's analysis of the symphony, but forget the nonsense about my use of Indian and American motives. It's a lie! I only tried to compose in the spirit of those folk melodies." *Korespondence* 4.

7   It would, of course, be a mistake to restrict all readings of this passage to a *Hiawatha* context. Some have noted that the chorale-like passage seems rooted in Dvořák's days as a church organist, showing how to get the choir from one key to another. The succession of chords also recalls the opening of Brahms's Symphony No. 4.

8   For more on this view, see Hepokoski.

9   This article appears in *Cesta* 1 (1918–19): 104–6, 134.

10   A recently located file card in Šourek's hand reads, and I translate: "Am. symphony/ According to the New Y. Herald in the Fall of 1893 it is said that the 2nd movement was composed under the influence of a reading of Hiawatha (funeral in the forest)." Under this is a reference to Emingerová's article in *Cesta*.

11   See John Clapham, *Antonín Dvořák*, 88.

12   In disagreeing with any scenario that involves the funeral of Minnehaha, Robert Winter writes that "Beckerman is forced to deal with an episode ten chapters after the wooing" in order to give credence to Emingerová, and Winter is troubled by the

twenty-five years that separate her article from the premiere of the symphony. But the idea of jumping ahead several chapters should in no way invalidate the funeral hypothesis. In Dvořák, we are dealing with someone who has known *Hiawatha* for close to thirty years. It is hard to imagine that he couldn't immediately make the jump from Chapter 10 to Chapter 20, whether in his imagination or by turning a few pages.

13   *Musical America*, 1924.

14   I am indebted to David Schiller for pointing this out. See his "Music and Words."

15   For a discussion of this view see Hepokoski.

16   These lines from Krehbiel's article raise additional questions. I have not found a way to connect the return of first-movement material with any idea or image from the poem. It may simply be Dvořák the symphonist breaking through with motivic reminiscences at the moment of programmatic sunrise. Carrying this idea expressed by Krehbiel to an extreme conclusion and seeing it in relationship to "Hiawatha's Wooing" would have grand ramifications, perhaps even implying that all four movements constitute a giant "Hiawatha Symphony." We cannot know whether Krehbiel's remarks about Indian "mood" refer to the middle movements only or to the whole symphony.

17   Published in *Korespondence*, 3:207.

18   "Goin' Home," from the Largo for the "New World" Symphony (Philadelphia, 1922).

19   Ivanov, 364.

Chapter 3: The "Local Color of Indian Character" and the Scherzo

1   American Sketchbook No. 5, p. 25. Also see Chapter 5 for more discussion of the *Hiawatha* opera and two illustrations with sketches.

2   In Dvořák, *Letters and Reminiscences*, 82–83, B. Fidler recalls Dvořák's fascination with birds, including the passage "You know, before I die, I shall write a fine bird symphony and I shall put my very best into it!" And in a letter to his publisher Simrock, Dvořák says, "I am spending the most wonderful days in the loveliest weather and am filled with ever new admiration as I listen to the enchanting song of the birds."

Chapter 4: A Nose for Hiawatha

1   See Hepokoski and Winter.

2   See Hepokoski.

3   Winter, in his CD-ROM, was aware of both my reading and Hepokoski's, while Hepokoski was not aware of either reading when he evolved his scenario.

4   Hepokoski, 687.

5   Šourek tells us (3: 195) that Act 2 of the first *Hiawatha* libretto (possibly written by Edwin Emerson), now disappeared, was supposed to end with the "treachery of Pau-Puk-Keewis," probably referring to both Chapters 16 and 17.

6   Quoted in Olin Downes, "A Dvořák Reminiscence," *New York Times*, August 12, 1934. Hopkins had come to Bohemia and tried constantly to get Dvořák to speak about the symphony "From the New World," but "regardless of every effort to make him talk, the subject was always evaded when approached. The endeavor might be made in a round-about way, such as a discourse upon modern instrumentation, or talks concerning the influence of newly composed symphonies upon present-day music, but he would detect the stratagem and gruffly brush the topic aside."

Chapter 5: Dvořák's Hiawatha Opera

1   Sychra, 328.

2   See especially Sychra, 313–18, 327–32, 336–51.

3   Clapham, *Antonín Dvořák*, 280.

4   Thurber, 694.

5   Ibid.

6   Quoted in Neilson.

7   Thurber.

8   James Creelman, "Does it Pay to Study Music?" in *Illustrated American*, August 4, 1894.

9   Here Kovařík is referring to the period after November 6, 1893. On that day Dvořák sent several scores to Simrock with a cover letter. Dvořák, *Letters and Reminiscences*, 221.

10   *Boston Herald*, May 28, 1893.

11   *Dalibor*, 1894, no. 233.

12   Thurber.

13   James Creelman, "Real Value of Negro Melodies," *New York Herald*, May 21, 1893.

Chapter 6: Two Who Made the "New World"

1   H. L. Mencken, "Huneker: A Memory," in *Prejudices* (New York: Knopf, 1922), 66–68. Quoted in Schwab, 235.

2   Schwab, 236.

3   Huneker 2:66. The reminiscence about Dvořák also appears in Beckerman, ed., *Dvořák and His World*, 181–84.

4   See Neilson, Chapter 4, p. 78.

5   Huneker, 2: 67.

6   In Schwab, 280.

7   Huneker, 2:67

8   Ibid., 2: 68.

9   As noted, Kovařík's reminiscences, written to Otakar Šourek in the form of letters, have never been printed in their entirety. This and other extracts are taken from the commentary to the "New World" Symphony edited by Jarmil Burghauser; see Dvořák, *IXth Symphony in E Minor*, 21.

10 In *The Musical Courier*, December 20, 1893, pp. 37–38. Also available in Beckerman, ed., *Dvořák and His World*, 159–65.

11 "Dvorak on His New Work," *New York Herald*, December 15, 1893. "I found that the music of the two races bore a remarkable similarity to the music of Scotland. In both there is a peculiar scale, caused by the absence of the fourth and seventh, or leading tone. In both the minor scale has the seventh invariably a minor seventh, the fourth is included and the sixth omitted." Compare with the second page of "Negro Music" in the Appendix.

12 I had determined that "Negro Music" must be the article in question for many of the reasons outlined above. I asked one of my students, then doing research in Prague, to see if he could find a copy in the archive. He did: a clipping of an article called "Negro Music." I knew at this point we had the correct article, since Kovařík spoke of a "cutting" in his recollection. I am grateful to both Diane Paige and Thomas Svatos for their help in tracking down the article.

13 *New York Daily Tribune*, December 17, 1893.

14 *The Musical Courier*, December 27, 1893, pp. 8–9.

15 Ibid., January 3, 1894, 22–23. The Bowery, Central Park, Harlem, the Elevated Railway, and the Belt Line were all features of the New York cityscape.

16 Ibid., January 10, 1894, 19.

17 From commentary to the "New World" Symphony, Dvořák, *IXth Symphony in E Minor*, 31.

18 Ibid., 31–32.

19 *The Musical Courier*, March 7, 1894.

20 *Musical America*, April 29, 1916, p. 25.

21 Huneker, 1: v.

22 This letter and the melodies are reprinted in Beckerman, ed., *Dvořák and His World*, 201–2.

23 Hill, 85.

24 Ibid., 85–86.

25 The article "Women Can't Help" appeared in the *Boston Post*, November 30, 1892. The composer was reported to have said: "Here all the ladies play. It is well; it is nice. But I am afraid the ladies cannot help us much. They have not the creative power."

Chapter 7: The Real Value of Yellow Journalism

1   The full text of this article appears in Beckerman, ed., *Dvořák and His World*, 177–80.

2   Most of this article is available in Tibbetts, 355–59. The various subheadlines for
the article are as follows: "Real Value of Negro Melodies/ Dr. Dvorak Finds in
Them the Basis for an American School of Music/ Rich in Undeveloped Themes/
American Composers Urged to Study Plantation Songs and Build Upon Them/
Uses of Negro Minstrelsy/ Colored Students to Be Admitted to the National
Conservatory—Prizes to Encourage Americans." The following passage, which I
consider to be quite interesting, is left out of this reprint and occurs directly following the ellipsis in Tibbetts, 359: "Already in the case of the grand opera private
subscriptions have been just as efficacious as public subsidies. But the ladies and
gentlemen who parade their public spirit at the opera house must not forget the
foundation of it all unless America is to remain forever a musical dependency of
Europe. It requires a strong and pure interest to carry on the slow beginnings of a
national school. People as a rule want to see results at once when they contribute
to a cause. A man will contribute to a hospital because the next day his self-esteem
may be ratified by the grateful smile of a sick child, but would he as readily contribute to a bacteriological institute where the doctor who saved the patient learned
to grapple with the disease! Americans vaunt their hospitals, and yet I have seen
the most extensive and most perfectly equipped bacteriological institute in the
world maintained by a few Russians without a word of boasting. Americans loudly
proclaim the generosity that upholds grand opera on a scale only equaled by
Vienna, Dresden, Munich and Paris, but where is the serious spirit that supports
the energy for producing operas and opera makers!"

This passage is followed by a list of 140 patrons of the National Conservatory,
and the long fascinating letter by Fanny Payne Walker, a black woman, to Jeannette
Thurber. She says, "Trouble and being poor have kept me from having my voice cultivated." She is a widow and speaks about how difficult it is to support herself. She
asks: "If I get my friends to give me a benefit concert after school closes, June 15,
enough to pay my fare, will you allow me to come to your conservatory and receive
musical or vocal instruction?" This letter is used as evidence for the need of such an
institution.

3   This article is also reprinted in Tibbetts, 359–61, but several interesting elements
have been omitted. First the headlines: "Antonin Dvorak on Negro Melodies/The
Bohemian Composer Employs Their Themes and Sentiment in a New Symphony/
Hints to Young Musicians/ Negro Melodies to Be the True Basis for a Distinctively
American School of Music/ Merit of American Music."

The following passage occurs before the printed portion of Dvořák's:

"Through the Herald today Dr. Antonin Dvorak, the foremost living composer
of the world, makes an appeal for a native school of music in America that ought to
awaken lovers of art from one end of the country to the other. This utterance, coming from a supreme authority, is the result of a judicial and personal examination into
the musical capacity of the American people.

"Dr. Dvorak's explicit announcement that his newly completed symphony reflects the negro melodies upon which he says the coming American school must be based will be a surprise to the world. Here is his appeal:"

The article contains two illustrations. The first is a drawing of Dvořák teaching a woman dressed in her turn-of-the century best, with hat and long dress (see Fig. 15). She is working at the blackboard, and Dvořák, seen in profile, is ready to correct her, with a serious look and his mouth half open. According to Maurice Peress, the woman is Laura Sedgwick Collins (1859?–1927), who was a student of Dvořák's at the Conservatory. Below it is a sketch of Harry Burleigh with the title "Harry Burleigh. Colored Teacher in the Conservatory."

The article concludes with another long letter, this time from a man named Gaius C. Bolin, praising Thurber effusively for her efforts on behalf of his race.

4   For a list of the articles that appeared in the *New York Herald* see the Bibliography. The following articles appeared in the European edition of the *Herald*: May 22, "American Music of the Future" (reprint of "Real Value"); May 26, "American Music (interview with Joachim); May 27, "Herr Rubinstein Is Skeptical" (interview with Rubinstein and Sally Liebling); May 28, "America's Musical Future" (interview with Bruckner, Mandyczewski, Richter). I am indebted to Maurice Peress for this information. There was also an article in the Boston edition of the *Herald*: May 28, "American Music. Dr. Antonin Dvorak Expresses Some Radical Opinions." Excerpts from this article have been reprinted by Adrienne Fried Block as "Boston Talks Back to Dvořák," *ISAM Newsletter* 18, no. 2 (May 1989).

5   There is no standard biography of Creelman. I have been especially lucky to have had extended contact with John Creelman, a distant relative, who is in the process of writing a major biography of James Creelman. He supplied me with articles, letters, photographs, and additional information. His knowledge of Creelman and his times has been invaluable. I have also relied on biographical information supplied by Ronald S. Marmarelli in *Dictionary of Literary Biography* 23: 56–67, which includes a comprehensive bibliography. There is also an illuminating article titled "James Creelman, the *New York World* and the Port Arthur Massacre" which appeared in the *Journalism Quarterly*, Winter 1973, 697–701. Several biographical sketches are useful; the most substantial, titled "Character Sketch: Mr. James Creelman, War Correspondent," appeared in the London edition of the *Review of Reviews* and was written by William T. Stead (1849–1912). Stead was actually publisher of the *Pall Mall Budget*, which might explain how Creelman's piece on Dvořák came to that newspaper. Stead was a well-known spiritualist whose fame rose even higher when it was noted that he had written a short story about a man traveling on a ship that strikes an iceberg. Stead died over a decade later on the *Titanic*.

6   Creelman, 5.

7   Ibid., 174. Creelman devotes an entire chapter to a defense of yellow journalism, "Familiar Glimpses of Yellow Journalism," which includes his most passionate

defense: "If the war against Spain is justified in the eyes of history, then 'yellow journalism' deserves its place among the most useful instrumentalities of civilization. It
may be guilty of giving the world a lopsided view of events by exaggerating
the importance of a few things and ignoring others, it may offend the eye by
typographical violence, it may sometimes proclaim its own deeds too loudly; but
it has never deserted the cause of the poor and the downtrodden; it has never
taken bribes,—and that is more than can be said of its most conspicuous critics"
(187).

8   Milton, 35.

9   Creelman, 233.

10   This article is really about the composer and journalist Ernest Reyer, although the
first part concerns Dvořák. When asked his opinion concerning Dvořák's ideas,
Reyer replied: "The popular melodies of a country have always had an influence
more or less direct on the style of the composers of that country; negro melodies may
have, therefore, also had an influence by their originality and native flavor. If they do
not serve as a foundation for a school which would arise in America, at least they may
give it a particular and well defined character." The article continues with a presentation of the salient facts of Reyer's career.

11   This is a long piece that quotes three identified sources and "one gentleman, who
does not wish to be quoted as criticising so eminent a musician and composer as Dr.
Dvorak." Those interviewed include the songwriter David Braham (1834–1905), his
partner Edward "Ned" Harrigan (1844–1911), a playwright, actor, and lyricist, and
composer Victor Herbert. Together Braham and Harrigan created sketches and plays
that portrayed the social conditions of immigrant families in New York. Harrigan
was immortalized by George M. Cohan's song of the same name, whose memorable
chorus begins, "H, A, Double-R, I, / G, A, N spells Harrigan."

The article starts by suggesting that the expression "Negro melody" in Dvořák's
famous proclamation is not exactly clear. Braham speculates on the musicality of
African-Americans and worries that educating them "will destroy the very charm that
his song now has for our ears." Harrigan too is taken with what he takes to be the
natural abilities of African-American musicians: "The fact that the negro race pos-
sesses a remarkable facility for music is so familiar to every one in this country that
I am rather surprised no great authority in music has thought before this of taking
the matter up." He agrees with Braham "in suspecting that a good deal of this musical taste may evaporate when an attempt is made to educate it." The following two
paragraphs describe Victor Herbert's reaction to the question:

"Mr. Victor Herbert, the noted 'cello player of the Seidl orchestra, who has been
looking up American melodies this last few months in order to write original music
for the use of the Mackaye Spectatorium that has come to grief in Chicago, tells me
that he doubts whether there will be found enough original material in negro melody
to warrant the hope of making much of it.

"When he was in Richmond last year conducting some concerts he was taken to several tobacco factories, where the negroes sang for him, and he was much impressed. It was often beautiful singing, of a weird, rather mournful character, but there was not much that could be made use of in music of a more ambitious type. According to Mr. Herbert, the melody is not so important a matter as the ability to develop it. This art is exactly what the negro fails in, and whether he will succeed in absorbing scientific instruction, while retaining his faculty for adapting what he hears, is a problem yet to be solved, but highly interesting and well worth solving."

The anonymous member of the quartet touches on Dvořák's theory only tangentially before digressing into a general discussion of song. The beginning of his remarks is worth quoting here, because he takes a swipe at his peers saying that "while he considered the scheme of educating the musical negro rather a fantastic one he hopes that some day the negro might give us a little better songs than we were getting from some white composers."

12   Dvořák's use of the world "friend" in inscriptions of this kind is quite unusual.

13   John Creelman has directed my attention to a letter to Creelman from the archbishop of Canterbury, which suggests that Creelman attempted to get the archbishop to attend the performance of the work. There are eighteen pages of notes in Alice Buell Creelman's hand that constitute a biographical sketch of her husband, probably written in 1894.

14   The article is preceded by two full-page pictures of Dvořák and Jeannette Thurber. We have evidence that Dvořák was given a copy of his remarks to edit. See Paige and Beckerman, "Does it Pay to Study Music?"

15   This article includes the first known public announcement that the symphony was complete. Dvořák had informed intimates of the fact in letters and, no doubt, in discussions.

16   The Creelman papers at Ohio State University include a program from Gilmore's Grand Concerts on July 31, 1892, that lists a performance of a "Mazurka" by James Creelman sandwiched between Mozart's "Non più andrai" and a cavatina from *Robert le Diable*.

17   "Men of Our Day," by George T. B. Davis, in *Our Day*, August 5, 1894, pp. 371–77; the quoted material is part of a section dealing with Creelman's interview technique, pp. 376–77.

18   I am grateful to both Maurice Peress and Robert Winter for providing me with the ideas and materials that led to this conclusion. Peress informed me about the articles in the Paris *Herald*, and Winter discussed the matter with me at great length. John Creelman also communicated the following to me in a personal letter : "The device of publishing a controversial article followed up with such reactions was fairly common. It was a means of lending credibility to articles and showing that notable people read the paper. From my research, it appears that such notable people were constantly being asked their opinion about articles and events. . . . Creelman's Papers

have many examples of where his publisher or editor directed him to get such reactions. He had many important contacts and was valued for this."

19   Bennett, the editor of the *Herald*, was in Paris at the time, and his was the only newspaper that was completely connected by telegraph. I am grateful to Robert Winter for bringing these facts to my attention.

20   It is not precisely clear how Dvořák and Creelman met, but it may have been through Jeannette Thurber at the National Conservatory. All of Creelman's articles on Dvořák have long passages dealing with the conservatory, and there is a long letter from Jeannette Thurber to Creelman dated July 2, 1894, that begins: "My Dear Mr. Creelman / The National Conservatory of Music wishes to engage a vocal teacher with a name as well known in this country as abroad—perhaps someone from Paris. *A man*—with a woman." The tone of political intrigue in this letter reveals that Creelman must have been a highly trusted friend of the institution. Letters in the Creelman papers from Alice to James in the year 1894 make it clear that Jeannette Thurber owed the Creelmans $500, a substantial amount of money at the time. Perhaps the money was a loan, but it is more likely that Thurber promised payment to Creelman in exchange for his help in publicizing the conservatory in general and Dvořák's visit in particular.

21   Clapham and Melville-Mason, "Dvořák in a New Role," 100.

22   A reproduction of this letter appeared in the *Herald* on the following day, December 18.

23   The editorial is titled "Dvorak Awakens the Musical World" and reads as follows:

"Dr. Dvorak's bold declaration that the negro melodies of America are to be the foundation of a great national school of music ranging through every stage of the art, from ballads to symphonies and oratorios, has aroused the musicians of Europe. The Commercial Cable brings us an interview with Ernest Reyer, the distinguished French composer, which we print to-day. He says that the negro melodies, even if they do not serve as the actual basis of the coming American school will determine its character.

"The presence of the great Bohemian master in this country is a blessing to art. And it is a remarkable thing that at the very moment Rubinstein, Richter, Joachim and other famous musicians were discussing Dr. Dvořák's discovery with HERALD correspondents in Europe, the composer himself was writing for these columns the gratifying announcement that he had just finished a new symphony reflecting all through it the negro melodies of the Western world."

24   Procter, 128–29.

25   The timing of Creelman's departure from the *Herald* is difficult to ascertain. Alice Creelman says he left the paper in the winter of 1893. His letter of resignation to Bennett was dated December 17, but since Bennett was in Europe, we have no idea when it took effect. As of now, the last article in the *Herald* written for certain by Creelman is the one that appeared on December 17, the same day of Dvořák's letter

to the editor of the *Herald* that is found among Creelman's papers. Dvořák's inscription to Creelman is dated January 22, so he probably remained in New York for at least a month after his resignation. The tone of the inscription and the inclusion of the Foster melody suggest that Creelman continued working with the clothing fund, either as a member of the *Herald* staff or through the National Conservatory.

26   Creelman, 5.

Chapter 8: Dvořák, Krehbiel, and the "New World"

1   In a practice quite different from today's concert life, there were, in effect, two premieres. The first performance, on December 15, 1893, was supposedly an open dress rehearsal, but many notables attended, and several newspapers reviewed the symphony. The "real" premiere was on Saturday.

2   I am indebted to Maurice Peress for his help in locating both this article and the Dvořák–Krehbiel correspondence. I also thank Marketa Hallova, director of the Dvořák Museum in Prague, for her assistance.

3   See Chapter 2 and also "Dvořák's 'New World' Largo and *The Song of Hiawatha*."

4   These biographical details are taken mainly from the obituary by Richard Aldrich in *Music and Letters* 4 (1923): 266–68 and the extensive coverage in Krehbiel's own *New York Tribune*, which ran a full page on the critic's life and contribution on March 31, 1923. Further material is available at the Music Division of the New York Public Library. The articles about Krehbiel in both *New Grove* and the *New Grove Dictionary of American Music* are based heavily on the writings of Aldrich. It is shocking that a first-rate critic such as Krehbiel does not have a more impressive entry in either publication. Although this study is not the place to supply a full biography of Henry Krehbiel, such a work would be both useful and rewarding.

5   *Music and Letters* 4 (1923): 266–68.

6   Krehbiel, 13–14.

7   Ibid., 323.

8   *Century Illustrated Monthly Magazine* 44 (September 1892): 657.

9   Ibid.

10   Ibid., 660.

11   See Chapter 2 and also Beckerman, "Henry Krehbiel, Antonín Dvořák, and the Symphony 'From the New World.' "

12   See Chapter 4, n. 6.

13   Jeannette Thurber wrote about her relationship with Dvořák, and particularly about the "New World" Symphony, in her 1919 article "Personal Recollections of a Great Master: Dvorak as I knew Him." In it she completely dismisses the connection between the symphony and *The Song of Hiawatha*.

14   Fletcher, *A Study of Omaha Indian Music*.

15   In the *New York Daily Tribune*, December 17, 1893, p. 7.

16   This article contains a substantial discussion of Dvořák's "American" Quartet, Opus 96, complete with six music examples. It has not, to my knowledge, appeared in any of the Dvořák bibliographies.

17   "Antonín Dvořák" in *The Looker On*, October 1896, pp. 261–71. This passage occurs on p. 261.

18   Ibid., 262.

19   The following articles concerning the premiere of the symphony appeared between December 15 and 20. The names in parentheses are those of the probable authors. Since only one story (in the *World*) has a byline, the writers had to be identified by other means. The *Tribune* articles can only be by Krehbiel. In the cited article in *The Musical Courier*, the author, almost certainly James Huneker, names the writers for the other papers who have written about Dvořák. He identifies Steinberg of the *Herald*, W. H. Henderson of the *Times*, Mrs. Bowman of the *Sun*, and Henry T. Finck of the *Post*. He also mentions an article by Spanuth in the *Staats Zeitung* and articles in the *Advertiser* and the *Recorder* that I have not been able to locate.

> *New York Herald*: December 15, "Dvorak on His New Work," interview with Dvořák; December 16, "Dr. Dvorak's Great Symphony" (Steinberg); December 17, "Dvorak's Symphony a Historic Event" and "Dvorak Hears His Symphony"
>
> *New York Daily Tribune*: December 15, "Dr. Dvorak's American Symphony" (Krehbiel); December 17, "Dr. Dvorak's Symphony" (Krehbiel)
>
> *Evening Post*: December 18, "A Notable Concert" (Finck)
>
> *New York Times*: December 17, "Dr. Dvorak's Latest Work"(Henderson)
>
> *Sun*: December 17, "Dvorak's New Symphony" (Bowman)
>
> *New York World*: December 16, "Dvorak's Symphony" (DeKoven)
>
> *Musical Courier*: December 20, "The Second Philharmonic Concert" (Huneker)

Chapter 9: Burleigh and Dvořák: From the Plantation to the Symphony

1   Letter to Karel Baštař, Dvořák, *Korespondence*, 3: 155–56.

2   Skvorecky, 325.

3   In *Musical America*, April 12, 1924, p. 21.

4   In Hazel Kinscella, *Music on the Air* (New York: Viking, 1934).

5   Victor Herbert, "Sketch of Antonin Dvorak," Library of Congress, 1922.

6   Miloš Šafránek, "Co vyprávěl Dvořákův černošsky přítel" (What Dvořák's black friend told me), *Lidová demokracie* 7, July 2, 1954. Also in *Ivanov*, 172–73.

7   Letter to Oskar Nedbal, written some time in February 1900, Dvořák, *Korespondence* 4:185.

8   In Jean Snyder, "A Great and Noble School of Music," in Tibbetts, 136.

9   Clapham talks about this in his article "Evolution of Dvořák's Symphony 'From the New World,' " 177.

10   See Jon Cruz, *Culture on the Margins* (Princeton: Princeton University Press, 1999).

Chapter 10: A Spillville Pastoral

1   For a discussion of these Spillville myths see Klevar and Polansky. For a treat, listen to the stories told aloud on Robert Winter's CD-ROM *Antonín Dvořák: Symphony No. 9, From the New World.*

2   Škvorecký, 158.

3   Reported by Kovařík. Dvořák, *Letters and Reminiscences*, 160.

4   Large, 280.

5   For a description of Vysoká see Dvořák, *Letters and Reminiscences*, 81.

6   Schick.

7   See Schick.

8   See Beveridge, "Sophisticated Primitivism."

9   Quoted in Burghauser's commentary to the "New World" Symphony, Burghauser, 21.

10   Ibid.

11   See Houtchens, 228–37, and Beveridge, "Sophisticated Primitivism."

12   Krehbiel in *New York Daily Tribune*, January 13, 1894.

13   Faragher.

14   Ibid.

15   Hepokoski.

16   *The Musical Courier*, January 10, 1894.

17   In Houtchens, 231. Translation is by the author.

18   Krehbiel in *New York Daily Tribune*, January 13, 1894.

19   Letter from Kovařík to Amy Balik, unpublished.

20   Ibid.

Chapter 11: Inner and Outer Visions of America: Dvořák's Suite and Biblical Songs

1   Dvořák, *Korespondence* 3:207; Dvořák, *Letters and Reminiscences*, 166.

Chapter 12: Some American Snapshots

1   See Tibbetts, 274.

2   In the *Decorah Republican*, October 19, 1893. Quoted in Cyril Klimesh, *They Came to this Place* (Sebastopol, Calif.: Methodius Press, 1992).

Chapter 13: The Master Is Not Well

1   Otakar Dvořák, 36.

2   Beard, *Practical Treatise on Nervous Exhaustion (Neurasthenia)*, 5.

3   Beard, *American Nervousness*. Later published in a larger format in 1881.

4   "In his classic work, *American Nervousness* (1881), Beard argued that America created a far more intense social milieu for its citizens, particularly those with the finest mental sensibilities, because it lacked the traditional forms of authority that stabilized European society, such as a state church and titled aristocracy." Gamwell and Tomes.

5   Barushka Klírová in Ivanov, 119.

6   Leitner.

7   Clapham, *Dvořák*, 104. The passage continues with further details: ". . . and when it was suggested that he should go to Moscow a little earlier than originally planned, he said: 'I have no objection to changing the date of the concert to February, although fear that the cold weather in Russia might affect my health. . . . He was disturbed by the report that there was an influenza epidemic in England three weeks before he was due to go to Cambridge, and he gave Stanford a fright when he wrote: '. . . on account [*sic*] of that I and my wife are afraid to come there. The journey from Prague to London is very long and if we had a bad weather we can easy take cold— and what shall we do then? Please tell me what is to be done.' Stanford immediately reassured him by saying that there was no longer any risk, that the weather in Cambridge was glorious, and as regards health we would probably be safer in Cambridge than in Prague. . . . "

8   *Diagnostic and Statistical Manual of Mental Disorders*, 4th ed. (*DSM-IV*), 396.

9   Ibid.

10   Ibid., 403

11   There is at least one recent study that is more skeptical about the connection between panic attacks and agoraphobia. See Paul M. Salkovski and Ann Hackman, "Agoraphobia," in *Phobias: A Handbook of Theory, Research, and Treatment* (Chichester: John Wiley & Sons, 1997), 27–61. "There is reason to doubt such an extreme conclusion," p. 29.

12   "As in all psychological problems, the specific pattern of fears is idiosyncratic." Ibid., 27.

13   *DSM-IV*, 398.

14   From Kovařík in Dvořák, *Letters and Reminiscences*, 187.

15   In the parlance of *DSM-IV* and other contemporary works this would be considered a "specific phobia."

16   Harry Patterson Hopkins in Downes.

17   See Hopkins, "How Dvořák Taught Composition," and "Student Days with Dvořák."

18   Dvořák, *Letters and Reminiscences*, 161.

19   Letter to Antonín Rus, Vysoká, June 14, 1889, Dvořák, *Korespondence* 2:370.

20 For another perspective on this issue, see Webster.

21 From the letters between Josef Kovařík and Dvořák biographer Otakar Šourek, quoted in Jarmil Burghauser's commentary to the "New World," Dvořák, *IXth Symphony in E Minor*, 29.

22 Dvořák, *IXth Symphony in E Minor*, 29.

23 See Chapter 7.

24 In *Steeplejack*, Huneker mentions that he looked after Dvořák at the request of Mrs. Thurber, but that after their bout of drinking together he informed Thurber that he "was through piloting him."

25 From Šubert's reminiscences, in Dvořák, *Letters and Reminiscences*, 202.

26 *DSM-IV*.

27 Otakar Dvořák, 52 This passage most certainly refers to the fall of 1894.

28 Ibid., 71.

29 Klevar and Polansky, "The Dvořák Myths in Spillville."

30 Dvořák, *Letters and Reminiscences*, 194.

31 See Huneker 2: 65–69. The episode is also reprinted in Beckerman, ed., *Dvořák and His World*, 181–84.

32 See Klevar and Polansky.

33 Clapham, *Dvořák*.

34 For a discussion of the general relationship between anxiety and alcoholism, see Vaillant. For more specific findings, see D. Baron, B. Sands, et al.; D. Johannessen, D. Cowley, et al.; M. Kushner, K. Sher, et al.; and M. Weissman.

35 Ivanov, 223.

36 Dvořák, *Letters and Reminiscences*, 190.

Chapter 14: A Cello Concerto, a Death—and Secrets

1 Dvořák, *Korespondence*, 3: 422.

2 Šourek, *Život a dílo Antonína Dvořáka* 3:236.

3 Looking further through the various editions of Šourek's biography does not shed any definitive light on the matter. The issue of Dvořák, Josefina, and the Cello Concerto potentially involves as many as four or five works: *The Cypresses*, according to Šourek, written with her in mind; *Silhouettes*, which contains similar material, and the songs of Opus 82 and Opus 83. Neither the first nor the second volume of the first edition of Šourek's work mentions Josefina. While the first edition of Volume 1 in 1916 mentions that Dvořák fell in love while teaching the Čermáková sisters, there is no special mention of Josefina, and those not familiar with birthdates (Anna was only eleven years old at the time) were left to conclude that he'd fallen in love with his future wife. It was not until the first edition of Volume 3, published in 1930, that Šourek made clear that Dvořák had been in love with Josefina, although he still doesn't make it explicit that she was fond of the song quoted in the concerto. On p. 227 of

the first edition, Volume 3, he writes that this assertion is based on "witnesses close to Dvořák," something he never mentions in subsequent editions. I am indebted to David Beveridge for his assistance in sorting out Šourek's various arguments and assertions.

4   Or as Antonín Sychra suggests, the composer was contemplating his youth at the time he wrote the concerto.

5   The possible exception to this is Otakar Dvořák, who mentions it in his memoirs. But he may well have gotten his information from Šourek.

6   Clapham, "Dvořák's Cello Concerto in B Minor: A Masterpiece in the Making." The letter is quoted on pp. 131–32.

7   Dvořák, *Korespondence*, 7: 287–88.

8   For more on this matter, see Palisca.

9   This figure appears throughout French Revolutionary music, but Frits Noske discusses related passages going back to the seventeenth century which he refers to as the "figure of death."

10   One possible source for the opening of Dvořák's *Holoubek* could be Berlioz's *Symphonie Funèbre et Triomphale*, the opening of which is a kind of mirror image of Dvořák.

11   Beveridge, "Dvořák's 'Dumka.' " See also Burghauser, "Dvořák and Janáček's Dumka."

12   Burghauser, "Dvořák and Janáček's Dumka," 42.

13   Unknown reporter in *The Musical Times*, May 1, 1890, p. 279.

14   Letters, Vol. 4, p. 138. Letter to Emil Heermann.

15   There is a discussion of this photograph in Jaromil Jireš's documentary film on Dvořák.

Chapter 15: Between a Ring and a Hard Place: Dvořák's Homeric Wagner

1   Cited in Sandra McColl, *Music Criticism in Vienna* (Oxford: Clarendon Press, 1996), 186–87.

2   *Die Reichswehr*, March 1, 1904, in Dvořák, *Letters and Reminiscences*, 223.

3   The article, originally published in the *Century Magazine*, is reprinted in Clapham, *Antonín Dvořák*, 296–305. Also see Beckerman, "Dvořák's American Schubert."

4   See David Beveridge, "Dvořák and Brahms: A Chronicle, and Interpretation," in Beckerman, ed., *Dvořák and His World*, 56–91. Beveridge translates and annotates virtually the entire correspondence between the two. Especially noteworthy are the letters on pp. 66–69.

5   "Enthusiasts Interviewed," *Sunday Times* (London), May 10, 1885, p. 6. Also in Beveridge, *Rethinking Dvořák*, 287.

6   Quoted in Vojackova-Wetche.

7   Clapham, *Antonín Dvořák*, 7, 50, 60, 65, 67, 70. Dvořák, *Letters and Reminiscences*, 170.

8   Letter from Kovařík to Šourek, published in Jarmil Burghauser's critical commentary for the facsimile edition of the "New World" Symphony (Prague: Pressfoto, 1972).

9   Masaryková, *Hudba ve Spillville* pamphlet.

10 Quoted in Dvořák, *Letters and Reminiscences*, 170.

11 I am indebted to my former student Paul Bertagnolli for his work on this subject.

12 *The Century Magazine* 26 (1894): 342.

13 Vojackova-Wetche, 135.

14 Alexander Poznansky, *Tchaikovsky: The Quest for the Inner Man* (New York: Schirmer, 1991).

15 Memoirs of Karel Sázavský, "Reminiscences of Master Dvořák," in Dvořák, *Letters and Reminiscences*, 194.

16 Horowitz.

17 Horowitz, personal communication to the author.

Postscript

1   Simeon Pease Cheney, *Wood Notes Wild* (Boston: Lee & Shepard, 1892).

Bibliography

The most complete Dvořák bibliography is found in Jarmil Burghauser, ed., *Antonín Dvořák, Thematický Katalog* (Antonín Dvořák, thematic catalogue). 2nd ed. (Prague: Bärenreiter Editio Supraphon, 1996).

Cited Works

Aborn, Merton Robert. *The Influence on American Musical Culture of Dvořák's Sojourn in America.* Ann Arbor, Mich.: University Microfilms, 1965.

Abraham, Gerald. "Dvořák's Musical Personality." In *Antonín Dvořák: His Achievement,* ed. Viktor Fischl, 192–240. London: L. Drummond, 1942.

Baron, D., B. Sands, et al. "The Diagnosis and Treatment of Panic Disorder in Alcoholics: Three Cases." *American Journal of Drug Abuse* 16 (1990): 287–95.

Bartoš, František, ed. Preface and notes to Antonín Dvořák, *Souborné vydání* (Complete works), ser. 5, vol. 4: *Suita.* . . . Prague, Artia, 1957.

Beard, George M. *American Nervousness.* Richmond, Va.: J. W. Ferguson & Son, 1879.

———. *Practical Treatise on Nervous Exhaustion (Neurasthenia).* New York: E. B. Ghent, 1888.

Beckerman, Michael. "Dvořák's American Schubert." In Studia minora facultatis philosophicae universitatis brunesis 39, ser. H 35. Brno: Masarykova univerzita, 2000.

———. "Dvořák's 'New World' Largo and *The Song of Hiawatha.*" *19th Century Music* 16 (1992): 35–48.

———. "Henry Krehbiel, Antonín Dvořák, and the Symphony 'From the New World,' " Notes 49 (1992): 447–73.

———. "On the Real Value of Yellow Journalism: James Creelman and Antonín Dvořák." *The Musical Quarterly* 77 (1993): 749–68.

Beckerman, Michael, ed. *Dvořák and His World.* Princeton: Princeton University Press, 1993.

Beveridge, David. "Dvořák's 'Dumka' and the Concept of Nationalism in Music Historiography." *Journal of Musicological Research* 12 (1993): 303–25.

———. "Sophisticated Primitivism: The Significance of Pentatonicism in Dvořák's 'American' Quartet." *Current Musicology* 23 (1977): 25–36.

Beveridge, David, ed. *Rethinking Dvořák: Views from Five Countries.* Oxford: Oxford University Press, 1996.

Block, Adrienne Fried. *Amy Beach: Passionate Victorian.* New York: Oxford University Press, 1998.

———. "Boston Talks Back to Dvořák." *ISAM Newsletter*, Institute for Studies in American Music, May 1989.

Burghauser, Jarmil. "Dvořák and Janáček's Dumka." *Czech Music* 20 (1997/98) 41–56.

Cheney, Simeon Pease. *Wood Notes Wild: Notations of Bird Music.* Boston: Lee & Shepard, 1892.

Clapham, John. *Antonín Dvořák: Musician and Craftsman.* London: Faber & Faber, 1966.

———. "Dvořák and the American Indian." *Musical Times* 107 (1966): 863–67.

———. "Dvořák and the Impact of America." *The Music Review* 15 (1954): 203–11.

———. *Dvořák.* London: David & Charles, 1979.

———. "Dvořák's Cello Concerto in B Minor: A Masterpiece in the Making." *The Music Review* 40 (1979): 123–40.

———. "Evolution of Dvořák's Symphony 'From the New World.' " *The Musical Quarterly* 44 (1958): 167–83.

Clapham, John, and Graham Melville-Mason. "Dvořák in a New Role." *Czech Music* 18, no. 2 (1994): 100–26.

Creelman, James. *On the Great Highway: The Wanderings and Adventures of a Special Correspondent.* Boston: Lothrop, 1901.

Diagnostic and Statistical Manual of Mental Disorders, 4th ed. (*DSM-IV*). Washington, D.C.: American Psychiatric Association, 1994.

Dorwart, Jeffrey. "James Creelman, the *New York World*, and the Port Arthur Massacre." *Journalism Quarterly* 50 (1973): 697–701.

Downes, Olin. "A Dvořák Reminiscence: The Man and Musician Recalled in Memories of American Pupil." *New York Times*, August 12, 1934.

Dvořák, Antonín. *Korespondence a dokumenty* (Correspondence and documents). Ed. Milan Kuna. 8 vols. Prague: Supraphon/Bärenreiter, 1987–2001.

———. *Letters and Reminiscences*, ed. Otakar Šourek. Trans. Roberta Finlayson Samsour. Prague: Artia, 1954.

———. *IXth Symphony in E Minor, From the New World, Op. 95.* Ed. Jarmil Burghauser. Prague: Pressfoto, 1972.

Dvořák, Otakar. *Antonín Dvořák, My Father*, ed. Paul Polansky. Spillville, Iowa.: Czech Historical Research Center, 1993.

Emingerová, Katerina. "Antonín Dvořák v Americe" (Antonín Dvořák in America). *Cesta* 1 (1919): 104, 134.

Faragher, John Mack . "Dvořák and the American Indian." In *From the New World*, a program book for the Brooklyn Philharmonic Orchestra, ed. Joseph Horowitz, January 1993.

Fletcher, Alice. *A Study of Omaha Indian Music*. Cambridge, Mass.: Peabody Museum of American Archaeology and Ethnology, 1893.

Gamwell, Lynn, and Nancy Tomes. *Madness in America: Cultural and Medical Perceptions of Mental Illness Before 1914*. Ithaca: Cornell University Press, 1995.

Grant, Mark N. *Maestros of the Pen*. Boston: Northeastern University Press, 1998.

Hepokoski, James. "Culture Clash." *The Musical Times* 34 (1993): 685–88.

Hill, Mildred. "History of Music in Louisville." In *Memorial History of Louisville from Its First Settlement to the Year 1896*, ed. J. Stoddard Johnston, 2:85–97. Chicago and New York: American Biographical Publishing Co., 1896.

Hopkins, Harry Patterson. "How Dvořák Taught Composition." *The Etude* 49 (1931).

———. "Student Days with Dvořák." *The Etude* 30 (1912).

Horowitz, Joseph. *Wagner Nights*. Berkeley: University of California Press, 1994.

Houtchens, Alan. "The F-Major String Quartet, Opus 96." In *Dvořák in America*, ed. John Tibbetts. Portland, Ore.: Amadeus Press, 1993.

Huneker, James. *Steeplejack*. 2 vols. New York: Charles Scribner's Sons, 1920.

Ivanov, Miroslav. *Dvořák's Footsteps: Musical Journeys in the New World*. Kirksville, Mo: Thomas Jefferson University Press, 1995.

Johannessen, D., D. Cowley, et al. "Prevalence, Onset, and Clinical Recognition of Panic States in Hospitalized Male Alcoholics." *American Journal of Psychiatry* 146 (1989): 1201–3.

Klevar, Harvey, and Paul Polansky. "The Dvořák Myths in Spillville." *Czech Music* 18, no. 2 (1994): 64–72.

Kovařík, Josef. A series of letters between Kovařík and Dvořák biographer Otakar Šourek. Some of these letters are published or quoted from in various places, including Šourek's biography. The original correspondence is in the possession of Jarmil Burghauser.

Krehbiel, Henry. *Afro-American Folksongs*. New York: G. Schirmer, 1914.

———. *How to Listen to Music: Hints and Suggestions to Untaught Lovers of the Art*. New York: Charles Scribner's Sons, 1896.

Kushner, M., K. Sher, et al. "The Relation Between Alcohol Problems and the Anxiety Disorders." *American Journal of Psychiatry* 147 (1990): 685–95.

Large, Brian. *Bedřich Smetana*. New York: Praeger, 1970.

Leitner, Karel. *Antonín Dvořák: Jak učil* (Antonín Dvořák: how he taught). New York: New York Papers, 1942.

Mahler, Zdenek. *Spiritual bílého muže* (White man's spiritual). Prague: Primus, 1990.

Marmarelli, Ronald S. "James Creelman." *Dictionary of Literary Biography* 23, 56–67.

Milton, Joyce. *Yellow Kids: Foreign Correspondents in the Heyday of Yellow Journalism*. New York: Harper & Row, 1989.

Neilson, Francis. *My Life in Two Worlds*. Appleton Wis.: C. C. Nelson, 1952–53.

Paige, Diane. "Dvořák in Spillville." M.A. thesis, University of Iowa, 1994.

Paige, Diane, and Michael Beckerman. "Does it Pay to Study Music?" *The Musical Quarterly* 81 (Spring 1997): 34–50.

Palisca, Claude V. "French Revolutionary Models for Beethoven's Eroica Funeral March." In *Music and Context: Essays for John M. Ward*, ed. Anne Dhu Shapiro. Cambridge: Harvard University Department of Music, 1985.

Poznansky, Alexander. *Tchaikovsky: The Quest for the Inner Man*. New York: Schirmer Books, 1991.

Proctor, Ben. *William Randolph Hearst: The Early Years, 1863–1910*. New York: Oxford University Press, 1998.

Schick, Hartmut. "What's American about Dvořák's 'American' Quartet and Quintet?" *Czech Music* 18, no. 2 (1994): 72–83.

Schiller, David. "Music and Words in Dvořák's Symphonic Works: A Nietzschean Perspective on the 'New World' Symphony and *The Wild Dove*." In *Rethinking Dvořák: Views from Five Countries*, ed. David R. Beveridge. New York: Oxford University Press, 1996.

Schwab, Arnold T. *James Gibbons Huneker: Critic of the Seven Arts*. Stanford: Stanford University Press, 1963.

Škvorecký, Josef. *Dvorak in Love: A Light-Hearted Dream*. New York: Knopf, 1987.

Simpson, Anne Key. *Hard Trials: The Life and Music of Harry T. Burleigh*. Metuchen, N.J.: Scarecrow Press, 1990.

Smaczny, Jan. "Dvořák and the Seconda Pratica." In *Antonín Dvořák, 1841–1991: Report of the International Musicological Congress, Dobrís, 17th–20th September, 1991*, ed. Milan Pospíšil and Marta Ottlová, 271–80. Prague: Ústav pro hudební vědu Akademie věd České republiky, 1994.

———. *Dvořák: Cello Concerto*. Cambridge: Cambridge University Press, 1999.

Snyder, Jean. "A Great and Noble School of Music." In *Dvořák in America*, ed. John Tibbetts. Portland, Ore.: Amadeus Press, 1993.

———. "Harry T. Burleigh and the Creative Expression of Bi-musicality: A Study of an African-American Composer and the American Art Song." Ph.D. diss., University of Pittsburgh, 1992.

Šourek, Otakar. *The Orchestral Works of Antonín Dvořák*. Trans. Roberta F. Samsour. Prague: Artis, 1956.

———. *Život a dílo Antonína Dvořáka* (The life and works of Antonín Dvořák). 3rd ed. 4 vols. Prague: Státní nakladatelství krásné literatury, hudby a umění, 1954–57.

Stefan, Paul. "Why Dvořák Would Not Return to America." *Musical America*, February 25, 1938.

Sychra, Antonín. *Estetika Dvořákovy symfonické tvorby* (Aesthetic of Dvořák's symphonic works). Prague: Státní nakladatelství krásné literatury, hudby a umění, 1959.

Tibbetts, John, ed. *Dvořák in America*. Portland, Ore.: Amadeus Press, 1993.

Tonsor, Johann. "Negro Music." *Music*, December 1892.

Vojackova-Wetche, Ludmila. "Anton Dvořák in the Class Room." *The Etude* 37 (1919): 135-36.

Webster, James. "Music, Pathology, Sexuality, Beethoven, Schubert." *Nineteenth Century Music* 17 (1993): 89–93.

Weissman, M. "Anxiety and Alcoholism." *Journal of Clinical Psychiatry* 49 (1988): 17.

Winter, Robert. *Antonín Dvořák: Symphony No. 9, From the New World.* CD-ROM. Irvington, N.Y.: Voyager, 1994.

Contemporary Newspaper and Magazine Articles, in Chronological Order

"Antonin Dvorak." *Century Illustrated Monthly Magazine* 44 (September 1892): 657–60 (Krehbiel).

"Dr. Dvorak's Reception." *New York Daily Tribune*, October 22, 1892 (Krehbiel).

"Women Can't Help." *Boston Post*, November 30, 1892.

"Real Value of Negro Melodies." *New York Herald*, May 21, 1893 (Creelman).

"American Music of the Future" (Reprint of "Real Value"). *New York Herald*, European Edition, May 22, 1893.

"American Music." *New York Herald*, European Edition, May 26, 1893.

"Herr Rubinstein Is Skeptical." *New York Herald*, European Edition, May 27, 1893.

"Antonin Dvorak on Negro Melodies." *New York Herald*, May 28, 1893 (Dvořák).

"Dvorak's Theory of Negro Music." *New York Herald*, May 28, 1893.

"Dvorak's American School of Music." *New York Herald*, May 28, 1893 (news brief).

"American Music. Dr. Antonin Dvorak Expresses Some Radical Opinions." *Boston Herald*, May 28, 1893.

"America's Musical Future." *New York Herald*, European Edition, May 28, 1893.

"Negro Melodies in America." *New York Herald*, May 29, 1893.

"Dvorak Awakens the Musical World." *New York Herald*, May 29, 1893 (news brief).

"Criticisms on Dvorak's Theory." *New York Herald*, June 4, 1893.

"American Music." *New York Herald*, June 15, 1893 (news brief).

"America's Musical Future." *New York Herald*, June 15, 1893.

"Negro Song Writers." *New York Herald*, June 18, 1893.

"The National in Music." *The Musical Courier*, July 19, 1893 (Huneker).

"Dvorak on His New Work." *New York Herald*, December 15, 1893 (Steinberg?).

"Dr. Dvorak's American Symphony." *New York Daily Tribune*, December 15, 1893 (Krehbiel).

"Dr. Dvorak's Great Symphony." *New York Herald*, December 16, 1893 (Steinberg?).

"Dvorak's Symphony." *New York World*, December 16, 1893 (De Koven).

"Dr. Dvorak's Latest Work." *New York Times*, December 17, 1893 (Henderson).

"Dvorak's Symphony a Historic Event." *New York Herald*, December 17, 1893 (Creelman?).

"Dvorak Hears His Symphony." *New York Herald*, December 17, 1893.

"Dr. Dvorak's Symphony." *New York Daily Tribune*, December 17, 1893 (Krehbiel).

"Dvorak's New Symphony." The Sun, December 17, 1893. (Bowman).

"A Notable Concert." *Evening Post*, December 18, 1893 (Finck).

"The Second Philharmonic Concert." *The Musical Courier*, December 20, 1893 (Huneker?).

"Why American?" *The Musical Courier*, December 27, 1893 (Huneker?).

"Music in Boston." *The Musical Courier*, January 3, 1894 (Hale).

"Music in Boston." *The Musical Courier*, January 7, 1894 (Hale).

"Hear the 'Old Folks at Home.'" *New York Herald*, January 23, 1894 (Creelman?).

"Dvorak Leads for the Fund." *New York Herald*, January 23, 1894.

"Grand Concert for the Fund." *New York Herald*, January 28, 1894.

"Largest Single Gift of Money." *New York Herald*, January 29, 1894.

"Something Startling." *The Musical Courier*, February 28, 1894.

"The American Symphony." *The Musical Courier*, March 7, 1894 (Huneker?).

"Dvorak's Negro Symphony." *Pall Mall Budget* (London), June 21, 1894 (Creelman).

"Does It Pay to Study Music?" *Illustrated American*, August 4, 1894 (Creelman).

"Men of Our Day." *Our Day*, August 5, 1894 (George T. B. Davis).

"Musical Matters." *New-York Daily Tribune*, March 31, 1895 (Krehbiel?).

"Dvorak May Not Return." *The Musical Courier*, October 16, 1895 (Huneker?).

"Antonin Dvorak." *The Looker On*, October 1896, pp. 261–71 (Krehbiel).

Index

CD Contents

Please note: Performer and label information is provided the first time a work is listed; subsequent performances of the same work are taken from the same recording. Unless otherwise noted, piano performances were recorded by the author.

Track	Page	Work, Movement: Measure Nos. (Performers). Label & No.	Time
1	30	"New World" Symphony (NWS) II: 7–12 (Václav Talich, Czech Philharmonic Orchestra, Prague). Supraphon CD 11 0290-2 001, Great Artists Series. ℗ 1988 by Supraphon a.s. Licensed with the kind permission of Supraphon, Prague	:40
2	30	Pastoral tone, series of examples (piano)	:37
3	33	NWS II: 46–49	:17
4	33	NWS II: 54–58	:26
5	34	NWS II: 68–79	:56
6	35	*Rusalka,* Act 3: "Milačku, znáš mne, znáš?" (Zdeněk Chalabala, Prague National Theater). Supraphon CD 0013-2 612, disc 2. ℗ 1962 by Supraphon a.s. Licensed with the kind permission of Supraphon, Prague	:50
7	35	NWS II: 90–94	:23
8	42	Melodrama, NWS III: 1–58	:43
9	46	"Onaway! Awake, beloved!" setting of text (piano)	:15
10	46	NWS III: 68–75	:23

Track	Page	Work, Movement: Measure Nos. (Performers). Label & No.	Time
11	46	NWS III: 176–191	:15
12	46	NWS III: 216–223	:08
13	49	NWS III: 192–208	:14
14	49	Melodrama, NWS III: 176–208	1:02
15	54	"Hiawatha," setting of word (piano)	:08
16	56	NWS IV: 1–17	:29
17	56	NWS IV: 42–53	:19
18	56	NWS IV: 65–79	:29
19	57	NWS IV: 320–325	:17
20	57	NWS IV: 313–320	:15
21	59	Melodrama, NWS IV: 1–17	:29
22	61	Melodrama, NWS IV: 42–53	:19
23	61	Melodrama, NWS IV: 65–79	:29
24	62	Melodrama, NWS IV: 126–136	:22
25	63	Melodrama, NWS IV: 172–224	1:39
26	73	"Onaway! Awake, beloved!" fanciful realization of sketch for tenor and piano	5:08
27	86	NWS, first melody; first American sketch (piano)	:17
28	86	"Negro Music," part of first example, metamorphosed into Scherzo of String Quintet in E♭ Major ("American"), Op. 97 (piano)	:23
29	86	"Negro Music": end of third example; NWS I: excerpt (piano)	:21
30	87	"Negro Music": part of third example; NWS opening (piano)	:12
31	132	NWS II: theme; "Steal Away" (piano)	1:04
32	133	"My Way's Cloudy," melody (piano)	:11
33	133	NWS IV: theme; "Don't Be a Weary Traveler" (piano)	:19
34	133	"Swing Low," melody; NWS use of melody; Burleigh's arrangement (piano)	:31
35	133	NWS I: melody; "Hard Trials" (piano)	:12

Track	Page	Work, Movement: Measure Nos. (Performers). Label & No.	Time
72	194	Concerto for Cello and Orchestra No. 2 in B Minor, Op. 104, II: 42–46 (Václav Neumann, Czech Philharmonic Orchestra; Josef Chuchro, cello). Supraphon CD 3093-2011. ℗ 1996 by Supraphon a.s. Licensed with the kind permission of Supraphon, Prague	:13
73	194	"Lasst mich allein," Op. 82, No. 1: 1–6	:15
74	198	Concerto for Cello and Orchestra No. 2 in B Minor, Op. 104, II: 1–9	:36
75	198	Concerto for Cello and Orchestra No. 2 in B Minor, Op. 104, II: 15–18	:15
76	198	Concerto for Cello and Orchestra No. 2 in B Minor, Op. 104, II: 38–42	:16
77	199	Beethoven, Symphony No. 3 in E♭ Major ("Eroica"), II: 1–8 (piano)	:26
78	200	*Holoubek,* Op. 110: 1–8 (Václav Talich, Czech Philharmonic Orchestra). Panton/Supraphon CD 81 1100-2. ℗ 1991 by Supraphon a.s. Licensed with the kind permission of Supraphon, Prague	:37
79	201	Piano Quintet in A Major, Op. 81, II ("Dunka"): 1–4 (Jan Panenka, piano; Panocha Quartet). Supraphon CD 11 1465-2131. ℗ 1994 by Supraphon a.s. Licensed with the permission of Supraphon, Prague	:10
80	202	"In the Sweet Power of Thine Eyes," Op. 83, No. 7: 3–7 (Zdena Kloubová, soprano; Věra Müllerová, piano). Supraphon CD 81 9008-2 231. ℗ 1999 by Supraphon a.s. Licensed with the kind permission of Supraphon, Prague	:23
81	203	Concerto for Cello and Orchestra No. 2 in B Minor, Op. 104, II: 28–33	:23
82	203	Concerto for Cello and Orchestra No. 2 in B Minor, Op. 104, II: 95–98	:16
83	204	Concerto for Cello and Orchestra No. 2 in B Minor, Op. 104, III: 421–435	:27
84	204	Concerto for Cello and Orchestra No. 2 in B Minor, Op. 104, III: 460–465	:12
85	204	"Lasst mich allein," Op. 82, No. 1: 26–29 (piano)	:15
86	205	Concerto for Cello and Orchestra No. 2 in B Minor, Op. 104, III: 468–473	:14

BAKER & TAYLOR